SISTER MOON
OF THE PHILIPPINES

Amidst a Culture of Terrible
Abuse and Poverty,
an Astonishing
Filipino Girl Rises Up

VICTORIA MULATO

Sister Moon of the Philippines:
Amidst a Culture of Terrible Abuse and Poverty
an Astonishing Filipino Girl Rises Up

Published by:
Victoria Mulato
www.VictoriaMulato.com

ISBN: 978-0692219638

ACKNOWLEDGMENTS

A special thank you to my mother, Anita, for reliving her story and providing such rich details of our lives as I wrote this book. I am also grateful to my sister, Bebeng, for helping me remember events of the past and supporting this project.

Very special thanks to my brilliant and talented publisher, Howard VanEs. President of Let's Write Books, Inc., whose time and effort, enthusiastic support, ideas and suggestions made the story where it is today. My book editors also deserve special acknowledgement: Marie Judson-Rosier for her style and organization, Robin Harnist for copyediting.

I would also like to extend my love and thanks to my Brother Di and sisters Wilma, Neneng and Weng for being available when I needed them.

And most importantly, my heartfelt gratitude to Dr. James R. Palleschi, urology surgeon, who believed in me, whose praise and questioning encouraged me to keep on writing.

RESPONSIBILITIES OF A BIG FOUR YEAR OLD SISTER

It was so long ago, but I still remember staring at
Moon-ay's milky white, silky skin. Her face was so perfect,
so round, like a tiny moon illuminating the dark skies.
Her delicate beauty shone, and her brown, slanted eyes
were perfection. Moon-ay lay in her crib, a "duyan", and
cried to be fed. I rocked my baby sister's hand-strung
basket. The cradle hung in the middle of the room tied
on both ends with sturdy, fibrous string, strong enough
to hold it like a tiny hammock. Even as a four-year-old, it
was my duty to make her happy, to help feed her, and to
rock her to sleep.

She was always in her duyan even when she was
awake. Sometimes when mom was doing laundry, the
baby was allowed to crawl on the floor for a couple of
hours to play with my three-year-old brother, Di. I'd
have to watch Moon-ay carefully, so she would not crawl
to the stairs and fall to the hard ground outside our
house. When she started to look sleepy and tired of
playing, I put her back in her duyan and lulled her back
to sleep. I'd push and pull the duyan to make Moon-ay
go to sleep. One time, I rocked it faster, using all my

strength to see how far it would go. I pushed it farther away from me, but as it swung back, it pushed me to the floor. I landed on my little bottom and hit the back of my head on the hardwood floor. The duyan slowed. Moon-ay gave a small cry as I crawled away from the duyan before it hit me again.

My other sister, Bebeng, who was two, played quietly nearby. She was never any trouble and almost didn't even get noticed.

A WALK

By late afternoon, after our nap, Dad would tell us to put on our sandals. "We're going out for a walk," he'd say excitedly. We walked away from the house, around the neighborhood, holding hands with Bebeng and Di as Dad carried Moon-ay.

We walked far from our house, up and down the street of our village, Paranaque. I had a sense of harmony within myself, being with my family, and feeling safe.

Dad pointed to the clear, blue sky. Moon-ay had to tilt her small head up to gaze. I, too, looked up and saw for the first time in my life, men in camouflage uniforms, jumping out from a small aircraft. We watched them fall through the sky, one by one, before opening their parachutes. I wondered what it would be like to be inside their flying machine. It looked daringly scary, but the display of bravery and wonder was quite a spectacular show for little spectators. I was sorry that Mom had missed out on our excursion and the show.

CLIPPED TOO CLOSE

I knew where the nail clippers were kept, so one day I got them and started clipping Moon-ay's fingernails. I clipped as quietly as possible, while she was still asleep with a bottle of milk in her mouth. At four years old, I already knew that the best time to clip a baby's nails was when she was asleep. When I got down to her pinky, I had such a hard time because it was too tiny of a finger and nail. Suddenly, she let out a loud cry, then went back to sleep, sucking the nipple of her bottle. I rocked her duyan gently and sang her a lullaby again.

It was the very first time I remember Father rolling up old newspapers in his hands, looking angry at me. As I watched him, I felt scared and started to cry. I knew he was going to come after me with it. I squirmed on the floor as I moved away from him while he slapped my bottom twice and once on each thigh. Then, he squatted in front of me, still holding on the newspapers on his right hand. I looked up at him, and he brushed a wisp of long, thick, black bangs covering my wet face. He looked angrily at me. I dared not move because he was still watching me, analyzing my behavior. Perhaps his gesture was to mean that I had to fear him as an authoritative figure.

When Mom arrived home, she went straight to look at the baby and noticed blood on her blanket. She panicked. Nervously, she inspected the baby's body from head to toe and noticed that the tip of her right pinky finger was clipped, red and swollen while a piece of muscle tissue and nail were cut off. She asked what had happened.

"I clipped her finger nails," I told her. I did not know I had clipped a piece of her pinky muscle off. She told me never to clip her fingernails again. She talked to my Dad, and he told her that I was already punished for it. Mom was agitated but understanding. She did not spank nor yell at me, but I had a bad feeling that there was something wrong with my tiny sister being entrusted to my poor, four-year-old skills.

DAD THE EXECUTIONER

One time we had a female dog that gave birth to four puppies. The puppies were rambunctious but a lot of fun to play with. They constantly demanded to be fed. My brother was very excited and asked if he could keep one for himself as his very own personal pet. Dad let him keep a black one. He showered his pup with unconditional love, playing with him all day. They

even slept next to each other, and my brother fed him
personally. No one was allowed to play with his pup
or even touch him without my brother's permission.
Whenever he was playing with his best friend in the world,
my brother was laughing and cheerful. The pup and my
brother never tired of each other. After playing, the pup
would lick my brother's face, which I found repulsive.
I watched them with envy. I was jealous but happy
for my brother.

"Eww," I said. I thought it was disgusting being
licked on the face.

But my brother liked it. In fact, he did not mind one
bit. He loved his pup more than he loved anyone else
in the household, it seemed. They were inseparable, day
in and day out.

Mom's business of selling fish and fresh produce
slowed. We must have been running low on cash because
Dad sold the other pups, including the mother, to his
friends. The pups hadn't even had their vaccinations
yet. One day, Dad came home and told Mom to take my
brother outside.

"What for?" my brother asked.

"Come with me, Sweetheart," Mom said. "I want to
tell you something."

I followed them downstairs but stopped and
looked back at my dad's face, as he hinted for Mom
to be quiet. I was confused as to what he was trying to
signal my mother. Somehow, I knew he was going to do
something unpleasant.

With a burlap sack on the floor next to him, Dad
started playing with the pup for a little bit. I hesitantly
followed my mom and brother outside. When Mom and

Di were far away from the house, I stopped again, still near enough to the house that I could hear the pup squealing. Mom and Di's figures disappeared into the distance, far away from the house.

Dad brought the pup outside and went in the opposite direction. He signaled for me to quickly go inside to keep an eye on Bebeng and Moon-ay. On my way up the stairs, I heard one loud yelp. I turned my head to the direction my mom and brother went. They could not have heard the noise I heard. I sat on the stairs outside, waiting for my mom and brother to return, or for Dad to return with the pup.

As soon as they returned, he asked, "Where's puppy?"

He called the puppy's name inside and outside the house. No answer. Usually, when he called out his pup's name, the pup would come running immediately and jump all over him, licking his face, and they would roll on the floor together, my brother giggling. They would play wrestle on the floor, ignoring anyone else in sight.

My brother was starting to worry. He called out his puppy's name louder and louder, but there was no pup in sight. The pup was nowhere to be found. Dad wasn't home either.

Depressed, my brother sat in the corner, anticipating Dad and pup's return. Mom tried to hug my brother close and explain that the pup had to go someplace. I could not quite make out the rest of what she was telling him. However, shortly afterwards, Dad came back, empty-handed and quiet. I looked up and saw a grin on his face. He walked around the house as if nothing had happened as I studied his every move. I knew what he had done to that little pup. He forced it into the burlap sac, held its mouth so it wouldn't bark loudly, and beat its head forcefully with a four-by-four or a rock. It only yelped once. I had butterflies in my stomach and a big lump in my throat. I cried uncontrollably in the corner. I looked at my brother and mom.

She had tears in her eyes, trying to appease my little brother who was gasping for breath. My brother was inconsolable as he tried to breathe. He cried his aching heart out for days, sobbing in his sleep. Mom and Dad started arguing in the middle of the night, at dawn, in the morning, at noon and at night.

ARGUING BETWEEN SLEEPS

At night, I saw my brother staring at the ceiling, most likely thinking of the good times he'd had with his dog. He woke up in the middle of the night, calling out his pup's name. Mom would get up and try to help him back to sleep. For a while he got up at dawn, sat alone while everybody was asleep (or he thought I was asleep), sobbing and calling for his pup. Dad finally had enough and got irritated. He crawled out from under the mosquito net, turned on the wicker lamp, and talked to my brother. He told him to stop crying now.

"Be a big boy," he told him. "Your pup was very sick and had to be put to sleep."

My brother let out a big howl. "He was a happy, healthy pup!" he protested.

"No," said my father, trying to be patient, "he was not. He was very ill and can't come back."

He told my brother to go back to sleep or he'll get a lashing. Di crawled back under the mosquito net, curled up on his side of the bed, bitter, with eyes of hatred and tears of pain.

"No more sobbing!" Dad shouted with a harsh and demanding voice.

I lay on my bed feeling sorry for my brother and resenting my dad, my pillow wet with tears.

But I heard my mother ask, "Why did you have to do it? He was just a little pup."

I never found out the reason, and Mom insisted the pup was never truly sick. All I remember now was my poor brother's heart-torn, wet face. He was withdrawn for a long time.

A few days after the disappearance of his beloved pup, my brother tried to save a sickly baby chick that wobbled as it tried to walk. It would just lay down all day long, too weak to get up to eat. The miserable little chick was breathing heavily, rapidly. Determined that he could make this chick strong again, my brother nourished it and gave it all his time and attention. He often, forcefully but gently, opened its beak widely and put drops of water into its throat, and he'd feed it grains of rice.

I watched with curiosity as my brother laid an empty half coconut shell over the chick and left it. After a half hour, he returned and started tapping the shell very lightly and slowly.

"Watch," he said to me eagerly. I watched anxiously. After a few minutes, he removed the coconut shell, and the baby chick stood up quickly, shaking its body, fluffing its wings and feathers as if it was just waking up from a long, deep sleep. I could not believe it! It was as if he had just performed a miracle on the baby chick. I could see my brother's smiling face, completely delighted. He repeated the process several more times, and the chick always emerged as lively as ever, as if it was just coming out of its shell for the first time, alive and ready to play. My brother played with the chick for a long time.

A couple weeks passed, and it too, vanished.

DAD THE SURGEON

I watched Dad burn the tip of a sewing needle. The tip turned from silver to an orange glow. He let it cool for a bit by placing it on a clean towel, then called my mom to hold me tight on her lap. I started to cry frantically, feeling scared. I did not know what he was going to do with the needle. They never explained. Mom just grabbed hold of my tiny four-year-old self, and restrained me with her arms and legs. I kicked and screamed as I struggled to escape.

Finally my dad exclaimed irritably, "We're going to get rid of your boil!"

I continued to cry loudly, calmed down a bit, after hearing what he had just told me, still tears falling down my cheeks. Dad explained again what he would do to me.

"So hold still!" he demanded angrily.

All I knew was I had a big boil under my chin. He said he wanted to drain the pus out and that I had to hold still. If I didn't, I would get a spanking. So I stopped struggling. I did not want to be spanked. I tried to sit still on my mother's lap as dad poked the boil with the needle and squeezed out the green pus.

Every day after that, I watched him burn the needle as it glowed into a magnificent neon orange, and I grew so frightened. I remember the pricking of the needle and pus being drained from under my chin with his fingers. I knew I had to sit still and be silent on my mother's lap and let him pierce the boil and squeeze the green fluid. They told me if I didn't, I would die of infection.

Because my parents could not afford to visit a doctor or buy medicine, they became our private doctors, sometimes using herbal leaves to patch up a wound or boiling special herbal roots and making us drink the juice to cure a stomach ailment or a fever. Mom or Dad never took any of us children to a public clinic for a check-up. They either had no means to pay the doctors, or they believed that herbal medicines were just as good if not better than any prescription medicine.

Like his father's father before him, my dad would consult with a shaman or a 'faith healer' for advice on a cure. He would always come home with some kind of remedy. My mom disagreed with his traditional beliefs and called his advisors 'quack doctors'.

TALK OF MOVING & GUAVAS

One day, Dad announced he had to leave for the province
of Bangar, La Union, where he grew up. Our parents
told us it was going to be a long eight-hour trip by bus
for Dad to visit his family, and while there he would
look for a house for us. My mother's cousin, Inday Mitos,
a daughter of upper class landowners, had decided
that it was time for us to move out of her house so she
could sell the property at a profit. She also thought we'd
overextended our stay. Mom said Inday Mitos only let us
stay for a while until we settled into a permanent home,
but unfortunately, we had stayed for almost a year. Now
she had a change of plan, or change of heart. Either
way, we had to move soon, so Dad left for Bangar the
following day.

He was gone for a month. When he had returned
home from the Province to Paranaque, he brought with
him a burlap sack full of ripe guavas he'd hand-picked
from his father's yard. They were green on the outside,
but sweet and pink on the inside. We devoured them
morning, noon, and night until they were gone. We just
helped ourselves whenever we wanted.

I noticed that, after taking a big bite into one of the
overripe guavas, there were tiny white worms wiggling
about furiously. Of course, that one was thrown out. I
picked up another, hoping it did not have worms.

A couple weeks had passed when our anuses began to itch like mad, especially at night. The itching woke us from sleep. I wondered if it was the worms I'd seen in the deliciously sweet guavas. We all scratched our anuses a lot during the day and more so during the night. It was especially annoying when I was in deep sleep.

One night, Mom decided to take a peek at Bebeng's anus while she was sound asleep and snoring—I could not believe she could snore through that terrible itching. Mom moved a jar lamp close to my little sister's buttocks and lifted one cheek to expose the anus. We saw that it was coated with a silky, white, wiggly pinworms. There must have been hundreds of them crawling out of her anus. Just one white, wiggling pest would have been enough to tickle her. But hundreds of them? I could only gape at them in horror. Mom wiped her anus with a clean towel. I guess she threw the infested thing away before coming back to bed. She told me to try to get some sleep, but I lay thinking about those same worms in my own butt and had a hard time sleeping for the tickling and itching.

The following evening, it was brother Di's turn. He slept next to Bebeng so he, too, was most likely infected. Sure enough, he had the same problem. My mom did the same, checked his anus. He had pinworms, but not quite as many as sister.

Early in the morning Mom left the house. Dad said she was going to buy us some chocolate. Boy, we were jumping with joy, with the pinworms catching a ride in our anuses. Mom came back with what she and Dad called "chocolate medicine". It was oval shaped, wrapped in foil and resembling Easter chocolate candy I'd seen in pictures. Dad unwrapped one and gave it first to Bebeng, since she had the most pests in her anus.

"Open your mouth," Dad instructed her.

Bebeng opened her mouth wide, and Dad popped in the chocolate medicine.

"There you go," he said, "Now chew slowly so you don't choke."

He unwrapped the second chocolate and gave it to Di. Then he gave me one.

"Swallow all of it," Dad demanded as he watched us chewing. It had a sweet yet bitter taste to it.

"It's delicious!" I said and eagerly finished mine. "Can I have another one?"

We loved the luscious chocolate and were excited for more.

"There's no more," Dad said and explained that they were not real chocolate candies. They were medicine to deworm us and too expensive to eat like candy. That was the very first time I ever tasted chocolate 'candy'.

A few days passed, and mom and dad decided to check our anuses once again just to make sure the medicine had worked. That night, one by one, my brother and sister and I had to drop our undergarments, turn around, and bend over in front of mom and dad to be inspected. Dad held a jar lamp in one hand and spread our butt cheeks with the other while mom watched. A quick check and once cleared from inspection, we hurriedly pulled up our trousers, feeling embarrassed.

THE MOVE

My aunt Li and cousin Violet visited for a short time, and after they left, Dad told my mom we had to leave for the Province soon. We did not have very many belongings. They consisted of five plates, two big bowls, a couple of mugs, a water jug, a washbasin, and the portable gas stove. We have only a few pieces of clothing to fit into a big canvas bag. We were to leave around midnight, sleeping throughout the ride and be in La Union by daylight. At the depot huge red and yellow buses lined up in rows. A cacophony of deafening roars from giant engines sent vibrations through my stomach. Earth-shaking to a small child. A tight grip on father's hand provided safety and protection as we passed a number of buses in search of ours.

I remember walking in the aisle of this big, red, crowded bus called *The Philippine Rabbit.* I thought I'd sit by the window so I could watch the grand views of countryside as soon as the sun starts shining. Like the other young children around, we tried to keep ourselves awake. We yawned a lot as we fought sleepiness and watched and waited for the grown ups, mostly male passengers, to finish loading their belongings. As soon as everyone was seated, the bus slowly drove out of the well-lit depot and out into the dark streets.

After having driven a couple hours, the bus pulled over to a public market with restrooms and allowed passengers to relieve themselves. A few men, including my father, and a couple of older women, smoked cigarettes on the side of the road. Dad couldn't afford his own, so he bummed them off other men.

When there wasn't a public market to stop at, the bus stopped by the side of the freeway and allowed everyone to do their business behind bushes or trees. Passengers on the back of the bus struggled to walk down the aisle on their way out the door due to all the baggage, including live chickens and ducks in cages, quacking occasionally throughout the ride. Even baby piglets were tucked under seats. Some passengers slept right through the stops, with their babies and young children on their laps.

Very early in the morning, the bus made a momentary stop for gas. Vendors carrying cola drinks and food items came inside the bus to sell to hungry, thirsty passengers. Hard-boiled quail eggs and *balut* (a fertilized duck embryo boiled alive that was served hot with salt) were favorite items. *Balut* was a most favored product. It did not matter what time of day it was. It could be eaten for breakfast, lunch, or dinner.

When my favorite, sweet rice wrapped in banana leaves, came, I asked my parents if we could have some. But alas, they said no. They did not buy one item from the vendors. I watched families sitting nearby us enjoying their purchased food. Even those who brought their meals prepared at home bought big bottles of Coca Cola or orange Fanta drinks. Mom took out our breakfast she had prepared the night before we left: steamed white rice and deep-fried fish. She spoon-fed me and brother Di. We had only a big jug of water to drink and a couple of milk bottles for the baby. I wondered if my parents really did not have enough money or if they were just being frugal. Oh, how I wished I could have just one *balut*, and of course, a sweet rice cake. I salivated, and with a jealous knot in my stomach as I watched other kids eat.

My parents took turns carrying the baby and watching us while the other took a brief nap. I decided to stay awake, enjoying the country scenes every moment of the way, whether dark or light out, until we got to our destination.

The rich green rice fields stretched for endless miles. We passed sparkling lakes and rivers, food stalls with fruits in hanging baskets, and beautifully crafted handmade products displayed in front of people's houses. Native Northerners walked along the sides of the busy highways carrying produce in big baskets balanced on their heads. I saw farmers riding on the backs of caribou. When they walked along the opposite side from the bus, they seemed very slow. I saw goats tied to trees as well as stray cats and dogs roaming the streets. The views of mountain ranges in a distance and breathtaking landscapes, of rice terraces, giant corn fields, and tall coconut trees farther up ahead gave my soul a deep sense of appreciation for the country.

As soon as we arrived in La Union—a province of small villages north of Manila—it was almost noon. The ride to our new house would be another ten to fifteen minutes. I was ecstatic to finally see what my father had built for us.

Mom carried the baby in one arm and held my hand with the other, while also carrying a huge bag. I held my

sister Bebeng's hand as we followed Dad. He held Di's
hand along with the big burlap bag of our household
items. Each one of us kids carried a small bag as we
shoved our way through the crowd to get to a tricycle
taxi parked in a row across from the horse carriages. Dad
loaded our heavy belongings on top of the tricycle. Then
he climbed in behind the driver and sat Di on his lap.
Mom followed, squeezing Moon-ay, Bebeng, and me on
her lap like sardines. The tricycle made a big U-turn, and
it slowly crawled into the traffic, constantly honking its
horn to warn people to move aside. The combination of
loud, chattering noises and humid heat was unbearable.
Sweaty people passed, and vendors fanned themselves
nonstop. Customers with umbrellas made the whole place
into a crowded, prickly quick stop.

We inched our way along in the traffic, watching all
kinds of exotic tropical fruits, tobacco leaves, string beans,
sweet potatoes, eggplants, and live and sun-dried fish pass by.

THE HOUSE DAD BUILT

With the help of my grandfather and four uncles, our
dad had built a tall house with a second story for us to
move into. It was a skinny house with walls and floors of
bamboo woods. It had a tin roof and a concrete floor on
the first level. The staircase leading to the second floor
was outside, in front of the house. We had no furniture,

no running water, no bathroom or electricity. Dad had built an outhouse on the backyard. It was six feet deep, covered with bamboo flooring with a foot long hole in the middle. It, too, was built of sturdy bamboo walls, with a white, tin roof.

Our new house was in the middle of lush tropical rain forest. Vegetation and trees were cut down to make room for the house and backyard. Some of the plants that thrived year after year on hot tropical heat, were just left alone. We were not allowed to wander into the jungle past the back yard, for fear of snakes or wild animals. But there was an abundance of delicious bananas, sweet papayas, guavas, durian, coconut palms, and Moringa oleifera trees on the property. There were also plenty of sweet potatoes, cassava, taro, and jicama plants at the far edges of the backyard. Even farther back were more fruit trees of various kinds.

LIFE AT THE NEW HOME

My family adjusted comfortably into our new home. One evening, before nightfall, I helped gather and light our three wick lamps. We used up kerosene quickly, and I was always told to go to grandfather's house to ask for more. Either Grandfather or Grandmother would give me the kerosene that lasted our household for a week.

Along with the kerosene, Grandmother sometimes gave me a potful of hot vegetable curry and a pot of steamed rice to take home. She always gave us a portion of their dinner when there happened to be extra food. Since we didn't have a table yet, we sat in a big circle on the floor with the plates of food and bowls of stew, and kerosene lamp in the middle. After supper, mom washed the dishes while my brother and I played with Bebeng and the baby.

When Mom finished in the kitchen, she would bathe Bebeng and the baby. She instructed me and my brother to wash our hands and feet, and to brush our teeth. We used our index finger and sea salt—not with toothpaste because my parents could not afford toothpaste. Then we made sure to lock the front door, and one by one we climbed up the stairs. I led the way with a lamp, my brother following with his own wick lamp. We remained upstairs until morning.

If we needed to use the outhouse during the night, we had to take a lamp downstairs and remember to bring a piece of paper or a bucket of water to wash our bottom. Then we had to climb back up the stairs again to sleep. Since that was too much work, none of us wanted to go down stairs in the night. Instead, one of us carried the big chamber pot upstairs and used it instead. In the morning or early afternoon, one of us was assigned to bring this loaded chamber pot down to the outhouse to empty it, careful not to spill its contents as we carried it down each step. Once emptied and cleaned, it was placed in the corner of the house to dry and be ready for use the next evening.

Since there was no running water inside the house, I helped Mom and Dad collect water from a hand pump between our house and my grandparents. I carried with me two empty buckets to fill and carry back to the house, to fill a tank. Every other day we took showers at the pump. We brought along clean clothes and soap. Our family owned only one big towel for everyone to share and always hung it to dry for the next person to use.

The pump never ran out of water. It filled from a river reservoir and pure rainwater during the monsoon season. We also washed our dirty clothes and dishes at the pump. It was also our vital source of drinking water. For a five-year-old, it was quite a struggle to grab hold of the long, wooden handle to get it to come down. Only when the handle was down would the water pour out, and I had to jump high to reach it. Then I needed to grab hold with both hands, not letting go. I wiggled my little body to pull the handle down using all my weight. When the water finally pumped out, I could let go of the handle and wait for it to go back up automatically. Then I repeated the process, jumping up high to get the handle to go down with me.

Sometimes I rode it like a seesaw, straddling the handle between my legs, climbing clear up to make the handle go down and climbing backwards to release it. As time went by, and I got stronger, I enjoyed going up and down with the pump handle. I did not mind at all that I had to struggle, wiggling my body, so the handle and I would come down together at the same time. It actually gave me a feeling of success whenever I saw water coming out. I repeated the whole process until I filled up the two buckets. Then I carried them home and poured them into a big clay jug, or the tank.

MY GRANDPARENTS & THEIR GIN

Grandmother was always walking home from the market tipsy, talking to herself, with a basket full of ripe Manila mangoes, milkfish, and fresh vegetables. She always hid an extra bottle of gin under the green vegetables balanced on her head. At home, she hid bottles of gin under piles of blankets, mounds of rice, and clothing inside a wicker chest in the living room, or behind a cabinet, or under bushes in her backyard.

She'd hunt up a bottle of gin, take a swig straight from the bottle, and then say "Just a little bit to whet my whistle." Then she'd recap the bottle and hide it, putting her finger to her lips to give me a sign to keep quiet. I'd nod. She did not want Grandfather to find out her secret hiding places. God only knew what would happen if he found out where the bottles were hidden. He would probably drink them all and put the empty bottles back.

When Grandfather and Grandmother were both drunk, they chattered nonstop, sounding as if they were arguing about nonsense. One would become annoyed by the other's chatter, and they would go on like that throughout the evening. When Grandmother was not around, Grandfather searched for a bottle, convinced there was always one in the house somewhere. More often than not, he found one and finished it. When

Grandmother returned, she, too, searched for her bottles, not remembering where she put them. When she found an empty one, she just kept quiet, not questioning who took them. She just looked for a new hiding place, behind a wall stuffed with old t-shirts, or in a wicker basket full of clothes.

Once, after digging out a bottle, she took one gulp of drink, turned around, hesitated for a moment, opened the wicker chest again, and said to me that she was going to take another small sip. "Just one drink," she would say reassuringly.

But I watched her pour a quarter of the bottle of gin into her mouth. "You're drinking like a thirsty horse, Grandma, looks like to me," I told her.

"Oh, be quiet. Shush your mouth," she'd say. "Ahhh! That's one strong bottle of gin!"

Satisfied, she shook her head as if to clear off the powerful burn in her throat and brain. She put the cap back on the bottle and hid it again. Then she got up, turned around, and headed towards the kitchen to prepare supper. I followed behind her as she tried to keep her equilibrium.

AUNT LI AND COUSIN VIOLET

Not too far from our house—about a quarter of a mile—was Aunt Li's house. It was in the process of being demolished to build a newer, modern, and more luxurious home than all the other houses in the entire village of Bangar. This new house would be specially designed and paid for by her husband, Uncle Pablo, who was thirty-seven years her senior and lived and worked in Hawaii.

He sent the funds via wire transfer to Aunt Li, who then paid the architect and the construction workers. Aunt Li, who was one year younger than my father, became like a second mother to me.

She often invited me to her house to give me hand-me-down clothes from her daughter. My cousin Violet acted different, quiet, as if she did not like me very much. Whatever Violet asked for, it was given to her. The maids called her to come to the kitchen table only when it was time to eat, and she was never required to do any chores.

One day, while I was over for dinner, my aunt asked me to call Cousin Violet to come to supper. I climbed the stairs to my cousin's bedroom and knocked on her door.

"Who is it?" she asked in an unfriendly voice.

"It's me. Xulli. Your mom says to come eat," I replied, irritated.

She did not open the door, but instead told me to tell them she would be down in a minute. Supper did not start until hands were washed, all were seated, and prayers given. We waited. Then I went back upstairs and knocked for a second time.

When she opened the door, she said, "It's you again? What are you doing here? You have no right to be staying here, you know? This is not your house! You can't just come and go as you please." She spoke harshly and, with her brows contorted, I thought she looked like a cow had just sat on her face.

"Auntie says it's time for dinner," I told her, hurrying to get as far away from her as possible.

Occasionally she acted in a good mood, when she wanted me to do something for her. Her harshness did not hurt my feelings. I knew it irritated her that I never took her mean words and criticisms seriously. I turned around, ignoring her comments, as her icy stare followed me down the steps. Aunt Li and the rest of the household ate meals in the kitchen.

After the meal, I went straight to the living room and played with my cousin's toys without her knowing—drew pictures with her crayons and so on. I changed into the hand-me-downs given to me by Aunt Li. I did these things without being seen by Cousin Violet, or she would have had a fit and start yelling and crying and saying terrible things.

"Just stay away from her," Aunt Li suggested to me. "Don't let her see you wearing her clothes. Take them home."

And I did. Nothing could stop me from going to Aunt Li's house, not even when my cousin pleaded with her mother, telling her she didn't want to see my face again. But it was no use. I still showed up.

WRITING PADS

Five days remained before the first day of school, so I went to Grandfather to ask for writing pads.

"School starts on Monday, and I really need writing pads. Can you please buy me some?" I begged.

He was reading a newspaper in his living room. He just was silent even though I knew he heard me. I turned and left his house, confident that he would buy them for me. The day before school started, I was so excited I could hardly stand it. I ran back to Grandfather's house, sure that I would find my writing pads there.

Confident, I climbed the stairs to his house and saw him waiting for me in the living room. Smiling, I continued toward him. He was seated in his chair. I noticed he held a tree branch in one hand. Interesting, I thought. Maybe he used it as a cane while he walked to and from the market.

He stood up and, as I came closer, he raised his arm and swung the branch across my little body, hitting me with great force. I crashed to the floor completely baffled. Taken utterly by surprise, I struggled to get up, but as I was trying to get my balance, he hit me again, and then again. I was struggling to get up, staring terrified at him. He swung again. This one to my thigh. It stung deep. Tears pouring down my face, I screamed and raised my arm to protect my face from another blow, but he switched hands, raising the limb again.

I crawled backwards as fast as I could to get away from him, screaming, "Stop!"

But the heavy branch came down on me again and again from behind. I tried to rub and comfort my arms and legs to soothe the pain as he kept hitting other parts of my body. I pleaded and screamed at the top of my lungs, begging him to stop.

"What did I do?" I screamed. "I'm sorry!"

He gave me another hit. When he panted, too exhausted to continue, I managed to pull farther away from him. I crawled on hands and knees to the farthest corner of the living room, huddled as small as I could get, knees to my chin, arms around my legs. He tossed the branch aside. It looked like he was done, but then apparently he changed his mind, for he retrieved the branch and came toward me.

"Nooooo! Please stop!" I begged, hands clasped as in prayer, beseeching. I cried, sobbing. "Whatever I did, I won't do it again. I promise. Just tell me!"

He finally decided to stop, turned around and walked away, still holding onto the tree branch. I stayed whimpering in the corner of the room, wondering what I had done wrong. The room became very quiet, except for my sobbing. It was just Grandfather and I in his house. Everybody else must have been away.

He came back without the branch, pointed his finger at me and said, "That will teach you a lesson, not to give away a single page of these pads to your classmates in school. Not one page, do you hear me?"

"Yes, Grandfather!" I nodded in agreement, still crouching with my arms around my knees.

"Here!" He held out a paper pad.

I looked up through a film of tears and reached out tentatively for the pad with a shaking hand. I wasn't sure if I should take it, if that might be wrong, or if I should shake my head and politely say, "No, thank you."

If by accepting it, I might bring on another rain of beatings. I took it cautiously. As soon as I had the pad on my hands, he turned and walked slowly away.

I cried in the corner as I leafed through pages of the pad, noticing that the one he bought me was the cheapest kind. The paper was dirty, light brown, and lined with purple ink that started off thick and became thinner half way across the page, not white and clean like Violet's. So this is what I suffered for? I questioned myself. One hundred pages of ugly writing paper that looked like someone spilled something on it and forgot to wipe it off?

Still sobbing, I felt like throwing the pad right back at him, but he might beat me again. Besides, I really needed paper for school or the teacher would probably become furious and send me home. I didn't want to wait another whole year to go to school. I knew students weren't allowed to come to school without school supplies. No borrowing, no begging, and no stealing. My brother had already told me all the strict rules.

Disoriented, my body was one big ache. I stumbled toward home, the writing pad in my hands. I told Mom what Grandpa had done to me. She was enraged with the old man and told me to stay away from him.

"I will have a good talk with him to stay away from my children!" Mom said, but she had to be very careful in her choice of words and approach because our family owed Grandfather so much. We lived on his land and ate his crops. He had basically built the house we lived in and used his own savings to lend my parents money. Our grandfather was the family's patriarch and was owed a noble degree of respect. And he knew it.

As children, we were taught to show reverence to those older than us. Not just with Grandfather, but also with all four of our uncles. Children must show their respect at all times. These rules were taught to us at an early age. All our elders were to be regarded as superiors. If they asked for help around the house, like cooking, cleaning, or going to the market, we had to immediately obey. We paid our respect by following their every demand.

MOON-AY

Moon-ay had been ill for two days. She was burning up with fever, whimpering in her sleep, until we had to take her to the hospital. We ran to Aunt Li's house, Mom carrying the baby. Mom asked Aunt Li for money for the hospital. Without hesitation, Aunt Li changed and readied to accompany Mother and Moon-ay to the emergency room. I begged to go with them, but Mom told me to stay put, be a good girl, and look after Bebeng and Di.

Later, Aunt Li came home alone. She explained that Mom had to stay with Moon-ay for a while at the hospital. I asked how long it would be before I could see my baby sister. Aunt Li just hurried away to her room, got something, and rushed right back to the hospital. I wished desperately for her to take me to the hospital.

Bebeng and I stayed at Aunt Li's. I did not know where father was. I had not seen him for days. Di walked to our grandparents. He felt most comfortable staying there. I waited and waited for Mother to return with the baby. I was so anxious to know what was happening to my dear, youngest sister.

Why did she have to stay in the hospital for so long? Why did she have to be taken away so suddenly? After about a week, my mother came briefly from the hospital. She brought home dirty clothes and took back clean ones. Aunt Ud said Mom was at Moon-ay's side at all times watching her and desperately trying to get her fever to cool down. I, too, was desperate to know what was wrong with my baby sister, but neither of the aunts knew. I was just constantly reminded to be a good girl. While Mom stayed at the hospital with the baby, Aunt Ud would go visit Di to make sure he was all right while she took care of Bebeng and me at her house. Bebeng, at four years of age, was easy to manage. She never cried and was always quiet, waiting patiently to be fed and cleaned.

I begged for days to be able to see Moon-ay. I cried, pleaded, screamed, pounded my fists on the walls and doors, begging to be heard, to be taken seriously. At night in bed, I sobbed myself to sleep, feeling panicked and longing to see sister Moon-ay, even for just one minute. I desperately wanted to touch her hands, her arms, and

her face. I wanted to be next to her, that's all! Was that
too much to ask? Anybody? I must have whimpered in
my sleep. I woke the next day with intense longing and
pain in my heart.

Finally Aunt Li said okay, but only if I behaved
and didn't run around the hospital. I would finally be
allowed to see her, for a short visit. I stopped crying
immediately. The feeling of jubilation instantly erased the
heartaches and despair that had been flowing through
my aching chest night and day. Dancing for joy to reunite
with Moon-ay was all I could wish for. In a moment, I
was dressed and leaping outside the house, waiting by
the gate before Aunt could change her mind. I just
had to see my sister. I waited and waited in front of the
house, watching cars coming and going. Finally Aunt
Li stepped out.

Please don't change your mind. Don't change your mind,
I whispered in my mind. We caught a tricycle to the
hospital. Walking through the long hospital hallway, I
could hear small children, some older than sister Moon-
ay, crying in pain. Others whimpered. I passed through
private rooms and peeked at their parents, mostly
mothers, sitting by their bedside. When we entered
Moon-ay's room, we found mom sitting by her bedside,
too. Moon-ay lay there, wearing only a cloth diaper, her
chest rising and falling rapidly.

I went closer and reached for her tiny, bony hands.
The same tiny hand I had held back in *Paranaque* when
I started clipping her little finger nails while she was in
her *duyan*. I stared at the same pinky where I had clipped
off a small piece of muscle tissue. I held that hand tight,
rubbing it, holding it so lovingly, as I looked at her face,

mouth open gasping in and out for air. I rubbed her right arm, so delicate and smooth, weak and dry. My eyes moved again to her chest, breathing so fast, still gasping for air. Her eyes stayed closed. Mouth opened but relaxed. She just lay panting, looking tired.

I was confused. I hardly recognized her. Her face was so thin and frail, without her usual energy. I sobbed quietly, tears filling my eyes. I tried to hide them so Mom and Aunt Li would not make me leave. I wanted to see Moon-ay's gorgeous eyes. I became depressed, seeing her this way.

Mom and Aunt Li talked behind me. I felt so sorry for her, wanted to hug her and kiss her, but I did not know if I was allowed to. I had promised to behave. And I did my best to. My hands still clung to Moon-ay's. I quietly called out her name, "Little Moon-ay."

She must have heard my voice, for she moaned a little. Aunt Li tapped me on the shoulder and told me it was time to leave. My heart sank. I did not dare leave my sister. I feared never seeing her again, but I had promised I would do as I was told.

"I wish I could kiss her," I wanted to say as Aunt Li was pulling me away. I wanted so much to tell Moon-ay I loved her. How I wanted to hold her, carry her like I used to do on my back like her horse. I wanted to play with her again. "Can I stay just a couple more minutes?" I pleaded.

But they said it was best not to get too close for too long at a time because I, too, might get sick. I had to remind myself of my promise to behave, so I could come back and visit her again. Aunt Li and I left the hospital. On the way home, I was quiet. At dinner, tears fell on my

plate. I could not hear anyone around me chattering. I
could not touch my food. My arms felt too heavy to lift.

"You better eat, Xulli, so you don't get sick,"
Aunt Ud ordered.

I tried to force myself to gulp the food down, but my
throat was too tight. It was impossible to swallow. I could
not stop sobbing, sitting there in front of my plate. I went
to sleep with a heavy ache in my chest. The following
day, a yellow taxicab pulled into my Aunt's driveway, late
in the afternoon. I stood at the front door searching to
see who was in it. It was Mom! I was excited. I smiled.
In her arms, she was cradling something. It had to be
Moon-ay, wrapped in a white blanket. Suddenly, I could
breathe easier.

"My sister! She's well now!" I exclaimed. "They're
home!" I was so happy. I was about to run towards them
with a great, big smile on my face.

But Aunt Ud, standing behind me, said, "Stay
put. Stay where you are." She rested her hands
on my shoulders.

I waited, trying to be patient, for my mom and baby
sister to walk up to the house so I could give them a big
hug. Especially Moon-ay! I would play with her more and
tell her I missed her so much! I could not express the
happiness I felt the moment I saw Mother climbing out of
the taxi, wearing a black dress, with Moon-ay in her arms.

"They're home now, and Sister is well!" I
cried out again.

The yellow taxicab slowly backed out of the driveway
and then drove off. As Mom approached, I watched her
face. Her eyes were red and swollen, as if she'd cried for
days. I followed her, towards the living room, Aunt Ud

next to me. Aunt Li hurriedly laid a mat on the floor for
the baby. Mother laid down the bundle, opened the white
sheet, and let out a piercing howl of pain.

"Oh God, No! Not my bbbaabbyyy!" She screamed
out to God, begging Him for answers. I stood, dazed. The
tears in my eyes fogged my vision as I came closer to see
the baby on the floor. Mother bent until her head lay on
Moon-ay's chest, mourning loudly, heart shattered.

I stood by her, struggling to make sense of it all, as
tears poured down my face. I stared at Moon-ay's frozen
face, her body not moving at all. She was dead.

My mother wailed on. Both Aunt Li and Aunt Ud
struggled to get her up and away from the dead baby,
but she fought them. She picked up my baby sister and
cradled her tight against her chest for one last time,
rocking back and forth on her knees, wailing to bring her
baby back to life. "Anybody. Please, I beg of you."

My eyes flooded with tears again, my face soaked.
I did not know what to do. I looked around me, and
there was Di and Bebeng behind me. They were not
crying. They were too lost and confused. I turned back
and watched Mother scream and weep. I moved out of
the way as Aunt Li and Aunt Ud tried to separate her
from the baby.

Two elder women neighbors must have heard, or
were invited earlier by the aunts, for they came over to
help calm my mother down. One woman spoke tender,
comforting words to my mother, trying to help her with
her grieving, while the other neighbor gently extricated
my baby sister from her arms. I trailed behind to the
bathroom where the neighbor woman bathed my tiny
sister, carefully washing her limp body and holding her as

if she had been her own child. She talked to her as if the child was only sleeping.

"You are an Angel from heaven. A very good little Angel. Won't you let *Lola* bathe you with this nice warm water?" she said lovingly as she rubbed soap on the baby's hair and body.

Moon-ay, of course, never cried or moved. She was so very silent, still, and pale. Not even the fast butterfly breathing woke her chest anymore. I could not help but sob as I watched.

As Lola dressed her lifeless body, in preparation for after life, she chanted a prayer for her spirit, a prayer that she would become an angel with wings, in her white dress and shoes, that she would be a guardian angel in heaven. I believe Moon-ay was listening, eyes closed and at peace, in her very deep sleep. When she was dressed in a long white dress, her fine hair combed, and a white bonnet placed on her head, Lola carried her back into the living room, set her on a mat until a male neighbor arrived with a small, elegant, white coffin, adorned with white silk ribbons and peonies. She was delicately placed in white silk blankets, in her white clothes and shoes. Baby Moon-ay looked very exhausted now in her deep sleep.

For a couple of days, her lifeless form lay there in the living room, while my mother, family and relatives mourned and prayed for her spirit to reach the high heavens. I slept on the floor next to her coffin and looked at her little white face first thing in the morning when I woke. I stood examining her little face and then closed my eyes with great sadness and grief burning deep in my heart. When I opened my eyes, I noticed

air bubbles coming out of her nose. I was alarmed.
I stepped back.

"She's alive again?" I wondered. I knew she was dead,
but I ran and told Aunt Ud there were bubbles coming
out of Moon-ay's nose! "I think she's trying to breathe!" I
panicked. Aunt Ud and I hurried back to the coffin, but
she explained that it was normal for fluid to come out of
her nose from her lungs after death.

THE FUNERAL

The day of the burial, all of us were dressed up for the
procession. Mom dressed in a black dress and veil. There
was a parade for my sister. Two men volunteered to
carry the coffin to the cemetery. Mother trailed behind,
then my family and all our relatives, with two drummers
and two trumpet players, walked behind the tiny coffin
to St. Christopher church. My father was not around.
Neighbors paid their respect by throwing coins in the air
as the procession passed by their houses. It symbolized
money she could take to heaven, so she would not be
poor. In the church, a special mass was given in honor
of her. After one hour of praying and saying our last
goodbyes, the priest gave a final prayer, a vigil. *Ave Maria*
music played in the background as we gathered, one by
one, to get another view of her in the coffin.

After the mass, we walked out of the church. Cousin
Violet, Di, Bebeng, and I were told to stand next to her
coffin and have a final picture taken with her, the very
last picture taken with those she left behind.

On our way to the cemetery, more prayers were
given. We said our final good bye as her coffin was
lowered into the ground.

Mom was inconsolable, with tears drenching her
face. The women soothed her with comforting words. We
rode tricycles back to Aunt Li's house. When we arrived, I
still did not see Father anywhere. I did not bother to ask
where he might have gone during all the time we were at
the cemetery, or whether he had ever visited Moon-ay in
the hospital. I never bothered to ask.

AFTER THE FUNERAL

My siblings and I stayed at Aunt Li's for a time, while
Mom recuperated. She still dressed in black every day and,
at times, was nowhere to be found. Both aunts looked for
her. Once they found her alone in one of the downstairs
bedrooms. Other days I heard her crying inside a closet.
She refused to eat. She mourned day and night, and she
was beginning to lose weight from depression. Constantly,
my aunts reminded her to eat and to live for the rest of
her children. But she remained silent, staring into space
as if she could not hear. The closet seemed to be her only

private grieving place. I guess it was comforting in the dark, closed space. I always heard her there, sobbing.

Every day, for several days, a candle vigil and prayers were given for Moon-ay at Aunt Li's house. The ritual went on from sunrise to midnight. Some old folks from the neighborhood were very traditional and superstitious. They were convinced that my sister's spirit was still roaming around the house, playing with us still. They chanted prayers, constantly reminding her, like talking to a living two-year-old, to go to heaven now where she belonged, a place where all the other angels like her were playing. I did not know whether these chanted messages made my mother happier, or if they depressed her more than she already was. But the old women claimed they could talk to my sister, feel her presence around the house, and would continue their chanting until she left.

As the chanting and praying continued, my mother slowly regained her strength. She started to eat again, eating the small portions given to her slowly. *Maybe Moon-ay will rest in peace with Mother happy again*, I thought.

GOING HOME

We couldn't stay any longer at Aunt Li's house. All of us had been living there for a while, eating her food and depending on her for everything. It was becoming overcrowded and somewhat uncomfortable for all of us. It was time for us to go back to our own house.

Late one evening, when everybody was lying in bed trying to sleep, a knock came at the front door. We froze, looking at each other.

"Who could that be at this time of the night?" Mom whispered.

My heart raced where I was, curled up under my blanket. I knew my brother and Bebeng were also scared. The knocking came again.

"Who is it?" Mom asked, raising her voice to sound as if she was a tough, strong woman.

"It's me. Open the door," a male voice answered.

It was Dad's voice. He had come back home! Mom recognized the voice and immediately opened the door. I did not know whether to be joyful or sad. I did not know what to feel or think. I decided not to get out of bed.

All the sudden we were no longer sleepy. We entered a somber mood, grieving all over again. It was an awkward time. Outside, all was quiet. We lay under our one big mosquito net. Dad came in, dressed up. He sat and gazed around at us. Mom, sitting next to him, started sobbing.

He asked, "Where is Moon-ay?"

My mother was silent for a moment, but then started to howl like a wolf at the moon, and whispered, "She's gone."

"Moon-ay passed away, Dad!" I exclaimed. "We buried her a week ago!"

As a child of six, I had not yet learned to tell time or the days of the month. It felt like only a week but had actually been over a month.

Dad was silent, his head bowed. The moonlight shone through the open window, illuminating the dim room just enough to see everyone. Everything seemed so silent, at a standstill in the dead of night. I could not even hear cicadas outside. The coldness of the evening felt eerie. Foreign.

I later learned that dad had been incarcerated this entire time.

DAD HAD CHANGED

Dad stayed away a lot, coming home drunk. He passed out in the corner, in the kitchen, or at Grandfather's house. His drinking seemed to get worse. Maybe it was his way of grieving over the loss of a child, or he was feeling guilty because he was not around when Moon-ay was sick, or when she was buried. It was hard to figure him out.

He seemed aloof from everyone who loved him. He was unpleasant to be around. He made us uncomfortable and nervous. Even his brothers refused to be near him. He picked fights with his sisters, his father, and even the neighbors. On numerous occasions Aunt Li threatened to have the police take him back to jail if he did not behave and leave her property immediately. I'd hear them arguing back and forth, shouting at each other, while Aunt Li waved her arms, lecturing him on what a bum he'd turned out to be.

"You're an embarrassment to the world, to the whole family," she'd say. "Why don't you do us all a favor and die? It'd save us all a lot of misery, not to mention our sanity!"

Cursing and pointing his finger at his sister, Dad told her to shut her big, fat mouth. Aunt Li had her maids behind her, keeping guard in case he laid a hand on her. He was well aware that he would lose this fight with his sister because there were five women against one foolish drunk. Dad would decide to leave and head home. I'd follow at a distance. At grandfather's house, he'd lie down on a bamboo bed on the first floor, with no pillow and no blanket, and the lack of netting left him undefended from giant starving mosquitos.

TRYING TO GET SOME DINNER

After school, I went straight home. There was not really enough time to play. Mom expected me to have a pot of rice ready before she arrived home from work.

She spent her days working at a tobacco factory, stringing bundles of tobacco leaves to hang onto long sticks for drying in curing barns. She left early in the morning for work and would come home exhausted very late in the afternoon, smelling of tobacco resin. She did not have enough energy and time to cook supper.

Sometimes there was nothing to eat with the rice. On those days, I ran to Aunt Li's house to see what they were having. I asked for food to take back to my family. Most nights I took home a bowl of pork or chicken soup, still hot, one hand holding the cover. Occasionally, the maids prepared roasted or barbecued chicken or a small portion of roasted pig for us.

At night, the streets could get pitch black very quickly. Only a few houses had electricity to help illuminate the streets and dark alleys. I walked on the side of the street to avoid being hit by tricycles, jeepneys, and trucks. But one night, a huge truck pulled over near me, making a complete stop. The two men extended their arms down, trying to pick me up. I could not see their faces, just that they were very close to my shoulders. I scooted as fast as I could away from their arms, while careful to not spill the soup.

I ran as if my feet never touched the ground. I did not stop and didn't look back. I ran down the block, turned the corner, and ran between houses, until I reached home, panting and struggling to catch my breath. I set the bowl of soup on the floor.

"What is wrong with you?" Mom asked. "What took you so long?"

"Two men in a truck tried to grab me!" I cried. "I ran as fast as I could." I was still panting and feeling panicked.

"It's good you ran away, but why did you leave so late?" Mom asked, worried.

"The soup was not yet ready, and I had to wait!" I cried, shaking, still in shock.

"You did the right thing. Don't go out late at night again. There are many evil men out there kidnapping children," Mom said.

When I settled in for dinner, I had lost my appetite and could not eat. I just watched my family enjoy their meal. The scenario of the truck stopping next to me on the side of the road,and the two men about to snatch me up, haunted my sleep for hours as well.

The next day, I told my best friend, Kristy, what had happened. "Oh yeah. Beware of those bastard rapists," she said. "If they catch a kid, they will rape and then sell us to China where they'll turn us into slaves or prostitutes."

EARTH WORMS

Later in the afternoon, I found Dad in the kitchen with his friends, Pamboy and Andres. They were discussing what to do with a bucket full of earthworms they'd collected.

"We could make teriyaki out of them," my dad said enthusiastically.

"But they taste better if we squeeze the guts out," Andres said, apparently an authority on the subject.

Pamboy, who lived nearby, went back to his house to fetch fresh garlic and scallions. Andres stayed with Dad to help squeeze each worm's guts out. They'd pick one up, squeeze it, clean it, and put it in a big pot for a final rinse.

All of a sudden, Dad told me to run to the store to buy a cup of vinegar and a cup of soy sauce. He handed me five pesos. That was the first time he had ever handed me paper money. I did not question how he got it.

While I was getting two empty jam jars out of the cupboard, he said, "While you're at the store, buy two bottles of gin as well."

I knew then why he handed me a large sum of money, what he was really interested in. I put on my flip-flops, put my empty jars into a canvas bag, and left.

Outside, I saw Pamboy coming back towards our house with cloves of garlic, a bundle of scallions, and half a bottle of gin. I walked to the store, asked Mr. Berney for the items I needed, and handed him the five pesos.

"Oh, now you have money, eh?" he remarked and then paused. After a moment, he said, "What is your father up to now?"

"He and his friends are cooking teriyaki worms," I replied.

'Is that so? Well, you tell that father of yours that your family owes me money. Tell him to pay his debt of almost fifty pesos worth of food." He sounded annoyed.

"Ah, that money belongs to Mr. Pamboy, Mr. Berney," I lied then, afraid to face my father with the message or without the gin. "It did not come from my dad. My family does not have any money to pay you right now, Mr. Berney."

"You just handed me five pesos, my dear. Your father must have money," he insisted.

"No, sir, it's borrowed money," I tried again.

"You just tell your father that I will not give him the bottles of gin, the soy sauce, or the vinegar until he pays the rest of his debt." He wasn't budging.

"But Mr. Berney, he really needs to have those ingredients to cook the worms he collected." At least I could try to get the other ingredients and forget about the gin.

"You tell your father I don't give a rat's ass about his worms, even if they came right out of his ass. You tell him that. And you tell him to pay his debt. Your family will not be sold any more items from my store until I am paid. Do you hear me?"

"Yes sir, I hear you," I said, but I did not dare go home empty-handed. Dad and his friends had already started preparing the worms. I didn't want Dad to get mad and cause trouble in the neighborhood. I did not want Dad to fight with Mr. Berney. On the other hand, I did not want Dad to drink more gin and maybe hurt my mother later. I felt trapped.

"Ok, forget about the bottles of gin, Mr. Berney. Just let me have the vinegar and soy sauce, and I will do my best to convince my dad to pay our debts." I swore and pleaded and promised, "I will convince Dad." I did not plan to leave his store until he agreed. I knew he would give me something, and I was determined to at least bring home the soy sauce and vinegar. I waited, and I kept badgering him, promising to tell Dad to pay up.

Finally, he gave in. "I will give you the soy sauce and vinegar, but no bottles of gin and no more borrowing from my store until you people pay off your debts." He was plainly irritated.

I left as soon as he handed me the sauce and vinegar, and I hurried home.

Dad and his friends were in the living room now, waiting for my return. The empty gin bottle and a shot glass sat on the floor between them. I handed my dad the jars of vinegar and soy sauce.

"Where are the bottles of gin?" he growled.

"They don't have any in stock, Dad. And Mr. Berney said you still owe him fifty pesos from goods we've gotten on credit," I blurted out in front of his friends, hoping their presence might stop him from smacking me. "He kept the rest of the money to put toward your debt."

He was quiet. Perhaps he felt embarrassed because I had put him on the spot in front of his friends.

Pamboy reached into his pocket and gave me twenty pesos. "Here, go to another store and buy a couple—no, make that three—bottles of gin."

I grabbed the canvas bag and the money and took off in the other direction, toward the market. The other store was located near the marketplace, but it was in a big house that was farther away, so I ran to make the trip faster.

The entire first floor of the house was packed with merchandise of all kinds, made to look like a mini mart, while the owner and his family lived upstairs.

I told the clerk I wanted to buy three bottles of gin, a popsicle, a toffee, and a cola. She gave me my order and the change, which I put in my pocket. I enjoyed the popsicle on my way home.

When I arrived home and opened the front door, the appetizing aroma of sweet teriyaki was already permeating the whole house. Dad had also deep-fried some of the worms to a crisp. I handed over the gin bottles and decided to be quiet about the change. Dad, Pamboy, and Andres took turns putting fried worms in their mouths followed by a shot of gin.

They called Mom to come downstairs and taste the delicacies. Mom politely refused. Dad asked her again to come down. She did. Dad handed her a shot of gin.

"No, thank you." Mom flatly refused. "I don't drink and you know it."

"Here, just one shot. Come on." He held out the gin.

"I better not," Mom said.

Both of Dad's friends encouraged her to just try it once in her life.

"It won't kill you," one kept repeating.

"It will calm your nerves," the other said.

"Come on. Here, try it," dad insisted. "Only one time. You just drink it fast."

"All at once," his friends chimed in.

Mom gave in and drank the shot really fast. Her face contorted. She turned and threw up. Dad and his friends started laughing.

"Don't throw it up," one of them groaned.

"How can you stand that bitter taste? And so strong!" she cried.

They offered her a worm again to taste. The food, the drink, and, most likely, the men disgusted Mom, so she went back upstairs.

Dad never bothered to ask my brother or me if we wanted to taste teriyaki worms. Not that it mattered. I would never touch one anyway. Dad and his friends hung out all night, chatting away until early in the morning.

I happily collected the four empty gin bottles to sell in order to add to my pocket money.

Mom woke up with swollen eyelids and lips, a reaction to the alcohol. She looked like a catfish, and she had red patches of rash all over her body.

DI

Most of the time, I wondered where my brother was. I never knew whose house he was visiting, or how he fed himself at lunch. One day, during recess in third grade, I looked for Di in his class. I wanted to see where he was and how he was doing. I saw father arrive at the school, unannounced and drunk.

"Where is my son's classroom?" Dad yelled in the hallway for everyone to hear. He just walked right onto the school campus. I could recognize his voice a mile away.

Swinging doors open in each classroom, he barged in while class was in session, demanding, "Where is Ferdinand? Is he here?" he asked the teacher. Di's legal name was Ferdinand.

A student pointed to the classroom where my brother was, and my dad invited himself in. I crept behind and watched, mortified. All eyes turned to him as he stood next to brother, leaning against the desk to stay upright. A student sitting next to Di stood up quickly to give his chair to Dad.

"Let me hear him answer a math question, Teacher!" he instructed the man. "Go on. Ask him a math question, and let me hear his answer. If he can."

All of the students stayed quiet.

The teacher was obviously unsure what to do with the drunken man in his classroom. "Brother, the class is in session. Please go home and get some rest," he politely reasoned.

He had never met my dad, and there was no security guard on campus to help him whisk a drunk out of his class. Adamantly, Dad demanded to hear one math question answered, and then he would leave. My brother, meanwhile, had turned pale white and was shaking. Encouraged by this promise, the teacher gave my brother a problem, one that would be easy to answer.

"Okay, Ferdinand," asked the teacher, "what is one plus one?"

"Eleven," my brother answered.

Gales of laughter filled the room and echoed out into the corridor.

Wham! Dad slapped the back of my brother's head with such force that his forehead hit the desk. Half the class thought the scene was hilarious. The other half did not. They sat shocked, staring in disbelief.

Dad stared at my brother for a while, his face showing his disapproval.

My brother stared straight at the blackboard, holding back tears.

The teacher was stunned, frozen. Dad still stared at my brother until the teacher asked him to leave again. I could stand it no longer, and squealed from where I stood watching from outside the classroom window. I saw tears or maybe sweat running down the side of brother's face. Di was still refusing to meet my father's gaze. I was so scared of what Dad might do next. The teacher walked to where dad sat and asked him again politely to step outside, that they could take care of the problem from there. Dad continued to stare at my brother as he rose from the seat and walked toward the door.

I ran in the opposite direction, towards the school's bathroom, miserable for my poor brother. In the bathroom, the stench of urine burned my nostrils. I pinched my nose so I didn't breathe in the fowl, strong odor. There were no toilets, no windows, just concrete walls and a concrete floor that dipped down a little towards the hole in one corner where urine escaped to the sewer. The girls had to just squat wherever there were the fewest puddles and do our business.

I could not stay in there all day, so I quietly peaked my head out to make sure I didn't run into my father. He could be heading toward my classroom, looking to humiliate me next. If he found me there in class, he might do the same thing he did to my brother. I did not see father anywhere in the hallways or yard, so I hurried back to my classroom. Luckily, when I got there, class had not yet started. The students were noisily gossiping. I sat dumbfounded, staring at the blackboard, my mind and heart focusing on nothing but my brother. *What might Dad do to him when we get home?* I knew he wasn't finished with my brother yet. That night I did not need to ask what was going on in my brother's mind. I could see by the redness of his eyes that he had been crying. I was petrified for him, yet helpless, powerless to do anything

for him. I went to the kitchen and started to cook rice.
But Dad did not come home that night.

The next day was humiliating for both my brother
and me. Kids were cruel, calling him 'eleven' and teasing
him. Some even laughed so hard they pissed their pants.
To his defense, I told brother I would kick their asses all
the way to China.

ANOTHER BABY

Mom was pregnant again. I hated her for it. I hated
being close to her and her big stomach, feeling sorry for
myself because I knew I would have to do extra chores,
like babysitting, which meant less time playing and
more time at home.

Custom dictated that, since I was the oldest, it
was my filial duty to tend to my younger siblings.
Since hospitals cost money, a midwife neighbor and
Grandmother helped with the birth. Dad was instructed
to boil water, fan my mother, and wipe sweat from her
brow. It was also his job to bury the placenta in the
backyard. Sober for once, he obediently followed all of
their commands.

"It's a girl!" exclaimed Grandmother, as if this was
some sort of miracle.

I was downstairs by the foot of the stairs, waiting, when I heard a tiny voice squalling. Then it stopped. I climbed the stairs and knocked on the door.

"Can I come in?" I asked, curious to see what the baby looked like.

"Hold your horses!" Grandmother warned from behind the closed door.

I descended the stairs again and went outside, where I tilted my head up to the sky, seeing shapes of the clouds. I studied a solitary coconut tree, tall and proud, sprouting husks with small nuts and larger nuts. Cast around on the ground were old, brown coconut husks, germinating, while others were ready for replanting. Dad opened the door with a big, silver bowl in his hands, a bloody towel hanging over the side. It must have been the placenta. I climbed back up the stairs and crawled next to Mother and the newcomer.

My new baby sister had very dark brown skin, big eyes and thick, black hair, as if she was wearing a toupee. Dad named her Wilma.

FIFTH GRADE & GRADUATION

By fifth grade, I was a Girl Scout leader and still ahead of the class. At the end of the year, my teacher announced that I was to be decorated with a special ribbon at our graduation ceremony. Everyone was talking about what a big celebration it was going to be, an occasion where all the students and teachers would wear brand new clothes and shoes. There would be music and dancing. The honor roll students would be called up onto the stage while proud parents and the entire neighborhood watched them claim their honors. The date and time of graduation and the names of students who would get acknowledged were announced in class.

I felt very proud of myself on my way home, and I told my mom the news. Dad was home, sober and quiet, listening. I told them I needed new clothes. Mom apologized and said we could not afford a new dress and new shoes, but said that I could go ask Aunt Li to buy me the things I needed.

Still feeling excited, I ran as fast as I could to Aunt Li's house. As soon as I got there, a maid stopped me and asked why I was barefoot. I told her I needed to talk to Aunt Li about my graduation and begged her to let me through.

"You are not to come inside the house until you get your feet clean," she demanded. She said she had just polished the floor and did not want my dirty feet leaving grimy footprints.

I ran at the back of the house and, sitting by the pump, rubbed the soles of my feet as hard as I could against the coarse concrete. I lathered a blue bar of Ajax soap onto my feet and scoured the soles again on the rough cement until the thick callouses and crusted dirt on the sides and soles of my feet rubbed off. It took me almost a half hour. I slipped on a pair of flip-flops that were by the back entrance.

I looked for the maid in the kitchen and showed her my clean feet. She gave me approval to be in the house. I walked carefully across the clean floors in my bare but clean feet and went to find Aunt Li. When I found her, I told her about my graduation, how I'd be called on stage as an honor student. I asked if she could act as my guardian to pin my honorary ribbon on me up on the stage.

Without hesitation, she told Aunt Ud, who was also there, to buy fabric and sew me a brand new dress. She also promised to buy me all the rest of a special outfit. My eyes went big and my mouth dropped open. I could not believe it! A dress made just for me—not a hand-me-down of Cousin Violet's! She also said she would buy my brother clothes and shoes for graduation. I was so overjoyed that I could not sleep that night. I was too excited to stop my brain from whirling, imagining graduation day. I couldn't wait.

Aunt Ud went to the store early the next morning and came back in the afternoon with brand new shoes for me. She had a new t-shirt and shorts for my brother, as well as socks and shoes for him too. I was so overwhelmed by her kindness that I could not stop thanking her. In her living room, Aunt Ud started measuring me for the dress and busied herself making it. Aunt Li instructed one of the maids to call the manicurist to curl my hair.

When graduation day arrived, my brother and I were so happy and excited that we could hardly stand it. All the students were dressed in their finest clothes and for once, we were, too. I was called up on stage two times because I received the highest honor. My chin high, and a big smile on my face, I walked proudly onto the stage in my beautiful yellow dress that Aunt Ud made especially for me. It was long, touching the tops of my shiny new black shoes. Aunt Li walked with ease and sophistication onto the stage in a stylish black-and-white checked dress with sunflowers here and there. It showed off her shapely legs.

"Look to your left. Smile for the camera and ignore your father," she whispered as she pinned on my ribbon. I looked the direction she said to, gave a half smile to the camera, and saw the bright flash, and then I looked passed the camera and saw Dad, looking tipsy, at the back.

The audience applauded and another flash illuminated the stage. I saw Dad approaching through the crowd.

"He'p, he'p, out o' my way!" He shouted loudly, drunk as a skunk. He was either proud of me, or just wanted to be a part of the scene.

Mom, in the front row seat, held the new baby, Wilma, on her lap, my brother Di and Bebeng next to her. I felt proud and courageous as I walked off the platform and sat next to my family, the ribbon pinned near my heart. It was the most wonderful feeling a child of ten could ever experience, and I've cherished the memory ever since.

Dad appeared in front of me. I looked up.

"Is Di graduating?" he wondered, uncertain if my brother had passed fourth grade. "Is he graduating?"

I felt mortified.

All students who completed the grade with satisfactory performance were then called to stage. At last my brother's name was called—the one my dad was waiting for. I gave a big sigh. I, too, was not sure if he had made it out of fourth grade. As soon as his name was called out over the microphone, he stood up to climb onto the stage. Dad walked away, in the opposite direction. He did not even stay to watch him go on stage.

After the ceremony, disco music blared into the night. Parents, teachers, students, and visitors danced while others helped themselves to refreshments. The school had invited parents to bring any special dish to share for the potluck. I forgot to tell my mother about that part—maybe afraid in my heart that she would say no anyway. We were the only family who did not bring food. Luckily Aunt Li donated cases of Coca Cola, orange soft drinks, and other treats. I figured my family could take some credit for her contributions. Since she was, after all, a relative.

DAD'S ALCOHOL

Around ten or eleven o'clock, as we were getting ready for bed, we heard Dad hollering "HEP!" as he kicked a big rock down the street on his way home. It seemed he wanted to wake everyone in our small community. As I heard him approaching our house, I lay wide awake and nervously anticipated what he might do to us when he got home.

A wick lamp in a jam jar sat on the table, giving off a weak glow. I sat up and stared around me. I heard

Mother snoring. Di's eyes remained closed, but he had to have heard Dad's voice. It was so loud. Our two sisters were deep asleep. The burning lamp was getting weaker, almost out of oil.

"*He'p!*" Dad yelled out again, followed by the sound of a big rock rolling on the road like thunder. Either dad was yelling for help, being a nuisance, or inviting someone for a fight. Whatever the purpose, his voice drew nearer the house and my heart thundered in my chest. As soon as I heard him climbing up the front steps to the house, I hurriedly lay back down and pulled the blanket over my head, pretending to sleep.

"*He'p!*" he called one more time as he climbed the stairs. "Di! Xulli! Get up! Get your books and start reading. Do you hear me!"

My brother and I lit another wick lamp that had a bit more oil in the jar, got out our books, and circled around the light. We started reading out loud so he could hear us. Our voices trembled as we read. I was so nervous that what I read made no sense to me. My brother read from his book while I read from mine, different stories. It was a jumble.

After three pages, I paused and peeked at him to see if he had passed out yet. No, he was still sitting by the door, leaning against the wall, head bowed. He lifted his head. I read aloud again, until I heard him snoring, head almost touching his feet. His body slowly dropped to the floor. I waited a couple more minutes, watching him to make sure he did not suddenly sit up. It was getting very late. Mom, who had woken, motioned us back to bed. We stopped reading. I blew out the lamp, and we hurried into our covers. We heard Dad snoring and hoped we were safe.

At times like those, Mom sat up all through the night, keeping vigil. I knew she would keep us safe, or try to. I woke up occasionally and saw her still sitting in the same position. She had not moved or changed position. I wondered if she had had any sleep at all. She worried that if she fell asleep, Dad might wake her with a big kick to her stomach or chest as had happened in the past. I dozed off again.

Morning came too quickly. I looked at my mother, head bowed to her knees, asleep in her sitting position. I got out of bed, took the covered pot full of urine downstairs and dumped it in the outhouse. Like the good little girl I was, I wanted to help Mother and not wait for her to tell me what to do. I rinsed the bucket and left it out to dry, to be taken upstairs later for use the next night. It was understood that if anyone of us needed to have a bowel movement, we had to use the outhouse. Mostly, we were able to hold it until morning. I hated going outside in the night, being feasted on by giant, hungry mosquitos while taking a poop. Besides, it was scary in the dark. Weird noises, movements in the bushes behind the outhouse, were enough to send the shit right back up the colon. We had no such thing as a flashlight, only two jam jars with wicks as lamps. Wick lamps don't give off bright lights that can be pointed at any distance like flashlights. It was hard to see even ten feet with them. Best to take a dump during the day.

QUEST FOR A MAGAZINE TURNS INTO MORE

Uncle Eddie once borrowed *Liwayway,* a magazine from a neighbor across the street. But he refused to lend it to us for fear he would never see it again. I really liked this magazine and asked Uncle Eddie for it, but he just scowled at me. I ran outside my grandparents' house and headed for Cousin Violet's. Once there, I roamed through the house, looking for a magazine. I searched in Aunt Li's room, where she was likely to leave one on her bedside table. Sure enough, I spotted one there. I looked around to make sure no one saw me, then hurriedly put the magazine flat against my belly under my shirt. I also found coins scattered on her bedside table. I hid four quarters under my tongue, and put dimes inside my ears. I walked out as quietly and calmly as I could, smiling and waving my empty arms as if I was just strolling along. As soon as I rounded the corner, I spat out the coins and ran as far as I could, then took the dimes out of my ears. I walked to the nearest Mom and Pop store, where I bought myself and my brother popsicles and sweets. I stuffed four popsicles and rock candy into my pockets. They bulged as I walked home, the magazine still safe, flat against my stomach, tucked down into my underpants. At home, I emptied my pockets and shared the popsicles and candies with my brother. I savored every bite, licking the dripping popsicles while I read, for the first time, a story about Kling-Kling.

KLING-KLING & A GROWING LOVE OF READING

Kling-Kling was a story about a baby mermaid discovered by a fisherman and brought home to his childless wife. The poor fisherman went about his usual routine: up at dawn to fish in the Pacific, when, late in the afternoon, while gathering up his fishing net, he heard a baby crying on the nearby rocks. He stopped what he was doing and looked around. There was no one around, and he could only see other fishermen far into the distance. He ignored the crying and continued what he was doing. He had caught a lot of fish that day. He and his wife would sell them to the market and whatever remained unsold, they would eat. When he was done gathering his things and had moored his boat, he threw strings of fish of all different kinds and sizes over his shoulders and headed for home. As he walked barefoot along the shore, he heard another loud cry which sounded like an injured infant. Again, he looked around him and could see nothing but rocks, could hear only the waves crashing onto the shore. There was nobody else around. The crying kept on, and he followed the sound. There, in between big rocks, in an oval tin can, lay a tiny child wrapped in seaweed and kelp. A perfect baby girl stared at him, her hands clasping and legs kicking the kelp away with her perfect feet. The fisherman, stunned and speechless, panicked. He did not know what to do. To be continued . . .

Man, the popsicles were gone and the story was not yet finished! I stormed out of the house and left my brother and sisters home alone. I must look for the magazine with the next part of the series. I promised myself I would return the magazine the next day. I would hide it under my shirt again and put it back where I found it. Returning to Aunt Li's, I looked around, trying to find where the next magazine might be. In Aunt Li's bedroom? The living room? The kitchen? I even snuck into the maid's room looking for it. No luck. I went home disappointed, but hopeful. I knew the continuation of the story must be upstairs in my cousin's bedroom. I knew she, too, would be following the story. As I walked home, I promised myself I would find out what happened next.

THE PAINS OF POVERTY & BULLYING

Poverty hurts. When you don't have a cent and everyone else seems to have more, it's painful. But bullying hurts even more, especially if the bully is an uncle or a cousin. It started when I was only five years old. I was called "scaly"

by two of my uncles. I was born with hyper-pigmentation
and had scaly, dry skin from my neck all the way down
my legs. My hands and feet are crinkled with lines that
resemble an old lady. My skin was not at all like my
brother's or sisters', cousins' or friends'. My legs were
so dry, they looked like road maps and resembled the
outside of a cantaloupe, only with big, white flakes. I
would wet them, but as soon as the water dried, the lines
looked dry and flaky again. I kept splashing water on
them. The idea was useless. I tried using the coconut
oil that Mother, and sometimes grandmother, prepared
especially for me, but it only made my skin look very
shinny, and just as lined and weird as ever. My parents
had no money to buy emollients or any type of special
hydrating lotion to prevent the scale formations. After
having played outside under the sun with the coconut
oil all over, my skin turned dark brown quickly, but the
mapping was still there.

I resented Mom for not being able to afford the
right lotion which would keep my skin, hands and feet
moist. Cousin Violet had plenty in her bedroom. Oh,
what a sight, whenever I saw her lather her beautiful,
perfect, creamy white skin with Johnson & Johnson's pink
lotion. The fragrance permeated throughout the house,
smelling of fresh, clean skin. When I'd ask for some,
"Just a little," she gave me a squirt. That's all. A squirt. I
spread that squirt as far as it would go on my arms and
legs, trying to make it cover my entire skin, and leaving
it without washing for two, sometimes three days before
I had to take a shower. Eventually, I stopped begging for
a squirt and started sneaking into to her room when she

was out shopping with her mother. I helped myself to more than a squirt, lathered it all over my body.

All year round, my dry, flaky skin was an embarrassment. I had no jeans or pants to wear when I went out, so it they just hung out there for the whole world to see.

"Hey, *Kaliskis* (scaly), you have the legs of a chicken. Sure do," Uncle Toy would greet me, while his brother, Uncle Eddie, laughed in the background.

As I looked up, he sneered, laughing in my face. I tried not to let their name-calling get to me, and walked away with a lump in my throat. But, it did get to me. I questioned God for giving me this curse, printed on my skin for all my life. I told my mother what the uncles called me.

"Mom, they are teasing me again," I cried.

"I'm so sorry, Xulli. What can I do? I don't know what else to do to change your skin. I would do it in a heartbeat if I could." There was pain in her voice. "Try to forgive them, Xulli. You must ignore them. They are stupid and ignorant and don't know any better."

Whenever the subject of my skin came up, she just apologized profusely and sometimes blamed herself for not knowing what to do. As a child, I heard her apologize a lot. Whenever the uncles passed by and saw Aunt Ud applying merthiolate on the infected cracks in the soles of my feet, or rubbing coconut oil on my arms and legs, they shouted, "Scaly!"

Then they'd sneer, "Not enough coconut oil in the world would get rid of your *kaliskis*."

Once, Uncle Eddie approached me. I feared what he might do. He slid his hand along the roughness of my arm and tried plucking the scales off with his nails as if confident he could solve my problem with one pricking. I pulled my arm away, pushing his hand from me. His mouth twisted with contempt as I walked away.

"Quit your teasing!" Aunt Ud said irritably. "She can't help being born that way!"

These defending words meant a lot to a child. A few kind, protective words against my tormentors meant brief freedom and good spirits to a child self's well-being. Momentarily, they gave me comfort. Unfortunately, the effects of her reprehension were short-lived. The uncles' brains could not grasp or process deep sympathy or the misfortune of others, despite repeated warnings and chastisements for their insensitive remarks. They continued their name-calling when I was alone, when they knew my protector was not around. How I wished I could make them or myself disappear.

At least, one bit of exhilarating news came one day. I found out my tormentors, Uncle Eddie and Uncle Toy, would be leaving for the big city, Manila. Uncle Eddie was to study at one of the universities and Uncle Toy was going to look for work. The great news gave me a big sigh of relief. I would not have anyone reminding me of my skin imperfections, making fun of them and calling me names. They wouldn't be there teasing and laughing at me anymore. What a joy it would be not to see them as often. They were to live with their oldest sister, Aunt C, in the Big City. This would leave me with only two uncles, the younger ones. I did not mind them because they were quiet types and never bullied or teased. They only spoke if spoken to. I could handle them better than the two bullies. Secretly, I was savoring the news and celebrating inside, feeling unutterably euphoric. I skipped, hopped, and jumped along the sidewalk, as if a heavy weight had been lifted from my shoulders.

PORK FOR DINNER

In the house, Dad was cooking supper. I was surprised. He said we were going to have a delicious dinner of roasted *adobo (teriyaki) pork*. I could not wait! I started salivating. Never mind where he got the meat. The fact that we had red meat for supper was all that mattered. Only once in a great while did we have red meat because it was expensive. I helped Mom cook the rice, then set plates on the floor, and a basin of clean water into which we wash our hands. Since we had no forks or spoons, we used our hands to pick up food.

We gathered in a big circle around the kitchen floor to eat. The washbasin was passed around from one person to the next to wash his or her hands before we ate. A bowl of steamed, white rice was placed on each plate in front of us, as we waited for our portion of roasted teriyaki pork. The aroma made our stomachs growl as we watched the steam from the rice rise up. We breathed it in. The meat had been chopped up into cubes. The teriyaki dish even had laurel leaves, giving off their aroma and blending with the roast pork.

Dad had already shared a portion of the meat with his two brothers and parents. The rest was left for us to enjoy. My brother and I were so hungry that we paid little attention to our parents talking. We ate as if we had never been fed before. We had such a delicious feast. At the end, our bellies were so full that all we could do was take turns burping.

After, I helped Mom collect and wash the dishes and then swept the kitchen floor. Out of the blue, Mom asked Dad where he had gotten the money to buy such delicious meat. He said he did not buy it, that he and his buddies killed and roasted a black Labrador.

I froze and stopped sweeping mid-swing of the broom. My mom went mute, and her mouth dropped. He kept going with this story, of how he had stolen the neighbor's dog, that the neighbor still did not know his dog was in pieces in our bellies.

"I don't want to hear anymore," Mom protested and walked out.

I wanted to throw up. My mind racing with thoughts of the dog's master or its family looking for him. Dad sat leisurely cleaning his teeth with a soft twig from a guava tree on the floor by the open kitchen door, inhaling the cool breeze coming in, belly full of dog meat and steamed rice. He was very well aware that Mom hated eating dog meat. I guess he figured the only way to get her to eat it was if she didn't know.

He continued picking his teeth with a wooden toothpick, seeming very pleased with himself. Occasionally he turned his head to his right and spit out extracted small pieces of food particles from between his teeth. As I watched him, my mind revisited the time when we were living in Paranaque. What had happened to Di's little pup? Did it also make it into our bellies?

CASSAVA AND TAPIOCA ROOTS

The following morning, Grandfather came over to our house and gave Dad a burlap sack full of cassava roots that grew abundantly in his backyard. Grandfather had harvested the cassava roots before they matured and went bad.

Mom washed them at the pump, scrubbed them with a brush to get the dirt off each woody shrub, and put them all to boil in one big pot. Once it was boiled, Dad helped peel the skin off and placed them into a grinder to make tapioca. Mom fed the roots in small pieces into the portable grinder as Dad cranked the handle. Beads of sweat stood out on Dad's forehead as he switched from one arm to the other. He continued cranking the lever until the smooth dough emerged. Mom then cooked the ground cassava tapioca with coconut milk and cane sugar. She sliced cakes of it into small pieces and wrapped them individually into heated banana leaves. Then she sent me to sell them door-to-door for cash.

"Don't give too many for a quarter," she instructed, as she showed me how much money I was to receive for a piece of tapioca cake.

Carrying the flat basket of cakes balanced on my head, I stepped outside. I walked for miles, yelling, "Cassava tapioca!"

I kept walking and yelling all the way to the river, where I boarded a bamboo boat with the basket of cassava on my lap, and crossed to get to the other side of town. I made sure no splashes from the river contaminated my product.

When we reached the other side, I paid the boat driver, stepped out, and walked farther north of the city of La Union, to the small town of Paratong to find more buyers. I knocked on people's doors and asked if they were hungry for cassava cake. I walked around the neighborhood of the small town of Paratong, determined to sell all the cakes. I rested occasionally to catch my breath under a shady tree, and let my feet relax in the coolness of the white sands before walking on. I appreciated the tropical tranquility of the bamboo trees, swaying in the wind, branches cracking, leaves fluttering soft melodies. Just a few steps away from me was the blue Pacific Ocean. I watched the waves come closer and then disappear in the white sands.

I knew going home with cakes unsold was bad business, so I pushed on, yelling even louder so my voice could travel far. Occasionally, I peeked into the basket to check the cakes. They looked and smelled delicious, and they made my mouth water. Finally I helped myself to one. A little farther on, I had another. I hated myself afterwards, and also wished I'd brought along a bottle of water to drink. By late afternoon, I had a third and a fourth sampling. When no other customers responded to my calls, I decided to go home.

Tired and thirsty, I crossed the river again, satisfied with the amount of money in my pocket. Mom would be very happy, a grin coming to my face. And Dad would be proud of me, I thought, as I watched the boatman push the boat against the current with a long bamboo stick. With both hands, he pulled up the long stick from under the deep water and plunged it in on the other side to propel the boat back across to my side of town. I tried to peer deep down into the water to see fish, like I had near my first home, but it was too dark and scary. I did not know how to swim. So I sat still in the middle of the raft, not wanting to fall over the side. When the boat reached land, I paid the boatman twenty-five cents and walked home, proud, with more than twenty pesos in my pocket.

As soon as I got to our house, I handed over the money and leftover cakes to my mom. She was amazed at how good a little vendor I was, and was happy that I made more money than she'd expected. Dad was not home. I was dead tired from all the walking. I headed to the pump to wash my legs and feet, feeling like a grown up.

FIGHTING AT HOME

One day, after starting the rice for our supper, I was downstairs playing with my brother and sisters. I heard Mom and Dad talking upstairs. Dad's voice sounded like he was questioning Mom. She was trying to reason with him, but it sounded like it was no use. Dad's voice got louder as he interrogated her. Mom stopped answering. I heard a commotion, a slap, and then a yelp from Mother followed by a heavy thud. The noises increased, as though my parents were wrestling on the bamboo floor.

Scared, I ran up the stairs. Mom was on her back. Dad was on top of her and was pulling her hair as she tried to get away from him. I jumped at Dad's back, but he was bigger and taller than me. He was lean, but strong. He threw me across the room, and I hit the wall, sliding to the floor on my butt.

Quickly, I got up. "Mom, fight back!" I cried. "Please!" I yelled loudly to make sure she heard me. I wanted to encourage her to stand up and punch him where it hurts. *Do something. Don't take it.*

He punched her face as she tried to kick him. She was still on her back. She missed.

"Mom, kick him. Try again!" I screamed from a corner, hysterical. I ran down stairs and started yelling for help. "Somebody, help!" I screamed at top of my lungs, hoping someone, anyone could hear me, since houses were only a stone's throw away.

"Please come help! HELLLPP! Anyone! Please come!" I screamed as loud as I could, but no one seemed to hear my little voice. Mom was not fighting back. I heard her wailing, telling him to stop. I heard a blow, another yelp. A slap, a cry, and more thuds.

No one wanted to get involved. Standing still on the top step to our house, I looked around the neighborhood. No one came out. It looked deserted. Not even a dog was outside, yet I heard barking in the distance. Mom

managed to get up and run down the stairs, past me. I
saw her running away from the house, barefoot, until
she disappeared into the darkness. Dad rushed past me,
running after her. He, too, disappeared into the dark.
I stood still, hands gripping the rails, crying. I slowly
walked back inside.

"Where's the baby?" I asked my brother. He pointed
to the corner where Bebeng held the baby. She was
wrapped in a white blanket, sleeping. She had no
idea what had just happened. I saw my brother's eyes
glistening. Bebeng was quiet as a mouse.

Later that evening, I instructed Di to stay with
the baby and Bebeng. "No matter what happens,
do not leave."

He nodded.

"I'm going to look for Mom," I told him. "Do not go
out, you hear me?"

I headed out to Grandma's house. The house was
dark, but then I saw a soft glow coming from the kitchen
where grandfather sat alone at the dining table eating his
dinner. I came in and sat next to him, sobbing.

"Mom and dad had a fight," I told him.

He was quiet. The house was silent. Grandmother
and the uncles must not have been home. I did not know
where they were and I did not care. I asked if he knew
where they went. He did not answer.

"Can you please help me find her?" I pleaded.

He scooped up a handful of cooked rice from
the small pot in front of him, made it into a ball which
he dipped into a bowl of anchovy paste with chopped
tomatoes, and stuffed it into his mouth.

"I want my mom back," I cried louder. "I don't know where she went. Help me find her. Please!"

He dipped another rice ball and ate it. He then motioned me to eat with him, continuing to chew placidly. Again, I told him I needed to find Mom, tears streaming down my face. Still, he did not answer. Low in spirit, I gave up and left. It was already dark out, but I could still see the pathway home. The surrounding trees and shrubs were as black as the night sky.

At home, I told my brother and sister that Mom and Dad were not at Grandfather's house. I did not know where they were. The baby was still asleep, and my brother had stopped crying. He and I decided to go upstairs to bed. It was too dark to look for Mom at this point. At dawn, a chill wind woke me. I sat up. I was sharing covers with my sisters and brother. I saw Dad's figure sprawled on the floor by the door, fast asleep. I had not heard him come in.

Mom was not around. My eyes felt heavy, either from too much crying or too little sleep. Three days went by and Mom still did not show up. I did not know where she was. I stayed home a lot, watching for her. My friend Kristy came by once in a while to visit, but I was too busy running the household to play with her. I made rice milk for the baby by boiling rice with lots of water, then pouring the juice into a big thermos through a clean t-shirt to strain it.

Once I collected enough rice juice to last a couple of days to feed the baby, I left the thermos lid off to let it cool while I added more water into the pot of rice, and boiled more juice for the next day. I kept refilling the thermos and filled the baby bottle from it, adding sugar, if we had any, to sweeten it a little. I always cooled the bottle off by letting it sit in cold water before feeding it to the baby.

When we ran out of sugar, the baby sucked the bottle only a second, then threw it away onto the floor. She then let out a loud cry. I picked up the bottle, and I forced the nipple back into her mouth. She choked and pushed it away. I put it back in her mouth. The cycle continued until I pick her up and tried to quiet her down, placing her head on my shoulder. It was no use. I was getting angry and irritated with her. Then I squirted some into my mouth. It tasted sour. The thermos of rice milk had gone bad.

"Now what do I do with a hungry, crying baby?" I asked myself.

Her piercing cries hurt my ears. I covered them and screamed at her to shut up. She cried harder. I screamed at her again to stop it. It was no use. She cried even louder. I got up, left her upstairs and went down to the kitchen and put on rice with plenty of water, waited for it to boil. With her crying, the time it took for it to boil seemed like an eternity. I cleaned her bottle and nipple with a brush and soapy water, rinsed it well, and poured the rice juice into her clean bottle. Then I waited for it to cool, fanning it with a piece of cardboard to speed it up.

While I waited for it to cool, I picked her up and carried her downstairs. I tried talking to her to let her know her food was coming.

"Just be patient, will you?" I finally snapped when she continued to scream. "You'll get your milk as soon as it's cooled!" I shook the bottle, and it still felt hot. I tried to play with her, banging dishes and cups to distract her.

I put her down on the floor as I made musical sounds with spoons in front of her. She liked this and stopped crying. Before the rice milk could cool, she sobbed herself to sleep.

On the third day, when we woke, there was no food left. Dad had not returned after that first morning. I told Di to keep an eye on the baby while I went to Aunt Li's. As I approached the front gate, a maid greeted and told me to hush.

"Your mom has been hiding here," she whispered. "Make sure your father does not find out, or he will come barging in here and cause serious trouble."

"I promise," I assured her. I was grateful to know my mother was safe. I felt somewhat relieved knowing that she was not far away from us.

The maid led me to one of the extra bedrooms. She opened the door. A woman sat on the bed. She looked up quickly, not expecting a visitor. At first I did not recognize her. I tried to hold back tears, but they rushed out, flowing down my cheeks at her appearance. Black and blue bruises surrounded her eyes, and they were puffy and red as well. Her lower lip was cracked and swollen. She had bruises on her arms and legs. The soles of her feet were caked with mud and dirt, as if she ran across a rice paddy and never bothered to wash them.

"Close the door," she said, with longing in her eyes and voice. "Come closer."

I did as she told me.

"How are you kids doing?" she asked.

I kept my head bowed and did not answer for fear I might make a scene. She asked how my brother and sisters were. I told her they were fine. We were all fine and eating well, I lied. I did not want to worry her and add more to her depression. She told me to take good care of my brother and sisters for a while and to be a good girl. I promised her I would. I longed to get close to her, to hug her, kiss her. Just put my arms around her for a while and tell her I miss her so much, but felt hesitant.

I had a river of tears on my face as I listened to her tell me I had to be a big girl and take care of my siblings, since she could not come home. Not yet. She had to think of a plan, she said. I stood quietly, near the door, wiping tears with my t-shirt. I stared at the doorknob as I opened my heart and ears to her voice. I nodded to her instructions to let her know I heard every word she said, my side to her so she wouldn't see my tears. She said to go now and do as I was told. I opened the door and walked to the kitchen, wiping off the tears from my eyes and cheeks.

Aunt Li and Aunt Ud gave me something to eat and had put together food for me to take home to my brother and sisters. They also gave me a can of condensed milk for the baby. I knew from watching Mom how much condensed milk to put into the bottle of rice milk. If there was no rice milk, I would fill the bottle with warm water, add a tablespoon of condensed milk, and shake the bottle to make a thin milk. With the food I had brought home from Aunt Li's house, I divided it among sisters, brother, and me. Not giving any to Dad.

SICK BABY

A couple of days after I returned home from visiting
Mom at Aunt Li's, the baby started crying, mostly at
night. I did not know what to do. She had been crying a
lot, and her body felt hot. Finally, I went out searching
for Dad. I found him at his friend's house. He had been
hanging out with Pamboy and his friends. I found them
chatting like nothing was wrong. I told him the baby's
body felt hot.

He happened to be sober that day. He got up,
excused himself, and walked home. I followed behind.
At home, he picked up the crying baby. I was crying, too,
because I felt sorry for her.

Dad tried carrying her on his shoulder, but it did
not help. He tried changing her nappy. She had not had
a bowel movement for days, I told him. I knew because I
had not seen poop in her nappies for a while. Dad tried
singing to her.

For the first time, I heard him sing. I was surprised
by the softness of his voice, how tender his words were
to baby sister. I thought to myself, *Why can't he be like
this every day?*

He was a cruel man when he was drunk, but
compassionate when he was sober. He laid the baby on
the floor mat, pulled down her nappies. He told me
to hold the baby's body to stop her from moving and

wiggling. I did not know what he was planning to do. But his tender voice was trying to appease her. He checked her tiny form, her buttocks, then covered her and told me he would be right back. I tried talking to her, asking her to tell me what was wrong, but she just sobbed. I could only carry her around until dad returned. I put her head on my shoulder and sang, rocking our bodies to a lullaby.

Dad returned and told me to put the baby down on the floor again. I did as I was told. The baby was not crying anymore, just sobbing. He undid her nappies, and told me to hold sister's arms, her small body. He reached in his pocket and pulled out a small bottle. Uncapped it. He put oil on his index finger and inserted it inside the baby's anus. She screamed, and screamed at the top of her lungs. He pulled out a small piece of fecal matter. He tried again. The baby let out a big scream, and cried more than ever.

"I know. I know," he kept telling her, as if he knew what it felt like to have a finger inside one's anus. The baby's face had turned red, as she gave a long cry.

Kneeling, I begged Dad to stop. "It's hurting her, Dad!" I pleaded, in tears. "Please don't do it again."

He stopped, and I put on another clean nappy on her and covered her tiny body. I picked her up and carried her close to me, rocking her to hush. She whimpered, as if too exhausted, eyes closed. I could smell the mixture of poop, blood, and coconut oil he used to grease up his finger, as dad wrapped the dirty nappy and placed it aside. Before going downstairs to wash his hands, he told me to get rid of the dirty nappy later. I nodded to express I would obey.

He stood up and said he would be right back. I managed to put Wilma to sleep and laid her down on the floor. I grabbed the dirty nappy, went to the backyard, and threw the fecal matter out. I buried it and washed the cloth nappy.

Dad picked up the baby, and he told me to go to the neighbor store and ask for medicine. "Put it on a credit," he said.

Our list of credit bills was piling up. When unfolded, the list extended to about twelve inches long. The owner of the market showed me. Three months worth of unpaid bills.

"Tell your mother or father, would you?" She said sternly.

"But can you just please give me something for my sick sister?" I pleaded.

She said she did not have anything for the baby, that we should take her to a doctor. I went home and told dad. The baby was calmer now, asleep in her crib and sucking her bottle. The crib was made of a white bed sheet tied at both ends with a rope to a four-by-four structure. Dad was quiet with the baby, gently swaying the crib. I went downstairs to see if there was more condensed milk left in the can. I found an old can that I had been using, but it felt empty. I tilted the can and blew air forcefully into one small opening to let out the remaining milk on the bottom.

Finding a little, I poured water into the can, shook it, and poured the resulting milk into my sister's bottle for later use. Dad was too proud to send me to Grandma's or Aunt Li's for food.

"No child or family of mine is going to beg for food," he said angrily.

I said nothing as my stomach met my backbone, I just turned around and went to play outside.

That evening, I asked Dad, "When is Mom coming home?"

"Your mom is never coming home," he answered without feeling. "She's gone. She's not coming back. I don't want to see her face in this house!"

I began to cry. "No. Please don't say that. She's my mother."

"If you know where she is, you better tell me," he demanded.

"I don't know where she is. I swear," I said, shaking.

"Go take care of your sister," he growled, and I ran up to be close to her. I took over pushing and pulling her cradle gently. I heard him leave the house.

Luckily, Wilma started to get better. When we ran out of milk, I fed her cooled, boiled water with a teaspoon of sugar in it. Her body was not hot anymore. I played with her, drawing smiley faces on the back of my toes and wiggling them like puppets in front of her, changing my voice for each toe, which made her laugh. I carried her around the neighborhood, changed her nappy, gave her a quick bath, and put her back in her crib to sleep. While she slept, I played outside, staying right in front of the house. I knew I could not stray far, or I would get my butt whipped if father found out I left the baby home alone.

I continued the chores around the house, getting up early in the morning to gather sticks for the fire and piling them up to heat water. I went out back with the machete and looked for ripe plantain bananas to boil.

If I spotted sprouting green plants, resembling those of sweet potato leaves, that was an indication that there were potatoes underground. When I could, I hiked for about a mile or two searching for potatoes to fill up a bucket that I carried with me. As soon as it was full, I headed to the pump to wash off the dirt, and then I went home and boiled them. Simple tasks like boiling and cooking rice were all I knew about cooking, but I made sure not to burn down the house at least.

MOM S RETURN

As I walked into the kitchen one day, Mom was there tending to the baby. She had decided to return home. I was so overjoyed that I felt like dancing. But the celebration was short-lived. Dad's voice echoed in my ears.

"I do not want to see your mother in this house. Do you hear me?"

My excitement turned to a sour stomach, as I conjured up an image of what might happen if he found out Mom was home. I didn't know what to do. All I could think of was that he would hurt her again. *He'll hurt her again.* I was scared for her, for both of us. But, I loved being close to her. Bebeng came and clung to her side.

I felt happy. I wanted to keep feeling happy. *Just let it be,* I thought. I did not tell her what Dad had said. I did not want to tell her that she was not welcome at home, that she had better leave now before he came. I thought I should, but I was engulfed with longing for security and my mother's love. No one had told her the baby was sick. Our condition was not communicated to her, even when she inquired. Her seclusion must have been subsumed with the desire to be with her children, but everyone was too frightened for her.

I wondered why she hadn't fought back when Dad was pounding his fist into her face and body. *Where was her confidence and strength then? Why could she not talk back and kick his ass to kingdom come?*

Mom cooked some rice, but we had nothing else to eat with it. She asked me to go to the store and buy two raw eggs. She gave me coins for them. I ran to the neighbor's mini-store. The owner reminded me again to tell my parents about the bills piling up, that they needed to be paid soon or we would not be given any more credit. I went home with the two eggs and gave them to Mom. She had already put the steaming white rice into a big bowl. She cracked the eggs over the top of the steamed rice and stirred it. She put some in two bowls for Di and me, and spoon-fed Bebeng and the baby, blowing to cool it.

"Aren't you going to eat some, Mother?" I asked her.

"Never mind me," she said impatiently. "Just finish your food. I'd rather you and your brother get fed, put some meat on your bones. I'm all right." She circled her thumb and forefinger around our thin arms and compared us to toothpicks.

In the morning, Dad and Mom were downstairs in the kitchen. They must have talked.

The following night, we all settled in for sleep except Mom, who sat next to the baby. She looked down at her, deep in thought. Worried, perhaps. Then Dad came home, excited. He'd been out all day and came back very late and surprisingly sober. He pulled delicate decaying bones from a paper bag. With dirty hands, he laid pieces of bone on the floor.

"Bring the jar light closer, Xulli," he said, "and we'll take a look at these." They looked like tiny human bones.

"What are those?" Mom asked as she drew the wick lamp close to Dad. She grabbed the jar lamp from my little fingers. Dad held a scapula with clavicle still attached. He gave the piece to my mother and picked up the humerus. He examined it carefully in the light.

Then he told Mom to take a look at it and said, "These are Moon-ay's bones."

Mom nearly flipped. She was shocked, speechless. I could see her heart beating fast in her throat as she stared at dad, stunned. Her eyes grew moist.

"What are you doing with Moon-ay's bones?" she croaked, barely a whisper. "What are you doing? For God's sake, please put them all back!" Angrily, she handed back the tiny bones.

"I just wanted to examine them to see what might have caused her death," Dad explained calmly.

"For the love of God, PUT THEM BACK. Exactly as you found them!" she demanded, tears streaming down her face now. I picked up the bones and tried to wiggle the fractured scapula Dad was talking about. The bones were wiggly between the long fissures and I showed them to my brother, who was watching over my shoulder, curious.

"Fracture of the scapula was probably what killed her," Dad explained to Mom.

"There's nothing we can do now. She's gone!" Mom said angrily and started sobbing. "Xulli, give the bones back to your father now!"

I did as I was told.

"Take those bones back to her grave this instant!" she cried. "And I don't ever want to see them dug up again!" She was very clear. I handed the bones of my dead sister, Moon-ay, to Dad, who gently placed them inside the brown paper bag, rolled the opening closed, and headed out.

"He has no right to desecrate a child's grave! My baby's grave!" Mom sobbed as we heard Dad go out the front door. "Go back to sleep!" she instructed us, while she slumped in the corner, sobbing.

I had butterflies in my stomach as I lay curled up in bed. I did not know what to do or to say to her. We grieved separately. We were close and yet so far away from each other, in a distant faraway place, in the dead of night.

UNCLE ED RETURNS WITH A SURPRISE

I was searching for a new *Liwayway* magazine at Grandfather's house, when Uncle Eddie, one of my

bullies, arrived back from Manila. The rest of the uncles, Grandmother, Grandfather, Aunt Ud, Aunt Li, along with a couple of her maids, and some of the neighbors gathered in the living room to celebrate.

Uncle Eddie looked so grown up. Like an adult. I did not know whether to greet him, be happy he came back, or run and hide. I remained, observing from a corner. He brought along a male friend. A male boyfriend. His name was Natie (a nickname for Nate). They brought with them boxes of new household items: a portable stereo, new pots and pans, designer clothes and shoes, boxes of chocolates, bottles of wine and champagne, and what looked like stacks of fashion magazines in designer bags. My eyes wandered over their stuff as I listened in on the grown up discussion.

Everyone in the family had uncomfortable smiles on their faces, looking curious, confused, and inquisitive about this new friend. But tried to be polite, respectful. What did a city boy want with a poor country boy? How did they meet? The couple wanted to stay and sleep in one of Grandfather's bedrooms. Everybody eyed each other. They all talked about his being a homosexual, about his going public with it. Everybody was quiet, listening attentively, with forced smiles on their faces.

"Okay," Aunt Li got up and signaled everybody, "let the couple rest. They must be tired." She got up and shook Natie's hands. Then she called her maids over to pay the same respect. The rest of the neighbors followed. Some bowed and other elderly folks gave the couple their blessings. Mom gave her biggest welcome with a friendly smile. They spoke the same dialect, being from the southern part of the country. Dad left without saying a word.

"He's finally done it," Dad said to Mom later that day at home, as if he'd suspected. "He doesn't give a damn what people think. He's not ashamed. He's proud—him and his boyfriend staying right here in La Union. My brother's so fucked up." He was furious, and it was the first time I heard him say a bad word. "After all these years, he proved me right!"

"There's nothing you can do about it," Mom said. "It's the lifestyle he's chosen. It's his life, not yours. Leave him be."

"My brother? A faggot? Unbelievable!" Dad exclaimed. "I had better have a serious talk with him and his *boyfriend*," he said, determined, as he dressed to return to Grandfather's house.

"Do it tomorrow," Mother suggested. "There's plenty of time for more talk. Let them rest." She seemed more amused than anything else by the phenomenon.

The next morning, my grandparents, aunts and uncles again gathered in the living room, to formally meet the new visitor. They wore polite smiley faces, which, I thought, concealed shades of unease, a blend of excitement over the newness and the discomfort of the unknown. Everyone acted friendly, ready to talk of plans for the coming days.

After the meeting, they went their separate ways, all except Dad. He just sat, not saying a word. His silence made the couple uncomfortable.

"Well, I'm tired," Uncle Eddie blurted out as he stood. "And you must be exhausted," he said to Natie. They excused themselves.

Dad appeared mute as they headed to their room. His eyes followed the couple as they got up and left him by himself. The rest had gone to the kitchen and were whispering about the couple coupling. As tradition expected, the new couple were very private in their affection, but obviously in love and inseparable.

One morning, while visiting Grandfather's house, I saw Natie cooking deep fried duck, sweet and sour fish, and vegetable curry dishes. He was very busy in the kitchen while Uncle Eddie waxed the floors in the living room, bedrooms, and kitchen. Apparently they wanted the flooring to shine and smell of fresh, sweet sandalwood.

"Make 'em spic and span," Natie instructed Uncle.

Every day after that, the boyfriend cooked delicious meals for grandparents and uncles, as his payment for their welcoming him to their home and allowing him to become a part of the family. Every day they ate home cooked fish, vegetables, pork, and beef in rich sauces.

Grandfather was not saying much. He relished being served exquisite meals, so he had no complaints. He just ate what was given to him freely and enjoyed it.

Every time I entered a room, the floors were spotless and polished to a shine. I was asked to wipe my feet before walking in. Curtains, with designs of palm trees and beaches, were laundered and ironed by hand, and hung back up at each window. The aroma of lavish foods coming from the kitchen was a constant temptation.

Natie was industrious and never ran out of chores. He even laundered my grandparents' clothes and hung them to dry on a special clothesline he connected up in the backyard. He did all this work to pay respect to

my grandfather for letting them live free at his house.
Natie shared small portions of his cooking with my family
because he enjoyed my mother's company. He liked to
gossip with her about movie stars, the latest fashions, and
the community, while hemstitching a sleeve or crocheting
a mantel piece.

One day, I got up early as usual to hunt for duck
eggs in Grandfather's front and back yards. But first, I
thought I'd go upstairs to see if I could get into Natie and
Uncle Eddie's room to see them sleeping. With all the talk
about them, I was curious. The house was quiet. Everyone
was still asleep. My grandparents were in one room, and
the three other uncles shared another room. I passed the
others' doors before entering Uncle Eddie's and Natie's
room. I found them wrapped around each other under
one blanket on a twin size bed that was situated under
a mosquito net.

I thought they were still asleep and was surprised
to see them cuddled up so close, like one body with two
heads. I stood quietly in one corner as I studied the shape
under the covers. Perhaps one was on top of the other,
but they were not moving. After a while, I tiptoed out.

FAMOUS

After three months of living together at my grandfather's
house, Uncle Eddie and his boyfriend were the talk of the

town. Relatives and neighbors asked when they would get married, if they were considering getting a place of their own, and how long they planned to live in La Union. They remained at Grandfather's house for another three months until pressure started to build up around them.

Natie was too strict, a stern disciplinarian of Uncle Eddie's three younger brothers. They were instructed to take on household responsibilities and chores, such us washing their own dirty dishes and clothes, keeping the floors clean, helping out with wood chopping, and fetching water. Most unpopular of all, he demanded that they stop drinking so much.

When Dad was drunk, he accused Natie of having an affair with my mother because he always found Mom and Natie enjoying each others' company, speaking in the same dialect (called *Cebuano*), and laughing together. For a while, Natie disregarded Dad's accusations as foolish and did not let it bother him, but as time went on, Dad's accusation persisted. Dad finally called Mother a slut.

"With God as my witness, I have no reason or desire to sleep with a gay man!" she cried out loud. Unfortunately, Mom's reasoning fell on deaf ears. Every night, when Dad came home drunk, he was yelling about Natie this and Mom that.

Natie's temper was volatile, and he did not appreciate being accused of going to bed with a woman, especially my mother. She was the wife of his lover's brother. Finally one day, Natie could not take the allegations any longer. In the midst of doing laundry, he dropped the soapy clothes into the bucket, rinsed his hands, and stormed out of Grandfather's house. He crossed the road toward our house. About two feet from

our house, he started yelling my father's name, telling
him to come out and talk to him face-to-face.

As soon as Dad came out the door, Natie confronted
him loudly, telling him to keep his mouth shut, pointing
his finger in Dad's face. He let it be known that he was
not afraid of my dad or anybody else. His grand finale was
to tell Dad to stop wasting his life drinking, that it was the
devil's gin that fogged up his thinking and made peoples'
lives miserable. He told him he did not wish to waste any
more energy on him and that he'd said what he wanted
to say. Then he turned around and left. Dad, who was
drunk, responded in a loud voice, shouting nonsense.
Nobody cared what he had to say.

A couple of days later, Uncle Eddie found a folded,
yellow piece of paper on his bedroom table. He unfolded
it and read the message. It was a goodbye note from his
boyfriend. After he read it, he folded it back up and
placed it on his breast pocket. He never heard from Natie
again. Uncle Eddie became moody, depressed, chewed
on fresh ginger root every day for several days until he lost
his voice, and his body started to smell of ginger. Nobody
knew why all the sudden he was addicted to chewing fresh
ginger roots. No more elegant dishes were cooked, and the
house returned to its usual disarrayed mess that it was before
Natie came along.

KLING KLING

Kling Kling began to crawl. She became a handful around the house, crawling with her human legs by day, and bathing in the sea at night. Her earthling parents hid her from the village and from visitors. At times, she made a high pitch screeching like a dolphin, but her parents mostly managed to keep her quiet. Her legs turned interchangeably into fish fins and tail at certain times of day. Her father kept a tub of seawater ready for her, fetching it by the gallon. He carried two full buckets at a time. Each bucket was tied to the end of a bamboo pole and carried on his shoulders. Kling Kling's parents adored her so much that they would never let her go, but they did not know how they could continue raising her, hidden from the village people. They talked about it long into the night and worried about her future. To be continued.

What? To be continued again? I hated the suspense. As a child with no other books to read around the house, this magazine was a special source of excitement for me. The suspense made me hunt for the next issue of the magazine, to read the next chapter. I knew Cousin Violet had the new issue of *Liwayway Magazine,* and I wanted to borrow it. I was headed for her house when an old lady sitting on her porch with a brown cigarette hanging from her mouth asked when Cousin Violet's father would arrive from Hawaii. I shrugged my shoulders, indicating that I didn't know.

THE WEALTHY UNCLE PABLO RETURNS

I kept hearing that when Uncle Pablo retired to Bangar, to his brand new house, that everything would be different. He was notorious for being an unfriendly, grumpy man. When he arrived from Hawaii, none of my family would be allowed inside his house, especially my father. According to Aunt Li, my father was considered an impostor, son-of-a-bitch, good-for-nothing bum. All he wanted was his gin and to cause trouble.

"Uncle Pablo doesn't want any trouble in his house. And that's that," Aunt Li declared. "He demands rigid adherence to his rules, or else he will call the police."

He hated my family so much for depending on Aunt Li for financial support. He knew we had no one else to depend on, which made him all the more bitter since it was his hard earned money that we came with our hands out for. He was indeed a very strict old man.

Once he arrived back, we hardly saw him. Only his daughter, his wife, and the servants ever saw him. Whenever he saw me wandering around his house, he raised his voice and asked what I was doing there.

"I don't want you or any of your family at my house. You're an impostor! Get the hell outta here!" He yelled, making sure I heard loud and clear, pointing his cane in the direction of my house, for he had grown old in Hawaii.

I'd look at him briefly, turn around. When he'd walk away, I'd hide behind a door, waiting for him to go out of sight. Then I'd go about my business. Uncle Pablo was thirty-seven years older than my aunt. He could have been my great grandfather. My cousin was more like a granddaughter in age.

We all gave him the highest respect. Not because he was a U.S. citizen and wealthy, but he was also revered for his dedication to supporting his wife and child in the Philippines, while he worked his ass off in the sugar cane fields in Hawaii.

The only way I could get to Aunt Li's front door, I thought, was to climb up the mango tree located near the wall around his front yard. Two big German Shepherds were tied to the gate and would not be able to see or bite me there. Still, I did not want to even startle them and have them bark loudly.

It proved to be a very difficult task. As soon as I made it inside the yard, I looked around to make sure no one saw me. I managed to sneak quietly into the kitchen. I opened the refrigerator door, ate whatever I could find. I stuffed my mouth with fried chicken and ripe fruits. I crammed popsicles into my pockets for later snacks and to share with my sisters and brother.

I closed the refrigerator door quietly and opened cabinets, took out some candies, mini boxes of Kellogg's rice crispy cereals, stuffing them into my shirt, and

took off the same way I came in. At home, I shared my
food with my brother and sisters, and tried to form a
plan for when I could go back and get further into the
house. Rarely did I see my aunt outside the house any
more, talking to neighbors. But if I saw her out and
about, I approached her. Those days, she would let me in,
shutting the dogs away.

My cousin, their only child, was always upstairs in
her bedroom reading her favorite magazines. She had
even more beautiful dolls now, a new music box with a
ballerina dancing in front of a mirror, a tiny piano, new
tropical dresses and shoes, and bags and accessories.
They were all expensive items from Hawaii, and I could
only admire them from a distance because she guarded
them with her life, even more than before.

"Don't you dare touch my stuff with your dirty hands,"
she would say.

I could only admire the way they worked as she
played with them. Most of the best ones were locked
in cabinets in her parents' bedroom. Since she was
always upstairs in her own room, I would sneak into my
aunt's room if I got a chance, and I would check to see
if they might have forgotten to lock the cabinet doors.
Sometimes they did! Then I would touch the little piano
with my dirty fingers, careful not to press keys hard
enough to play a note. I'd stare at the music box with the
ballerina dancing in front of the mirror. Could I open
it and see her whirl around? No, I'd better not, for fear
someone might hear me. I held the dolls and stroked
their long, silky hair, and then put them back as I found
them. I could hear when Cousin came down to eat, or to
be taken shopping for more chocolates and toys. A maid

would call her name from downstairs. She'd answer back, "Okay." In about five minutes, she would come down.

Whenever we accidentally met in the hall, near the kitchen or the living room, our eyes would meet, and her hostile stare penetrated deep into the core of my existence. A sense of shame traveled through every fiber of my being. I knew what those looks meant. I was an impostor, unwelcome. Better get the hell out of her house, and now. She meant it. Her eyes skimmed me head to toe, as she mumbled something in disgust, and then she'd turn and walk away.

I tried to tell myself that it meant nothing.

One time, on the way to their house, I saw Violet, Aunt Li, and a maid in a taxi. They were most likely heading for the nearby town of San Fernando to do their shopping. San Fernando had bigger malls and more sophisticated, imported items than Bangar's markets. Cousin Violet saw me. Her eyes squinted in a warning.

So I went straight to their house and raided the refrigerator, especially Violet's favorite food items. She ordered the maids to watch out for me and not let me in.

One time a maid greeted me at the gate. She handed me a dish of porridge through the metal bars. "Go home now and eat. Share this with your sisters and brother," she said as I accepted the bowl of steaming porridge.

"Aunt Li would let me in, if she saw me," I told the maid. "Well she's not here right now. Run along before your uncle sees us." She'd shooed me away with her hand, like one might shoo an animal.

LOVE IN DIFFERENT FORMS

When Aunt Li was around and saw me by the gate,
she invited me in and gave me hand-me-down clothes,
including underwear and shoes that had been worn
but were still in good condition. I hurriedly grabbed
the bag full of her clothes to take home and share
with my siblings.

She was very caring, loving to everybody. I envied
her relationship with my cousin Violet. I most envied
their closeness, hugging and kissing. She even carried
Violet on her back, even though she was almost as tall. I
envied my cousin's relationship with her dad. They joked,
and he made her giggle. He played with her and gave her
piggyback rides, too.

I watched from a distance and then thought of
my own mother and father who could not show the
same affection toward anyone, let alone express their
love in words. I was painfully shy with my mother, even
embarrassed to hold her hand.

But I knew the feelings were there, just shown
differently and never expressed in words. When Mother
told me, "Come over and look for lice on my head," or
"Come pull any white hairs you find," I knew she wanted
to feel closeness.

At times I hated her for letting the things happen
and for not always being there. I hated her for being

rougher than Aunt Li, but, at the same time, we bonded in our own ways. Those moments were my only way to get close to her. My only chance to touch her.

"I help you clean the house," I said to her silently, with my actions. "I cook rice, fetch water, wash dirty dishes, and clothes, hang them on the line to dry. I sweep the floor for you, babysit when you go out to look for a job, or when you go to the market." This is my way of saying, "Nay, I love you so much."

A SACK OF CORN

I woke up late one morning and found that Dad had brought home a sack of corn on the cob.

"Where did you get these?" Mom asked suspiciously.

"Nevermind where I got them. Let's start boiling," Dad said as he dumped the corn onto the floor. "First, make sure we shut all windows and doors so no neighbors see and smell the steam."

That made Mom all the more suspicious.

Dad told me to bring upstairs a bucket of water and a big pot from the kitchen. I opened the door about ready to leave when he said, "Close the door quickly!" I did, and ran downstairs and brought what he had asked.

He was pumping air into a portable, one stove burner and lit it up with a match. He then filled the big pot with corn, not bothering to remove the husks, and poured water over them to boil.

"The corn tastes better when boiled with their husks," he commented. Our room upstairs became a hot, humid sauna. There was so much corn that we had it morning, noon, and night for a week. We were not allowed to eat it outside the house for fear of being seen.

Kristy, my best friend, came by and knocked at the front door. Immediately, I recognized her voice as she called out my name. I hurriedly went outside to meet her. I asked to go to her house and play. On our way, she told me her dad was very upset because somebody had broken into his cornfield and had stolen two huge sacks of corn. My stomach jumped into my throat.

As we approached her house, she walked me through to her backyard. Sure enough, rows of corn plants looked harvested. I felt badly for Kristy's dad. He had worked very hard to tend the perfect corn we had enjoyed for breakfast, lunch, and dinner for three consecutive days. I heard him threatening the bastard who robbed him of his crop. He had only a bucketfull of corn left for his family.

"Whoever stole it will pay," Kristy's father yelled. His angry voice carried from the kitchen to the backyard where we stood. I pictured Dad, creeping in there at night and stripping the stalks while Kristy's family slept. He could not have done it alone. He only brought home one of those burlap sacks full of corn, but I could not snitch on my father.

Kristy might have planned to bring me over to her house to see if I would talk, but I remained silent, too embarrassed to say anything. In the late afternoon, I

climbed up the stairs and saw dad boiling another pot
of corn, fanning the steam with a piece of cardboard to
clear away the smell of boiled corn.

MORE PLUNDER

Another month passed and Dad came home with another
surprise—a live, fat hen. He made sure we didn't get
too excited, and kept our voices low. He was going to
cook *Tinola* chicken soup, a special recipe that called for
ginger, unripe papayas, and herbs. Our father repeatedly
reminded us to stay quiet and not to ask questions. The
message was clear that there was a scandal afoot. I was
especially warned to keep my big mouth shut, or I would
get the taste of his lashing as opposed to his cooking.
Dad made sure to establish eye contact with his message.
He sure looked dead serious. Mom chastised Dad and
made it known she did not want any part of his stolen
chicken from another poor family.

"If you want to eat, keep your mouth shut. It's done,"
Dad snapped at her and remained silent throughout the
rest of his cooking. Mom complied, quiet as a mouse.

The front door and all the windows were kept shut.
The steam coming from a boiling pot of *Tinola* had
nowhere to escape to, but Dad used cardboard to fan
the steam out, as if to neutralize the air before it escaped
through the cracks in our walls. He did not want anyone

outside the house, especially the chicken's rightful owner, to smelling the soup.

We had a scrumptious meal that lasted two days. A couple of days passed, and I heard a neighbor complaining that one of his chickens was missing.

"Xulli, have you seen a hen wandering around?" the owner asked me, as he was heading towards our property.

"No. I have not," I replied. I lied.

He said he would report it to the police if he found out who stole it, and then walked away. The chicken was one of his egg laying ones, and he sold the eggs in the market to feed his family.

My dad gave excuses. "Well, they've got too many chickens anyway. One missing won't make any difference." Mom complained that he should not have taken the chicken from the neighbor. He was just as poor as we were, and if Dad got caught, he would spend more time in jail. Dad mumbled something to Mom, turned around, and left. I knew he would be gone the whole day and return drunk later that night.

Sure enough, in the middle of the night, Dad came home drunk and yelled for everybody to get out of bed. "Get up you little bastards! Up! Up!" His voice grew louder. "What did you do today? Huh?"

"You are drunk again. Leave the children be!" Mom told him.

Whack! Dad's hand flew across mother's face. I was stunned. Wide awake now, I began to cry. I knew where this was leading.

"What did you do that for?" asked Mom. "What did I do to you to treat me this way? It's very late, and the children were already asleep. Why wake them up?"

Dad pointed his finger at her. "You. You just shut your mouth."

There was silence for a minute. Then suddenly he kicked her on the stomach.

"NO, DAD!" I screamed at the top of my lungs. "Stop! Please don't fight!"

But it seemed the more I pleaded, the more he punched her. He hit her on the head, the stomach, her face, and all over the rest of her body. I heard heavy thuds as his fists hit her. All of us kids started screaming as we watched in horror. I yelled out for help, but nobody came.

Dad pulled Mother by her hair and dragged her outside the house, down the stairs, struggling to go down every step. On the ground in front of the house, she tried to get up.

She resisted the whole time, taking cover with her hands, when he kicked and punched at her. He let go of her hair. She got away once, but he chased and caught up with her. I ran to them, wrapped my arms around his waist, and tried to pull Dad away from her, but he was too strong for me. He came toward me and slapped me. I tried to protect my face and body. I curled up, chin pressed to my knees.

From the corner of my eye, I saw Mother get up and run. He turned from me and chased her down the street. They disappeared into the dark shadows of midnight.

FRIENDS AND ENTERPRISE

Kristy was always there for me. We were inseparable.
We had been in the same classes since first grade, and
we were close friends. We played together and shared
secrets. We could talk about anything. We even explored
each other's body parts as we took showers naked at
the water pump.

    She would even get up early in the morning to help
me collect banana leaves in our backyard, and then we
collected them from hers. We collected young fresh
ones, folded neatly to sell to vendors who passed by our
street in the early morning on their way to market. Just
before the sun rose to the north, Kristy and I were ready
with our merchandise for sale, all piled up neatly on a
table. We had many competitors on the street before the
vendors reached our spot, but they favored our banana
leaves over the others because we selected them carefully
from young trees. They looked fresh, clean, and we
offered the right price.

    We would run toward the buyers, even as they were
still inside the tricycle. They'd make a quick stop to
tell us the number of leaves they needed, and they had
money on hand, ready to pay us. Some gave signal with
their fingers as they approached, to give us a moment to
get our merchandise ready for them. Vendors used these
banana leaves to wrap fresh anchovies—marinated or raw.

They used them as wrappings for rice cakes and other fresh fish as well. They preferred them to a plastic bag or old newspapers.

Kristy and I would make ten pesos each in a day, and we would give seventy five percent to our parents. We kept the rest to buy popsicles and candy. By noon, the number of buyers would die down. Kristy and I would save the remaining banana leaves for the next day.

Then she and I would play with our friends, and sometimes we would get invited to others' houses. Sometimes, I lost track of time.

One day, one of the girls we were playing with said that my dad had been looking for me all day, calling out my name. I knew then that trouble was on the way. I knew what was going to happen, that I was going to get a lashing.

"Maybe you should put cardboard in your pants, so when he smacks your bottom, you won't feel a thing," Kristy had suggested. "Just tell him the truth."

"You lost track of time," my friends protested. "And promise him you won't do it again."

"It doesn't matter," I told them as I hurried outside to go home. "He will still hit me."

As soon as I arrived outside my friend's house, I saw Dad approaching with a belt. I could tell he was drunk. As soon as I was close enough, he started to whip me with his long belt. It hit me across my mouth, and then it struck my shoulder as I tried to walk away from him. He followed behind, hitting my back, my thighs, and my legs. I kept walking away fast, but he kept pace. People passing by watched in disbelief, but no one tried to stop him. I ran towards a tree, to hide behind its wide trunk.

He cornered me. I circled the trunk, letting out loud
piercing cries. I tried to run, but he blocked my path. I
ran the opposite direction and he chased after me. I saw
a bush ahead and plunged into it for protection, but Dad
caught up and yanked me out by the arm. I noticed now
he had a long branch in his hand. He used it to hit my
ribs, gripping me by the wrist. I heard a *thunk* and felt
a burning pain.

He struck me over and over on my ribs as I tried
with all my strength to pull away. He lost his grip, and
I ran towards Grandfather's house. I climbed the stairs,
sobbing, yelling for help. I glanced back and saw Dad
had thrown down the branch and picked up a large flip-
flop from the bottom of the stairs. He came after me up
the steps, I found Grandfather lying in bed in the living
room. My screaming had interrupted his nap.

"Grandpa! Help!" I pleaded frantically as Dad
approached. "Please stop him! Please!" I shook him,
trying to get him to help.

The top of my head took a powerful blow. He kept
hitting everywhere with the flip-flop, alternating with
right and left hand. Grandfather just stayed motionless
and silent, lying on his bed. I crawled on the floor on
hands and knees and kicked at him. I heard Grandfather
say something, but I could not make out of his words.
Maybe he said for Dad to stop, but he just lay there.
Dad stopped, turned, and walked away. I was relieved
momentarily, sobbing, holding my body where it hurt the
most, but he came back with another flip-flop.

He struck me all over again, fuming, murderous. He
did not like it when he missed, or when I managed to
avoid his swings. It pissed him off all the more. He was

outraged. One more hit to my face caused the flip-flop to break in half. I pressed my hands to my cheeks. He threw the broken halves to the floor and went down stairs. I thought he was done with me. I sulked in the corner of Grandfather's living room, my face wet from crying, my nose running, and my skin burning all over. I didn't bother to ask Grandfather to help. He wouldn't get up. Not the first time I begged, not the second time. It was clear he would not help me.

Dad came back carrying two long sticks, one in each hand. He threw one on the floor while gripping the other. I tried to escape, but he cornered me and pounded my back with the branch, wherever he could hit, while his father watched. Grandfather did not appear affected or bothered at all.

I pleaded and screamed for Dad to stop. "I promise I will never do it again!"

"Promises. Promises," he said as he continued to hit me with the stick. I begged for mercy.

But *wham!* The limb hit my hand. I thought it crushed the bones of my left pinky. It hurt so badly. I held it with my other hand. The branch broke as it hit me again, and he grabbed the other one.

He hit my face. I covered it with my hands. He hit my thigh. I covered that. He went after my head, and I tried to cover that. Wherever he hit, I covered with my hands. I curled and he beat my back until that limb broke. I could no longer hear my own voice. It felt like I had been screaming for hours.

I lay there, eyes squeezed shut, my whole body inflamed. My head felt like it was splitting in half. It hurt to breathe. My chest squeezed tight. I felt blow after blow until I was numb, blurred visions of Grandfather fading. At some point I stopped resisting, struggling. There was nothing more I could do. I no longer had feeling in my body. Numb.

Grandfather said something. Just mumbled. It must have affected Dad for he grabbed a handful of my hair and picked me up. He seemed determined to kill me, the same way he had killed a dog. He clubbed and beat me, dangling me by my hair. My voice grew hoarse. I was too weak to keep resisting. I saw his one hand going up with his weapon as it came down to some parts of my body, but, it seemed, my body could no longer feel anything. It developed immunity to pain. Numb. I prayed that he would finish, but he just kept right on. It was getting dark outside.

The next thing I remember, I was slumped in the corner of the room. I knew because a chill wind passed through me. I tried to open my eyes. It was pitch black all around me. My lids were stuck together. I could see red through slits in them. I was no longer being hit, but my body was jerking uncontrollably. I was gasping but couldn't even get enough breath. I could not move much. My throat was dry and hoarse. My body was on fire. My tongue was all tight and swollen. My arms and legs too heavy to move. Stinging, burning all over.

I thought I heard my mom's voice. She'd been gone. She sounded far away, but I recognized her voice, asking me what had happened. I tried to answer, to open my mouth, but it was too hard to talk. Everything around me was black. *She came back for me?* I wondered.

I tried off and on to wake up, to open my eyes. I could only make out darkness, and silence. Except the crickets, I could hear them. I took short breaths, still shaking as though I was crying. It seemed like this repeated—waking to hear Mother's voice, trying to move. I tried to speak, but it hurts to open my mouth, to move my jaw. Tears welled up in my swollen eyes. I forced to open my eyes just a little and turn my head. I saw Dad passed out in the corner, lying on his stomach, snoring.

Mom told me I had been in bed for three days while she nursed me. After, I remembered her waking me, tapping my shoulder, to eat, but I only fell back to sleep again. My face remained swollen. My skull felt like it was about to explode. I was thirsty all the time. Mother spoon-fed me soup, lifting the back of my neck as she placed a glass of water to my lips to drink. I just wanted to sleep more. My eyes felt heavy.

I wanted to pee, but ignored it. I woke up again with Mom rubbing my back. My hearing came back. I heard footsteps approaching. It was Dad, walking past me on his way downstairs, never saying anything. He walked around the house as if nothing happened, except we didn't speak.

Slowly I regained my strength, but I did not speak to Dad for weeks. I avoided him whenever possible. Whenever I heard him coming, I rushed to hide or went in the opposite direction. He owed me an apology. I knew what he did was wrong. I waited for him to say he was sorry, but the wait turned into days of silence.

He was my dad. I had to do what I was told, so I forced myself to be around the house when he was there. He spoke to me only to tell me to go fetch water, gather wood for the fire, or buy something at the store. I refused to speak to him or even look at him, but I had to obey. I kept up my duties. I cleaned the house, cooked rice, bought foods at the market, and helped my brother and sisters with whatever they needed. Another week passed, and I was strong again.

MANILA

Early one morning, he told me to write down on a piece of paper what he said. "Dear Aunt C, I will be in sixth grade soon, and I need a dress and a pair of new shoes. Please, Auntie, help me."

My dad said he was going to Manila to look for work and for a place for us to live. This letter, supposedly written by me, would be delivered to her. Aunt C was older than my dad by a year. She bought and sold designer clothing, and she was successful. I was happy to hear Dad was leaving us for a while because peace would be restored in our household. There would be no beatings to dread and no parents fighting. Secretly, I felt freedom and peace settle over me, overjoyed by the idea that he would not be living with us for a while.

No doubt Di was rejoicing, too. I did not know about Mother, if she felt the same. I heard her remind Dad not to forget to send his salary as soon as he got paid.

"Don't spend the money on booze," she said.

The tobacco factory had laid off workers and did not pay enough. There would not be enough money to sustain us unless he found a job within the first week.

But three weeks passed, and we had heard no news from him. However, by the following week, a telegram arrived from Aunt C saying Dad was creating havoc at her house, disturbing the peace, arguing with her children and her husband. He was getting drunk and passing out on the floor. His drinking was making him fight with Aunt C every day. So, she had told him to get the hell out of her house. Dad stayed with his friends who lived within walking distance.

Aunt C's husband worked as a foreman at a construction company. He asked his boss if he could employ my dad, and the boss agreed to it on a trial basis. Aunt C looked for Dad, giving him another chance to better his life and support his family.

All she had to do was ask one neighbor. He had not been difficult to find. He was already famous as a drunk, hanging out with the men in town and drinking late into the night with them. He would pass out in one house or another. Sleeping by day and socializing by night. He and his friends drew more men to join them, hanging out and drinking like there was no tomorrow. Perhaps, work would get him out of his drinking binge. A neighbor pointed his finger to the house where dad was staying and Aunt C rushed in that direction. When she found him, she told him to get his gear together. It was time to go to work, make money to feed his family, and become a useful citizen.

On their way to her house, she told him to quit drinking. He had a family to think about, and he needed to be a responsible husband, father, and so on. Dad, sober at that moment, remained quiet as he followed his sister home.

Dad worked building houses for a month, and sent most of his first paycheck to Mother. When a courier notified her that she had funds to pick up, she was thrilled. She paid our debts first thing, and budgeted the remaining money, awaiting the next transfer.

Along with the money, Dad sent Mother a letter. In it, he told her that he'd been working hard, trying to be a responsible citizen, with hardly time to write, that he was too tired after working all day. He told her he had not been drinking as much and, by living with Aunt C, he was able to save a little money to build a small house for our family. It was Aunt C's suggestion that Dad should go back to La Union and bring all of us to Manila to live with him in a one-bedroom house that he would build.

When the day came for the move to the big city, everyone went but me. They left me behind at Aunt Li's. I waved goodbye as the tricycle they rented moved off toward the bus depot in town, disappearing in a cloud of dust. I went inside Aunt Li's house, feeling strange, confused, and lost. I missed my family already. I looked around, feeling like a stranger. Though I'd stayed there before, things had been hostile lately. This did not feel like home.

MY NEW LIFE

One day, I went to Grandfather's house for a shower. He
had a pump in the washroom. I gathered a bucketfull of
water and used a blue bar of Ajax soap to wash my hair
and body. Then I poured the water over my head and
body, and soaped again, making sure no passers-by on the
street could see me. Of course, I kept my underwear on.
There were big spaces between the logs, so I could see
people passing.

I accidentally dropped the slippery soap. Damn!
It fell between the floorboards to the big, moldy rocks
below. With hair and body dripping wet, I put my dirty
t-shirt back on. I went through the kitchen and dining
room to the outside stairs, and climbed underneath to
find my bar of soap. I didn't dare step onto those big
slimy slippery rocks. Barefoot, I balanced along the side.

Ow! I stepped on a rusty nail that stuck out of a
four-by-four. I did not see the nail protruding as I busily
searched for the damn soap. I lifted my foot and saw
that two inches penetrated the bottom of my right foot.
Gritting my teeth, I pulled it out. It felt weird pulling a
rusty nail off the bottom of my foot. And, it hurt so much
I gave a loud yelp. Then it started to bleed heavily. The
bright red blood sickened me.

I went on hunting for the soap and finally saw it.
Holding a beam, I reached and picked it up without

stepping on the slimy stones, then went back upstairs, blood trailing behind to give myself a final rinse. I finished my bath and wrapped my foot with the same t-shirt I'd been wearing earlier. I kept my foot wrapped with the same t-shirt all night and day. The next night, I was burning up in bed. My whole body felt like it was on fire. I called out for anyone who might help me. I was murmuring in my sleep. I felt hot and then cold, shivering throughout the night.

Uncle Eddie, who had gone on living with his parents, came to my room. He unwrapped the now filthy t-shirt from my foot and discovered that the bottom of my foot was rotting. He asked me what happened. I told him the story of the nail under the house. He rushed to Aunt Li's and told her, then came back with a candle, a big needle, and a clean towel. "We have to drain the pus ," he told me. My foot was swelled up twice the normal size. I screamed, remembering Dad and the boil, and begged him not to touch my already painful foot. "It hurts so much," I cried. I went on screaming. He told me that I might lose the leg. I passed out.

Next morning, I woke still feverish. I had been burning up and sweating all night. My entire leg was still swollen, and the bottom of my right foot was throbbing and hot to the touch. It was also red and purple. My body still felt on fire, and I could not move. I knew I was going to die. It was a struggle to get up to go to the bathroom. I had to walk with a long branch I used as a cane that Uncle Eddie got for me so I could move around.

"Here," he said. "This will help you get around easier. But remember, we have to drain the pus out if you want to keep your leg."

For the first time, I felt his compassion. I was scared.
I wanted my mother to hold me, but she was not around.
She was far, far away in Manila. I missed my family. That
night, I cried, longing for her. My leg was getting worse,
black-colored on the bottom. Uncle Eddie told me he
was going to take me to see a doctor.

"No! I hate doctors!" I said.

"Oh, I see. So you want to die then? Very well, if
that's what you want. So be it."

"But if I go to the doctor he'll chop off my leg!" I
cried. I begged and pleaded not to be seen by a doctor. I
screamed until I grew dizzy and passed out. I was in and
out of consciousness.

I woke briefly to find Uncle Eddie sitting on
the bottom of my foot, lighting the point of the
long needle. Thankfully, I slipped back into sleep or
unconsciousness. When I awoke, I was pouring sweat.
He was still poking the needle into my foot, pressing
out green pus. The room stank like a rotten egg. He
continued to squeeze the pus out every night and put
a patch of ground up green, herbal medicine on and
around the wound. During the day, he collected fresh,
young guava leaves and mashed them up into a paste
to be used every night before I went to bed. Slowly but
miraculously, I healed. After that, I never bathed at my
grandfather's house again.

MISSING MY MOTHER

I longed to be with my mother. Every night I cried myself to sleep, waking, calling out for her. I pleaded with my aunt to let me send my mom a letter to come get me. She relented. We sent the letter, and then I waited. One day passed, no response. Then another. I became depressed again and pleaded with anyone who would listen to let me see my mother. Another day passed.

No one in Manila seemed to have heard my plea. Nobody listened. No one cared. I kept begging to go to her. It had been three days, but it seemed like forever. Finally, Aunt Li explained that it would take a day or two for the letter to arrive there, and who knew how many more days for my mom to be able to come.

"Just be patient, Xulli, and she'll come," my aunt assured me.

With this explanation, I stopped crying and begging. But I watched each day for a letter or my mom to appear. I tried to keep the faith that my mother would come for me. I kept hoping.

As I began to feel a bit better, I explored Aunt Li's house, parts I'd never been before. I discovered a basement storage area. It was dirty, and thick with cobwebs. Searching around, I found gourds of wine. There must have been over a hundred gourds in the basement. My aunt had been in the business of making rice wine. The storage must be the wine cellar. I squeezed between sections of gourds. Some of them had a strong vinegar odor.

I felt something cold under my bare foot. A silver coin! I picked it up and happily left the house for the mini store.

When I returned, Aunt Li said, "Look who's here."

I came around the corner into the living room and there sat my mother. And Bebeng with her! I dropped my popsicles and screamed, "Mom!" I ran to her and hugged her.

She was in tears. I knew then that she'd missed me, too. I wanted to hug Bebeng, too, but I was too shy. I sensed she, too, was shy to show affection towards me. So, we looked each other eye-to-eye, beaming with big smiles on our faces. We knew we missed each other very much. I sat in the middle, between them, holding their hands, and I asked mother if she had come to take me with her.

She said, "Yes."

It was the happiest moment of my life. I could not let her out of sight. When we separated for a few minutes, I stopped what I was doing and ran around the house looking for her. Even when she went to the bathroom, I searched for her. When she went to Aunt Li's bedroom, I followed her. I wanted to make sure she did not leave without my knowing. I tracked her every move. If I saw her coming down the hallway smiling at me, I felt such love. I spent as much time as I could playing with Bebeng. I played with her at Aunt Li's house and climbed guava and mango trees in the yard. But after a couple of days with her, I noticed she preferred spending more time with Aunt Li, following her wherever she went, sitting and eating in the dining room next to her, and watching television by her side. She even slept in the same bed as Aunt Li. They bonded quickly as if Bebeng was Aunt Li's second child. I returned with Mom, and Bebeng stayed with Aunt Li.

MANILA AND SIXTH GRADE

The house that father started building in Manila was nearly finished when a flash flood swept it away. We were to stay temporarily at Aunt C's house until the weather calmed. I would be continuing sixth grade in a big city. Mom enrolled me and my brother at Tatalon Elementary School. It was about a mile walk from our house. Three of my cousins had attended the same school since they were in first grade, and were comfortable with the environment and the teachers. They also knew which streets to take for a shortcut.

Aunt C told me that our cousins would accompany Di and me, and they would show us around our new school. Like her children, we should study hard and always listen to our teachers. A stern disciplinarian, she made sure we listened to every word she said and that her words registered in our little heads.

"Don't talk when the teacher is speaking," she instructed us. "Pay attention at all times." Every day she tried to ingrain these ideas in our memory. She ended her lectures by telling us she wanted to see straight A's and awards. The heat was on. We had competitions at home and at school. We were to be the best of the best.

I was both excited and nervous to be in a new school. We were the new kids on the block. We had new students, new rules, new strict teachers, and a new environment to get used to. On top of all this, we had to prove to our parents and Aunt C that Di and I were just as smart as, if not smarter than, our cousins. Aunt C told us that students in our new school wore uniforms. She bought us matching clothes. The girls wore brand new black shoes, white t-shirts, and freshly ironed blue skirts, while the boys wore white t-shirts and brown khaki shorts.

Aunt C, having her own business, buying and selling the latest fashionable clothing, was just the right person to order uniforms and school supplies. She understood city life. With brand new socks and shoes, I thought I had better keep my feet clean at all times. I swore I would not look like a poor peasant. When it came time to put on my new clothes, they felt weird. The brand new crisp, white t-shirt and stiff blue skirt felt foreign, as though I had never worn anything brand new in my whole life. I hardly had. These new items felt harsh and scratchy against my scaly skin. The socks, though, felt soft and gentle on my chapped, hard soles. My brother looked handsome in his brand new shirt, shorts, socks and shoes.

Monday morning came, and all the kids in the house were up at six to have enough time to eat, shower, and get dressed for school. Di and I beamed with pride, dressed in our new fine clothes, but we were nervous about how hard our new classes would be here. The maid had woken up around 4 AM to start deep frying milkfish with garlic and fried rice for later meals. We ate an early breakfast of fried eggs and rice with orange juice! What a treat for me and Di. Out the door we went, in our fine new clothes, and carrying our lunch boxes. Di and I had food our mother prepared the night before. Our cousins had lunch boxes prepared at dawn by the maid because Aunt C always came home very late at night after selling her products, and was too tired to get up.

As soon as we were out of the house, the maid could go back to sleep. But later in the day, when the house was quiet and everyone was at school or work, she would clean, cook more, and wash the family's dirty clothes. Oh, how I wished we could live permanently at Aunt C's. I loved being cared for. I never wanted to leave.

We gave ourselves ample time for the mile walk. We had to be at school at 8 AM sharp. Gina, a year older than me, was our guide. We climbed a hill, turned a corner, and walked straight ahead for half an hour. We learned how to cross the busy highways, with buses, jeepneys, and tricycle taxicabs rushing both directions. The girls held hands as we waited for the opportune moment to run for our lives to cross on the other side, sometimes having to dart through the spaces between vehicles. Occasionally, a driver cared enough to stop and let us pass. Most times we had to be very alert or risk being hit. After we'd crossed, we still had to walk another five minutes.

By the time we arrived at school, we were panting and sweating. When the weather was hot and humid, we were soaked in perspiration, like we just came out of the shower, not bothering to dry our face and bodies.

Our new school was far more spacious than our old one in Bangar, with bigger buildings and less trees. My

brother and I stood close together, not knowing where
to go. Our cousins, Pet and Zack, left us for their classes.
Gina found out my brother's room and took him there,
telling him to pick any seat and to listen to the teacher.
He nodded. We left him looking disoriented and scared.
Next Gina stopped a teacher and told her I was new.
She found out where I needed to be and walked me to
the classroom. She helped me find a seat and then said
she had to get to her own classroom before she got a
tardy and detention.

In class, I felt shy and nervous, as if I had never
been to school in my life. All the other students looked
clean, showered, and well-equipped with shiny lunch
boxes and school supplies. I listened intently to the
teacher, determined not to miss a word she said. Miss
Orchid embodied the quintessential, self-contained,
classy, traditional yet westernized, young Filipino woman.
I admired her—her shapely figure, feminine and fragile,
yet empowered and confident. She had short hair in
a stylish cut, highlighted in shades of brown. The suit
uniform of the teachers gave her a professional look. She
wore a nice watch and pearls around her neck and ears.

Independent with money, I thought. She wore very little
make up, but looked like an actress. She looked like she
was in her early twenties.

At the end of class, Miss Orchid introduced us to
our next teacher, for math. Mrs. Mimosa, a skinny woman
in her early forties, was very strict and expected all her
students to be prepared with answers in class, and to
turn in completed assignments on time, or we would be
scolded in front of the class. I hated math. We had to

memorize multiplication tables and learn division. I had to get straight A's like my cousins.

Often during class, I wondered how my brother was doing. I wondered which subjects he was liking, and how he liked his teachers. Were they treating him nicely? Di was always so quiet and so painfully shy. I worried about him.

In class, I sat next to a boy whose morning breath smelled like he didn't brush his teeth for weeks. His hair was unkempt. I thought he must have gotten out of bed and come to school without looking at himself in the mirror. Perhaps, his family had no mirror. He told me he knew his multiplication very well.

"Better watch out," he said with a grin. "I'll answer all the math questions in a flash—as fast as lightning."

"Show off!" I said. "Shut your smelly mouth! You ought to brush your teeth. And stay far from me!" I turned my head back to the teacher.

Mrs. Mimosa told him to stand up. He did it in a heartbeat. I thought he must be in trouble for talking to me. *He should have kept his mouth shut, should have known better,* I thought. But no. Mrs. Mimosa asked him five math questions. He stood up straight, chest and chin up, and answered all of them correctly and quickly! The teacher told the class to give him a round of applause. The thunderous clapping must have sent his ego sky high. He sat down looking proud and beaming with excitement, his chin still up. He looked my direction with a smug smile. I gave him an icy glare.

"Next!" I heard the teacher call.

She was looking at me! I did not know she called names randomly. My mind went blank. A flush crept up my neck and face. My heart hammered at three times the normal rate. *Oh, no. Not me. Not yet . . . Oh please, don't call my name,* I thought to myself. She called out my name.

I stood up quickly, trying not to piss my pants. "Yes, Ma'am!" I replied, loud, as I looked straight at the blackboard. She asked the first question. I answered slowly, with a questioning tone, as though unsure of the correct answer. Yes. It was correct! Then she asked the second question. I hesitated momentarily, but answered correctly again. She asked the third question. I hesitated, feeling numb. The teacher looked impatient. My mind was blank. I could hear my heart beating faster. I could not think. All eyes were fixed on me. *God help me,* I thought. I knew then.

I was about to give the answer, opened my mouth to speak, when she said, "Sit down."

No clapping for me. My heart sank into my seat and coiled there, shrunken, diminished. I wanted to run outside, go home and study hard.

She called another student and he answered all of the questions without hesitation. I cringed at my stupidity, avoiding eye contact with the math genius next to me. Out of the corner of my eye, I could see him, though, still wearing that radiant expression. I wanted to punch him in that smug mouth.

A few weeks passed. I studied hard, excelled at reading and spelling, and even improved in math. I became more confident in all my classes, and was nominated by Miss Orchid as a class leader.

The math genius with the bad breath said spitefully, as he passed me in the hall, "I know more math than you.

I have better grades than you. For the life of me, I don't
know why the teacher chose you as class president."

"Maybe I have leadership qualities," I countered.

Lacking a response, he turned and left without a
word. I felt kind of guilty, even sad for him, but brushed
the feeling aside. As class president, I helped the teacher
plan lessons and write them on the board for students to
copy. I was in charge of daily attendance and helped the
teachers correct test papers. I even took home test papers
to correct and brought them back the next day.

WHILE IT LASTED

While living at Aunt C's house, Mom helped the maid
prepare and cook meals for everybody in order to relieve
the maid of the burden and responsibilities of serving
two families. Mom contributed by sweeping, washing
clothes, and ironing them every day. Aunt C also had a
toddler about the same age as Wilma. The maid helped
with babysitting. Aunt C's husband, Uncle Fred, was tall
and slim, with neatly combed, shiny hair. He worked as a
foreman at the construction company and earned a very
decent income, or so I heard. He was a hard-working
man, the kind of husband any woman would want to
have, who focused on his family's needs, owned a jeepney,
and never drank. But he never spoke to any of us unless
we approached him and talked to him. Either he was a

quiet type, or he did not like us living in his house. Their house had two bedrooms upstairs, a small kitchen leading to the dining room on the first floor, and a living room with a colored television and stereo. There was a small washroom equipped with running water and a modern toilet that flushed.

Aunt C, who stood about four feet tall, always wore freshly ironed blouses and pants. She worked through the evening, leaving the house early in the afternoon. She came home just before midnight, tired from walking to find buyers for her products and was ready for bed as soon as she got home. On weekends, she worked only half days, collecting debts from creditors. Her attentive husband always picked her up around midnight on a designated corner with his jeepney, not wanting her to walk home at the mercy of muggers and rapists in dark streets and alleys. Aloof as he was to all of us, he was a kind husband and a responsible father, and was friendly when we talked to him.

Early in the morning, Uncle Fred blasted his Barry Manilow music collection. *Somewhere Down the Road* could be heard for miles. The music would wake us all up and get us started for the day. He played the same record nearly every day, so that the songs became engraved in all the cells of our brains. Since it was his house we were living in temporarily, he could play any music at any time he pleased, whether the guests liked it or not. He had an LP stereo player in his living room and no one was allowed to touch it, not even his own children.

One weekend morning, Gina got close to her dad, who was sorting his LP collection, when she asked for money to buy treats at the mini-mart. Without hesitation,

he reached into his pocket and pulled out coins. Then
Gina asked for an extra ten cents to give to me. Again,
he reached into his pocket and handed over the coin.
Gina and I ran from the house, giggling, on our way
to the store to buy ourselves treats. We walked along by
a creek, stopping to watch tadpoles at the edge of the
waters, then skipped on to the store. I was in heaven,
though it occurred to me that this was just normal life
for other kids.

THE NEXT MOVE

While we stayed at Aunt C's, Mom and Dad scrubbed
the mud and filth out of our new house. It was a box on
four wooden poles, about the size of a one-car garage.
The house was one that had been swept away by a flood
during heavy storms. The river had swelled, swallowing
it along with a number of others. It had been moved
far down the river. There, our house rested until the
flood subsided. Families with no relatives slept in
churches or stayed with friends. They, too, waited for the
floodwaters to sink below ankle deep before hauling
their homes back to their original spots. Children in the
neighborhood thought it was quite a spectacle, watching
a house being moved.

One at a time, four or five strong men carried the
house, with sturdy bamboo poles on their shoulders.

They lifted the house and marched forward, with children trailing behind as though it were a parade for their amusement. Once the dwellings were settled on the original spot, women armed with mops, sponges, buckets, and detergents started scrubbing, soaping, rinsing, mopping, and splashing the thick, foul-smelling mud off, inside and out.

Dad made a new ladder and placed it at the front door so we could get inside. It looked clean except for traces of black mud in cracks. The pungent smell of decay still lingered, wafting from the walls and floors. The musky odor burned our nostrils the first night. It was so strong I could taste it as I tried to get to sleep. On one wall was a small window whose wooden flip-cover stayed propped open all day and night, for fresh air. She spread a mat on the floor and threw a couple pillows down. I used a rolled up towel as my pillow. We all lay on the mat under a large, green mosquito net.

Dad still had the job at the construction business, so he was able to buy tools and tar to patch and repair holes in the tin roof. He spent some of his salary on whatever needed repairing. He came home from work tired, but still had time to do repairs. He had not been drinking, and he handed over his salary to Mom each week. Only once in a while he asked Mom for one or two pesos to buy a pack of cigarettes. Mom did the budgeting, making sure we had enough to eat until the next payday.

After that, on occasion, I visited Aunt C's house to play with my cousins, jumping up and down on their queen-sized mattress upstairs in their bedroom. We ate lunch that the maid prepared. But, over time, the maid began to complain about my dirty feet on

the newly cleaned, concrete floor, which she had just
swept and polished to a shine. She said I was leaving
dirty trails, and she was tired of cleaning after me. She
said I had no consideration for the hard work she had
been put through.

"Butt off, all of you, you ungrateful scoundrels!" she
shouted. "Stay off the clean floor, or at least learn to wipe
your feet before entering!"

Her reprimands left me with the impression that I
was still welcome to come in any day, anytime, as long as
it was with clean feet. Then Aunt C angrily warned all of
us kids to stop jumping on her queen-size bed.

"Now it's lumpy in the middle, and the legs are
breaking. It's not a trampoline! Out, all of you! Go
play outside and never set foot on my bed again!" She
screamed this loud enough for neighbors to hear.

I kept my feet clean after that, but the maid glared
at me as soon as I entered. She inspected my feet and
then let me in. I headed straight for the refrigerator, a
habit I had not broken from my hungry days prowling
Aunt Li's house in Bangar.

"I have not cooked anything yet," the maid said.

I looked for my cousins to play with, but they were
doing homework. Feeling guilty, I settled to do mine.
They started to seem annoyed with my presence. They
preferred playing and studying with their friends. They
spent less and less time playing with me. I did not
understand their new attitude. Either they were told
by their parents to stay away from me, to discourage us
from coming around, or they really didn't like to have
anything to do with unruly, disheveled country folks like
my family and me.

THE CLUSTERS

Under Marcos' government, land was distributed freely to disadvantaged families in some parts of Quezon City. It was rather a quick move by the city government officials to aid families living in low-lying areas affected by floods to move to higher ground. The land given away to families was divided into clusters or subsections. Five to eight families lived in a cluster. Every single family had packed up their belongings and moved up to their designated plot of land assigned to them to build new homes. My family included. In the community, each cluster had a playground encircled by five to eight houses. In these playgrounds, birthday parties, community dances, meetings, late afternoon movies and even funeral events took place. Sometimes foreign missionaries invited the residents to come out in the evening and gather for a prayer or to have birth control discussions.

WATER

The government supplied fresh running water for a number of subdivided clusters. They installed refilling stations within a mile radius of subdivided clusters that provided our community with clean, fresh drinking water all the time. People lined up with their buckets as soon as the first water flowed, and the lines were always there after that. If the water was shut off for repairs or quality testing, everyone invaded another water station. People would get up before the roosters crowed, or stay up until three o'clock in the morning to take their turn filling their buckets. They'd fill two, carry them home, fill their tanks or stock up by the gallons then go back, put more empty ones at the end of the line to start the process over. The rules of the game were that no one would sneak and jump. But people started to scorn such courtesies. Sometimes, due to desperate circumstances, there were people who cheated. When no one was guarding, they moved up in line, and then there would be arguments. Mother and father brought soap and towels along with their buckets, and they bathed on the street by the water station. It did not seem to make sense, collecting water to bring home to shower when they could just clean themselves by the station. They did not seem to care who was around, but they did not get completely naked.

Dad would shower wearing his boxer shorts, while Mom draped a thin cloth around her chest, covering herself down to her thighs. Some days there were groups showering, young and old, married or single. It didn't matter. Personal hygiene is of high importance to Filipinos no matter how deplorable one's living circumstances. Children as young as four or five were taught the value of cleanliness. The flow of water was strongest at three or four in the morning, with water not in use at other clusters. Since very few were willing to stay up until then, one could have the place to oneself without waiting in a long line. Few people had that patience. Children and teens showered in broad daylight, after school or before bedtime. Some women brought their laundry to do right in the street. Once finished, they took it home to hang out and dry in front of their houses, from balconies, or windows, on lines tied up neatly, swaying in the wind. To a foreigner, it might look like a huge clothing sale.

THE AMERICANS

One day, the school principal announced that there would be a group of foreigners from the United States selling used, but still good items such as clothing, shoes, and household items at the school.

"So ask your parents for money. The school will be having a huge garage sale on Saturday."

That's two days from today, I thought. I felt excited as I started for home. I'd never met Americans in my whole life, and I wondered what it would be like to talk to them.

I told my mother about the Americans coming to our school. She, too, was excited, and said she would borrow money to give to me. I must make sure to buy important things we needed for the house and to get decent clothes. I couldn't wait. I tried to prepare something nice to say in English. Saturday came. I was up and ready to leave the house at seven in the morning. Mom handed me twenty pesos in paper money. I put it in my pocket and headed for school.

There were rows of tables with clothing, shoes, and household items piled up. People scavenged, looking for useful items for their homes. Other tables held gardening and construction tools. All of it was being sold for very cheap prices. I could not believe my eyes. I picked up a brown shoulder bag and examined the zipper. In an inside pocket I found a ten cent American coin! I sure lucked out on this one, I thought. I'd better hold on to it so no one else buys it, while I continue to look around for clothes for my brother, dad, sister, and me. I told a lady with blonde hair and blue eyes that I wanted to buy the purse. She ignored me, or did not hear me. She was busy chattering and bargaining with adult customers.

"Excuse me, Ma'am," I interrupted in a loud voice. "I want to buy this purse!" I hoped I impressed her with my English.

"Oh, ok, my dear. Just hold on one minute," she said nicely.

I waited patiently in front of her while she counted out change to a customer. I told her, "Ma'am, I've been waiting for a long time now for my change."

"Did you pay me yet?" she asked, unsure. "Yes, ma'am! I gave you twenty pesos, and I have been waiting for my change."

"Oh, I'm so sorry. Let me give you your change," she said apologetically.

"Ahh, it's all right, ma'am," I said.

"Is that all you want? Just the purse?" she asked before giving me my change. "Yes, Ma'am. Thank you," I told her as she handed me my change. I proceeded to the next table and bought my mom a blouse, and good clothes for my dad and siblings. I was feeling happy as I walked home with the purse, with the good luck coin still inside.

When I got home, I told my mother I had only spent ten pesos and handed her back the change. I realized I had never paid for the purse at all! I thought I handed the lady the twenty pesos! Holding the money on hand, I was staring at it, in disbelief, thinking I came home with more money and goods than I bargained for. I handed over the money to mother and explained what had just happened. Deep inside, I was feeling very lucky. Mom said I should go back and give the lady the twenty pesos. I could not believe I had not paid her at all, that I still had the twenty pesos, plus the change I got back after paying for the clothes.

"No way!" I cried. "It's a long walk back and forth, Mom. My feet already hurt so bad. Couldn't we just consider the extra money as a miracle for the day?" I pleaded. "Besides, we need the money. Can we just consider it a donation from the Americans?"

Mom did not say anything. She stepped out of the house and returned the twenty pesos to the person she borrowed it from earlier. I had the purse with the ten cents inside, clothes for my family, and ten pesos still in my pocket. And Mom owed nothing to the neighbor.

OUR NEW HOUSE

Our flood-surviving house protected us from gusts of angry winds and from the rain, though the plywood walls swelled up from the slashing and pounding rain in storms. Patches bulged everywhere. They'd swell and then shrink, leaving fissures where we could see through to the street and the neighbors' houses. We did not have much privacy, as the neighbors and passersby could see inside as well. Sunshine made its way inside the house through these cracks.

The downstairs floor got muddy during the rainy season because it was not yet cemented. We walked on the muddy floor with flip-flops. The bottoms stuck to the wet floor, and it was a struggle to take the next step forward. When the lower floor got muddy, my siblings and I were not allowed to go down there. Mom did not want us tracking mud upstairs, and it was upsetting for her to see our bottom feet caked with mud when we went to bed. Oh, how I envied houses with floors cemented in red, green, or blue. Some people placed real paper money, coins in different denominations and sealed them with lacquer. I longed desperately to have a floor adorned with real money. Owners proudly showed off their spotless, shiny, rich floors. But, over time, when life became harder and they were short of cash, some of these households became desperate and started drilling the money up, leaving holes and patches on their cemented floors.

On rainy days, Mom and Dad cooked downstairs and brought the food upstairs where we all ate in a big circle on the floor. But Dad built a wooden table resembling a picnic table, with long benches attached on both sides. So when the weather was dry, we ate downstairs.

A VISIT

Grandmother and grandfather came to visit Manila from Bangar Province. They stayed at Aunt C's house for a week. They felt more comfortable at her house than at ours because Aunt C's house has cemented flooring throughout the first floor and a bathroom with a flushing toilet, while our family used one chamber pot upstairs. Mom, Di, or I would take it downstairs to the outhouse to empty. Other days, we threw the collected urine into an open sewer outside, behind the house.

My grandparents came to see how we were doing, and sat on a long wooden bench downstairs in the early evening when it was pouring rain. The rain on the tin roof and thunder were deafening, like a steel band played right outside. Mom and Dad cooked supper, and the grownups talked downstairs while my brother, sister, and I hung out upstairs.

I came onto the stairs. I thought I'd sing for Grandmother, to entertain her. I wanted her to hear me sing. After all, she came to visit from far away and might be happy to hear her granddaughter perform. So I started singing songs I made up, raising my voice when a gust of wind lashed the walls or heavy rain hit the tin roof. The gale whipped against our plywood walls with wind at ninety miles an hour. The metal roof leaked in several places. Drops of rain falling from the tin rooftop splashed into several bowls and buckets placed on the upstairs floor. We put buckets and bowls all over the place to catch the water. The wall by the stairs leaked as well, causing slippery wooden steps, and creating small puddles everywhere on the dirt floor.

Mom asked me to get a bowl from upstairs. I forgot about the slippery stairs and, returning with the bowl, still singing enthusiastically, I slipped, tumbled, and came crashing to the bottom. I was in a state of shock and gave out a loud cry. Dad rushed over, picked me up, rubbed my back and sides. Grandmother and Grandfather just watched, witnessing such an unexpected show. Then they stood, mouths open, not knowing what to do. Perhaps they were torn about whether to give a standing ovation for my singing, or my tumbling performance. Dad's show of affection felt foreign to me, and yet it was clearly

understood that it was his duty as a father to appease
his hurt child.

Could it be he actually felt sorry for me and thought
I might have broken my bones?

After Dad rubbed my back and checked to see if
I'd broken anything, he told me to go back upstairs and
continue my singing up there. He picked up the bowl
floating on a puddle and took it to the kitchen, while I
climbed back up the stairs cautiously, achy.

"That was a good song, Xulli!" Grandma
called after me.

"You might have just angered the rain god to push
you off the stairs!" Grandfather speculated.

"You have such a marvelous voice!" Grandmother
added. "Go on upstairs and sing some more, won't you?"

"Your singing might only call for more rain,"
Grandfather remarked as I started to climb slowly up the
wet stairs, whimpering and feeling sore all over as if I had
been beaten. Luckily I had not broken any bones. I sat
quietly in a corner, upstairs, watching the dripping rain
as it fell into pots, creating its own musical rhythm. I did
not feel like singing anymore. Di and Wilma were busily
threading colorful rubber bands.

BIRTH CONTROL

Early Sunday morning, we were awakened by a knock
on the front door. I got up and opened it, still sleepy-
eyed. I thought the Jehovah's Witnesses had come by, as
usual, requesting time to talk about Jesus and God, and
giving us pamphlets. They were the most respectful and
polite homo sapiens I had ever met on this planet. They
were always dressed up, and always gave us something—
brochures and booklets that we used as toilet paper. But,
this time, it was people from the Birth Control Mission
inviting all the neighbors, husbands especially, but also
wives, to attend a community meeting that evening in the
cluster. They wanted to speak to Mom and Dad personally,
one lady told me.

"We want to ask them to participate in this very
important meeting," she said. I told them to wait outside,
and I would ask my parents if they could come in. Mom
came down and was respectful and friendly as she
listened to the female leader explaining the purpose
of their visit. Dad, still feeling groggy from his night's
drinking, got out of bed, came downstairs in just his red
cotton briefs, and said politely, "We'll think about it."

I was mortified with shame for Dad's outfit. No
doubt the guests felt uncomfortable seeing dad almost
naked, and they were probably as shocked as I was. Before
the missionaries left, they gave Mom a big, brown paper

bag with "gifts" inside. I closed the door as soon as they left. I stayed downstairs while Mom and Dad talked upstairs. Mom had to get ready for work. A neighbor had gotten her a job as laundry woman for a well-to-do family. Two dollars a day for a week's worth of laundry.

I went back upstairs, and joined my brother and sister who started blowing up balloons of different colors they found in the big brown bag of gifts from the Birth Control Mission. They were wrapped individually. We tore open the pouches to get the balloons out and blew up as many as we could. They were covered in a slippery substance that tasted bad, but the unpleasant taste was forgotten the minute we started bouncing, throwing and catching them outside in front of our house—staying within the cluster, of course. We tossed and kicked them, catching and chasing them, which led us farther and farther away from our house, toward busy streets. We laughed and ran back to the cluster, not thinking about time. Our giggling drew other children our age to join us. Since we did not have a television or toys, anything new was of great delight.

Our next-door neighbor, Mr. Garry, paid us a visit in the early afternoon. He was a tall, skinny man who walked around the neighborhood with no t-shirt on, sometimes just in his boxers. Dad invited him in and offered him a chair.

"So I see you don't like using the condoms the Birth Control Mission gave you," he said and chuckled. "Instead, you give them to your children to make balloons out of." They were both now laughing, but I could see Dad's face turning red. He played along with Mr. Garry's questioning, as if he had known all along. My cheeks grew hot as I realized what they were supposed to be used for.

MOM WAS PREGNANT AGAIN

We used up all those condoms as balloons. The Birth Control missionary group never came back, and Mom was expecting again. One morning in February, Mom woke up at 4 AM. She told Dad that her water broke. Dad was grumpy, irritated that he had to get up and take Mom to the hospital so early in the morning.

"I can't help it. My water broke," she said. "It's time to go."

Dad, at last, got up out of bed, got dressed, and said he'd call a taxi.

Meanwhile, Mom was folding baby clothes to take with them. I, too, got up. Still sleepy-eyed, watching mom folding baby clothes she had saved from when Wilma was born.

"Make sure you keep an eye on your brother and sisters," Mother said. "I will be back in a couple of days."

"Yes, mother," I said sleepily. I did not know whether to feel excited that another baby was going to join our crazy family, or not. Mostly I wanted some more sleep. Dad came back from calling the taxi. Mom was already packed and ready to go. Our eyes met and communicated

love. She descended the stairs where Dad waited. A
taxi pulled up.

The following day, in the late afternoon, Dad
came home from the hospital and announced, "It's a
girl." Then he mumbled, "Another girl. They will be
home tomorrow."

I was anxious to see what the new baby looked like,
but I did not know what to think. I also felt concerned
about the situation. Di was 10, Bebeng was 9, and Wilma
was 4. With the new addition to this family, there were too
many of us already. I brushed the thought aside. There
was nothing I could do but welcome her. I did wonder
about Mother's health. Dad hadn't mentioned whether
her delivery went well. I assumed she was alive. He would
have told me otherwise. I went back inside to clean before
Mom and the new baby came home. I fetched water,
swept the dirt floor, and cooked rice. I heard Wilma
crying and ran upstairs. She was sitting up. She pointed at
poop on the floor.

"You have to tell me when you have to poop!" I
snapped at her. She backed away, looking afraid. I ran
downstairs to find newspaper, ran back up, scooped her
poop with folded newspaper and took it outside. Threw it
in the garbage. Then I scrubbed the floor clean with soap
and water. She was too small to go out to the outhouse
alone, but I reminded her again to tell me if she had to do
number two as she watched me scrub her mess with her
big, round, black eyes.

She nodded, looking ashamed. I explained to her
that I would spread out old newspapers on the floor
and let her do her business there. I told her she could
wake Di as well to help her. She was crying. I took her

downstairs. I told her to bend over. With soapy left hand
and a jug of water to rinse on the right, I washed her
bottom with soap.

Wilma's skin resembled mine, dry and flaky from
the shoulder down, but because she was darker, the
flakes and dryness were less obvious. I wished I had good
lotion to put on both our skins. Di slept on, so I did the
chores by myself, telling Wilma to play in a corner while
I cleaned. Then I looked in the kitchen for something to
feed us. I sprinkled white sugar over cold white rice and
gave her a teaspoon to eat it by herself.

Mom arrived home, as expected, with a brand
new baby girl. Dad named her Neneng. Dad picked out
the name in memory of his High School girlfriend, he
announced. Nobody was paying attention to him at this
point. All eyes were on the brand new baby. The baby had
a tan complexion and very slanted eyes. I could not keep
my eyes off her. She was a cute little thing. My frustration
vanished the moment I laid eyes on her innocent face.
But I also knew I would have to take care of her.

GARBAGE

Garbage was a growing problem in our neighborhood.
There was garbage everywhere, piled high on street
corners, in back and front of neighbor's houses. Some
of it was burning, giving off a stench. Those passing

by had to cover their noses or inhale it into their lungs. Scrawny dogs scavenged for scraps on the piles along the streets. Horse flies buzzed around them. Maggots crawled in and about. Hungry cats and rats come out mostly at night, having a grand feast.

On a still night, the smell was unbearable, especially when the temperature was in the triple digits. It was hard to breathe, much less sleep. We kept the windows open for a breath of fresh air, but that brought the smell with it. We kept the inside of our house clean, but had no choice but to dump garbage outside, since no one picked it up.

Dad tried digging a hole in the backyard and burning the garbage, but it filled too quickly. We went down the streets looking for places to throw our garbage. We just found more garbage from other people piled up on the street and added ours to theirs.

"Something has to be done!" I heard neighbors say a lot. People in the community called a meeting to talk about Tatalon's garbage problem. City officials filed petitions to ask the government for funding to employ people to dig more dump sites. The city had no desire for Tatalon to be compared to Tondo, which was internationally famous for its smoky garbage mountains and squalid shantytowns, but it required money to pay for materials, equipment, and manpower for a garbage system. The meeting reached an impasse.

Garbage dumping continued. It kept getting piled up in the streets and in people's yards. Now the blame was aimed at the country's president, who was well aware of Manila's garbage crisis. The smoky garbage mountains piled up, and there were problems with the sewers, sanitation, and water. People were crying out for help.

"But most of what he promises is garbage! Get it? Ha ha ha," My father joked, drunk at one of the cluster meetings.

No one laughed.

Our community leaders had gathered a second time to educate and ask residents to volunteer in the effort to make our streets clean. They asked that people try to dispose of what they could properly. "Cleanliness starts at a grassroots level," one official said.

As a result of the petitions being signed in the clusters, the government finally started employing thousands of citizens to work around the clock cleaning the streets of Manila. These new employees of the government project could be recognized anywhere by their bright yellow t-shirts and orange pants. They were called Metro Aid. Their jobs were to sweep and collect garbage from designated streets around Manila. Once a week, a garbage truck came to Tatalon to pick up garbage. A big, yellow garbage truck arrived around midnight and hauled away garbage from each home.

For a couple months, the new garbage collection seemed to be working. Slowly, the streets of Tatalon started to look cleaner. No foul odor rose from mounds of refuse, no more choking smoke. Everyone was encouraged to resist throwing things in the streets, on the sidewalks or any other public place. Designated trashcans were installed to maintain cleanliness at all times.

City officials announced that the Philippine president, Marcos, and his wife would be visiting Tatalon to see the progress. A judicial mandate was then issued requiring every single person in the community, including the young and the very old to keep the roads and streets clean at all times until the visit was over. Residents worked diligently to keep their yards free of debris. Citizens were encouraged to plant flowers in their front yards, to paint rocks white and line them up neatly around plants and along walkways. Rocks painted white could be seen for miles, in everyone's front yards. It was unbelievable! No garbage could be seen anywhere. Green shrubs and flowering plants appeared where garbage used to be.

The officials further announced that whichever cluster looked the cleanest and neatest would win a prize in order to heighten people's morale. Every morning and evening, men, women, old and young, swept their front yards and walkways. They even dressed to impress the President in case that was the day he came. They added even more plants and were considerate of their neighbors. The night before the president's visit, city officials gathered one last time in preparation for the next day's big event. They announced over a microphone that they wanted the Philippine president to give our town two thumbs up.

Dad said, "Better if the President stuck his two thumbs right up his ass because sanitation and sewage problems are in dire need of attention." He stood up and walked out of the meeting. Mom, mortified, made no comment about Dad's behavior. Before going home, everyone was given a stick with a little paper flag of the Philippines to wave around upon the Marcos's arrival.

The big day came. Everyone came out of their houses wearing their best outfits. They inspected their yards one last time, marched up to a designated place, waited, and watched for the President and his wife. A huge crowd, thousands of people, gathered to await the President and his wife, Imelda Marcos. There was talk of gifts being given out to everyone. I was excited about the gifts. My family would receive a gift from the most important persons of the country. I wondered what the gift was.

When the limousine arrived, the crowd cheered loudly, proudly waving the flags in the air. The driver stepped out to open the door. The President came out first, raised his right hand and waived at the cheering crowd, some of whom screamed their devotion and love for the President, other's in tears for having seen the most important person of the country. Then his wife stepped out. A goddess of all goddesses stepped out. The cheering doubled! Everybody wanted to be near, get closer to the beautiful first lady and shake her dainty hands. The crowd continued cheering as they stepped onto the stage. I was too far away to really see. People stood in front of me and were bigger, taller than me. Some stepped on my toes. I pushed them away. I wanted to see what the President and his wife looked like in person.

The cheering crowd became wild, pushing and shoving closer to the stage. Guards pushed them back and asked them to keep calm. I stood, squeezed in the solid crowd, hearing the President give his speech, thanking the people for their time and efforts in making the country a better place to live. He did not speak too long. When he was done, he gave the microphone to his wife, and she took over. I heard a soft, feminine voice, followed by earsplitting thunderous claps from the audience. Then she was asked to sing a song. She was famous for having a beautiful musical voice. She did. When she finished, she gave a speech, but I could not understand what she was talking about.

After her speech, one of the guards, standing behind her, handed her a bundle. She threw a white plastic bag into the air, with the "surprise gifts" inside. The crowd went wild, raising their arms up in the air, vying to be the one to catch it. People fought over it. The first lady threw another white plastic grocery bag up in the air, and another, and another while people were fighting to catch and pick up the pieces of gifts on the ground. So many hands had ripped the plastic bags and grabbed the first item that came out. She kept throwing the gifts in the air while people cheered, screamed, shoved, and cried. Then she announced she would give one last very special gift. Everybody who was bent over, still fighting to get the last thrown bag, stood up straight. There was a brief hush in the audience, anticipating, wondering what that special gift was. All of a sudden, the special gift came flying over the crowd. All eyes followed it coming down. I heard a man yell, "It's a watch!"

The crowd went crazy, raised their hands up, and fought to catch it. When the crowd in front of me tried to move in the direction of the watch, falling through the air, I was able to finally see Imelda Marcos for one fraction of a second. The wife of the Philippine president stood calmly facing the frenzied crowd, in her elegant long white, sequined dress. Her manicured hand, with brightly painted nails, held the microphone firmly, her hair perfectly groomed. It was only a brief moment, but

for me, it was an image to last a lifetime. Soon it was over.
They thanked everyone for coming, waved good-bye to
the crowd, and left the stage.

That's it? I thought. *They're not going to step off the stage
and look around the neighborhood, after all that preparation?
And where is my family's gift?*

We walked home, leaving the cheering crowds
behind. I wondered if my family would ever get a gift
as promised. Behind me I heard someone saying the
President and his wife had to visit another town and did
not want to be late. So, half of the crowd decided to head
in the same direction as the President, to catch more gifts
from the air. Houses on both sides of the streets seemed
deserted, with their fresh paint and newly planted
gardens, bare of any garbage. I felt I was in a twilight
zone, walking into a different country, and wondered if
the place was going to stay this way forever.

The neighbors talked about the Marcos' visiting in
other places, other subdivisions, and schools. A large
entourage that had come with the President remained to
survey the town. They passed through in their limousines,
pausing occasionally to talk with a few residents and
shake hands. I worried, hoping they would not come
across my father who might be drunk and say something
to get himself arrested. Luckily, he stayed sober that day.
He came home with Mom, my brother and sisters. They
did not bring home gifts from the Marcos's. Dad was very
disappointed at the city officials making such a big fuss
about the visit and the prize giveaways.

"They were nothing but a bunch of propagandists,"
he grumbled. "They just talk big and do nothing." Mom
told him to be quiet, that the officials were still around,

and someone might hear him. He said he did not give a
damn, and the Marcos's could kiss his ass.

SUMMER IN MANILA

The mid-summer heat and humidity were unbearable.
It was oppressive and made everyone sweat. We were
constantly thirsty and longed for a cold drink. Since we
did not have a refrigerator, Dad would send me to the
store to buy a block of ice. When I returned with it in the
wagon, he put it in a pitcher of water. We then cooled
ourselves with glasses of ice water. We reveled in it, while
fanning ourselves with cardboard.

Aunt C came over to the house, panting. "Hurry,
Xulli! Get bags and bowls, as many as you can carry.
There's a ration of food being given away. Come quick!"
she announced frantically.

Mom hurried to the kitchen and gave me big bowls,
empty jars and bags. I grabbed them and ran as fast as
I could, following my aunt. The line was a couple miles
long by the time we arrived. It was blazing hot, and I had
neither hat nor umbrella. But I had to get this free food.
I stood and waited in line not knowing where Aunt C
had gone. Since I ran faster than her, I'd left her behind.
I thought she probably did not need the food anyway
because she could afford to buy anything she wanted for
her family. But, no, I saw her walking in the distance and

waved. She joined me, rather than having to start at the
end of the line, which kept getting longer every minute.
She brought her own big bags.

She started talking to the women behind us in
line, as I thought how nice it was going to be to have
free ration food.

"The government should do this more often," Aunt
said. She wondered what they were giving away and
who was giving it. People who had already gotten theirs
passed us. They had sardines, rice, pinto and black beans,
oatmeal, and packets of Top Ramen noodles. Aunt C
worried that there might not be anything good left by the
time our turn arrived.

After nearly an hour in the beating sun, it was our
turn to pick up our rations. I saw big boxes of canned
goods being opened and more inside a big military van. I
received my share and, leaving Aunt C, went home.

As I set the goods out, Dad said, "Go back for
another round."

He said to take my brother with me, and to bring
extra bags. I did.

NEXT YEAR AT SCHOOL

I was voted class leader for my dedication as a student
again. I was serious about my studies and helped other
students who were lagging behind, especially with

English. I helped others with their homework and was even starting to like math and science a little bit.

The more time I spent learning at home, the more prepared and confident I was in school. One day, I was busy writing when Gina paid a surprise visit to my classroom. I looked up and watched her approach my teacher who was seated behind her desk. She spoke with her in a low voice. I tried to figure out what she wanted with my teacher. I knew I was not in trouble, but I had never seen her talk intimately with my teacher before. She was never as close to my teacher as I was with hers.

Then she came to where I was seated, bent, and whispered in my ear, "Grandfather is dead. Come with me."

I looked at my teacher at front of the class. She nodded. I packed up my things, and we left.

"Hurry up!" Gina urged. We headed for my brother's classroom, pulled him out and then ran home, making sure to cross safely, and sometimes fighting our way between cars. Images of Grandfather crept into my mind. I was not close to him, and his death did not have any effect on me. He was an old man, and it was time for him to go. Gina blabbered on about getting ready for the Province.

"We will not be taking the bus," she said. "We're going to ride in my dad's jeepney."

It was big enough to fit thirteen people, including luggage. "We leave tonight," Aunt C announced when we reached her house.

I was excited to see the countryside again. It held a very special place in my heart, the place I grew up, with so many good memories along with the bad. I will

soon see Kristy again. I missed her, and I could not
wait to leave.

"Let's go!"

I went home and helped my family pack. By the time
we were ready, it was very late in the afternoon. We went
to Aunt C's and picked out seats inside the jeepney. As
always, we all sat and waited for Aunt C. I thought she
was putting on makeup, like normal, and couldn't believe
she would at a time like this, but it turned out she was on
the phone, talking to relatives in La Union. Gina went
back inside the house to find out what was happening
and then came back out. She announced that it was not
Grandfather who died. It was Grandmother.

My heart fell to the ground. My body went numb,
and my mind went blank. I looked up to heaven. A dark
cloud hung over the horizon. A cold chill brushed me,
clouding my eyes with tears.

"No! I did not hear that," I whispered to myself.
My head spun and my heart raced. I wanted to scream.
The one person in the world who showered me with
respect and love was dead. I wanted to slap Gina to
her senses and tell me she made a mistake, to tell me
it was Grandfather who died and not my grandmother.
How could she have been so wrong? A silent scream
formed inside me.

All my sweet memories of grandmother spun
through my head, making me dizzy and sick to my
stomach. I wanted to climb out of the jeepney and throw
up. Gina took her seat as the jeepey's engine started to
roar. She apologized for getting the news wrong. She
must have seen my reaction. I shrunk in my seat.

Everybody had to be retold the correct news. When Aunt C hung up the phone and came to the jeepney, she confirmed it and said it hadn't been Gina's fault. Even the telegram read, "Grandfather passed. Come home." That's what had been written. The person who relayed the news must have been drunk, utterly confused, or the telegrapher heard and typed the message incorrectly.

On our way out of Manila to the Province, I kept wiping tears off my cheek and swallowing back my vomit. I did not want to ask Uncle Fred to pull over for me so I could throw up and mourn on the side of the road. I was just a passenger. We had to keep moving. I wanted so much to hug Grandmother right then. It would be an eight hour drive before I could see her for the last time. No one spoke a word for hours, mute in our mourning and disbelief, and each of us somber and grieving in our own way. The jeepney made occasional stops at gas stations and for us to relieve ourselves.

When we were about thirty minutes away, Aunt C decided to shop for a big tin of biscuits and a jar of Nescafe coffee for neighbors and relatives who might call to pay their respects to Grandmother.

As soon as the jeepney parked in front of Grandmother's house, I was the first to jump out of the seat and run up the stairs. There she was, in her white coffin in the living room with a glass window showing her face. I stared at her as tears flooded my eyes. I could not believe she was dead. "I miss you and I love you," I whispered.

Grandfather opened the casket cover for everybody to touch her hands.

Aunt C walked towards the coffin, calling out, "Mother! Mother!" She wept her heart out, her head resting on her mother's chest and her arms wrapped around her body as she wailed and cried. A neighbor placed a chair behind Aunt C for her to sit on and continue her mourning. Her children and husband gathered next to her.

My dad and brother came next. Mom stayed at a distance, holding the baby and my younger sister, Wilma, next to her. She was superstitious about dead people. She would dream of them for days, she had told me. Aunt Li and Cousin Violet joined us around the coffin. Aunt Li's eyes were red and puffy. Cousin Violet did not cry, but she was abnormally quiet. All of my aunts stood around their mother's coffin. I backed away and sobbed in a corner. More people came—relatives I had never met along with neighbors here to pay their respects. They brought fruit and money offerings. They gave Grandma a quick look and then sat chatting. When everybody was seated, Dad came closer to his mother's side. He put his hand on her head and cried like a little boy.

"You're going to Heaven now, Mother," he said, as he patted her head, smoothing her hair with the palm of his hand. He was sober. He was emotional. He was in tears.

I was taken aback to see an emotional side of him. So, he had feelings—for the dead.

"I'm so sorry for all the troubles I put you through," he sobbed. "Please know I have always loved you." Everybody heard him speak with such tenderness in his voice and stopped talking. They could not believe what they had heard.

Dad closed the casket cover, pulled out a handkerchief from his pocket and blew his nose. Then he left the room. I went back to see Grandmother's face one more time. I stared at her a long while. Aunt Li, Aunt Ud, and Aunt C placed chairs around their mother's coffin to recite a special prayer for her. Everybody else joined in, including all four uncles. Dad was no longer around. He had left the house. I did not know whether or not he would ever come back.

Mom helped serve biscuits and coffee to all the visitors and relatives. She helped in the kitchen, cooking dinner for everyone. Aunt Ud made *Arros caldo* in a giant pot to feed the clan. It was a special sweet rice soup, sautéed with fresh garlic, ginger and chicken meat. It was an easy meal to serve.

In the evening, the adults placed a soft mat on the floor in the living room next to the coffin where the children would sleep while the grownups played mahjong until their eyes were too heavy to continue. By dawn, when it was still dark out, everyone went to bed.

I was haunted by images of Grandmother getting out of her coffin and touching me. The more I thought the idea, the faster my heartbeat. The post lamps standing at the foot of the coffin stayed on all night and they were very bright. They lessened my fear of a grandmother zombie. Dad was still not home. I did not know if I had been awake all night. I could not sleep. I tried not to close my eyes. Even though I loved Grandmother so much, there was still a possibility she could turn into a mean zombie.

On the day of the vigil, late in the evening, a Bingo game started. Dad and his drinking buddies came over to pay their last respects. Pamboy put on a great show, crying out loud, wrapping his arms around the coffin, saying sentimental words of farewell, and wishing he was the one who died instead of Grandmother. He was so drunk and out of control. The words coming out of his mouth sounded convincing enough to pull everyone into his depressed mood. He had even written a special note for Grandmother to take with her to the afterlife. He took it out of his pocket and read out loud:

Sister. Sister. Oh Sister.

Your life has been cut short in this world (a cry of despair). I hope you find happiness where you are going, Sister.

Oh, how I miss you.

Why . . . Why do you have to leave? Why . . . (sobbing)

The chattering of the crowd died down to an expectant hush, waiting to see if there was more.

Take me. YES! Take me with you, Sister! (Wailing) I want to go with you in the afterlife! (More crying) Here . . . take this letter I have written for you.

"Does anyone have a pencil?" Pamboy asked.

One of the uncles walked over to where Pamboy was sitting comfortably, and gave him one. He started adding to his special message, signed his name:

Here... Sister, take this letter with you . . . just so . . .

He folded the paper, opened the coffin cover and tucked the note at Grandmother's side and then closed it again.

You will not feel so lonely anymore.

We shall be together . . . soon.

Read it while you're in Heaven, Sister . . .
(more sobbing).

You and I can be together in Heaven . . . (Pause . . .
silence . . . sobbing).

I will meet you in Heaven, Sister . . ."

Dad interrupted Pamboy and tried to pull him away
from the coffin.

"For crying out loud! Does he even know what
he's talking about? He is too drunk to know what he is
talking about," Aunt Ud commented. Aunt C was getting
angry and ordered Dad to take his drunken friends
outside to cool off.

Pamboy, still crying, stumbled and refused to get up,
sobbing uncontrollably. As Dad struggled to help him get
up, Pamboy accidentally kicked the coffin stand. It shook,
tilted, and was about ready to topple onto him. A great
'ohhh' went around the room as everyone prayed for the
coffin to right itself.

"Oh Christ Jesus! Somebody help!" Aunt C
screamed as the coffin slid slowly off its stand to join
Dad and Pamboy on the floor. Guests in the living
room anticipated, and prayed simultaneously to the
Almighty and Mother Mary not to let the coffin spill
over its contents onto drunken souls. One elderly
relative nervously gave a quick cross sign, and prayed
hard to stop any accidents from happening. Dad tried to
get up but lost his balance and stumbled on top of his
friend as he tried to lift him up.

Pamboy looked too heavy for Dad to manage. He
had not been home for two days and looked like he had
not had a wink of sleep. His eyes were bloodshot. He
tried to pick himself up first while Pamboy continued

wailing. Andres, another friend, who was also drunk,
came in to the rescue. All three, with arms on each
other's shoulder, careened out the door.

Guests, holding mugs of coffee poised midair, stared
in disbelief, jaws dropped, as their eyes followed the three
drunken men out the door. The professional mourner
continued her prayers, head bowed, murmuring,
and now praying for the three alcoholics to come
to their senses.

Aunt Ud told me to call my uncles to come up and
help straighten the coffin back onto its stand.

Chaos always followed Dad wherever he was drunk.

FINAL GOOD-BYES

On the fourth day, at eight o'clock in the morning, we
said our final good-bye to Grandmother. After breakfast,
we all gathered in the living room, kneeling in front of
a crucifix hanging on the wall at the head of the coffin.
When we finished our prayers, everyone had another
glance at Grandmother's face. Then her coffin was closed
for good. Dad, who had a hangover and still hadn't slept,
dressed up neatly, hair combed back with greasy pomade.
He lifted the coffin with his brothers.

On the street, the three sisters huddled close, crying,
next to the two drummers, a trumpeter, and a horse and
carriage that waited, ready for the procession to

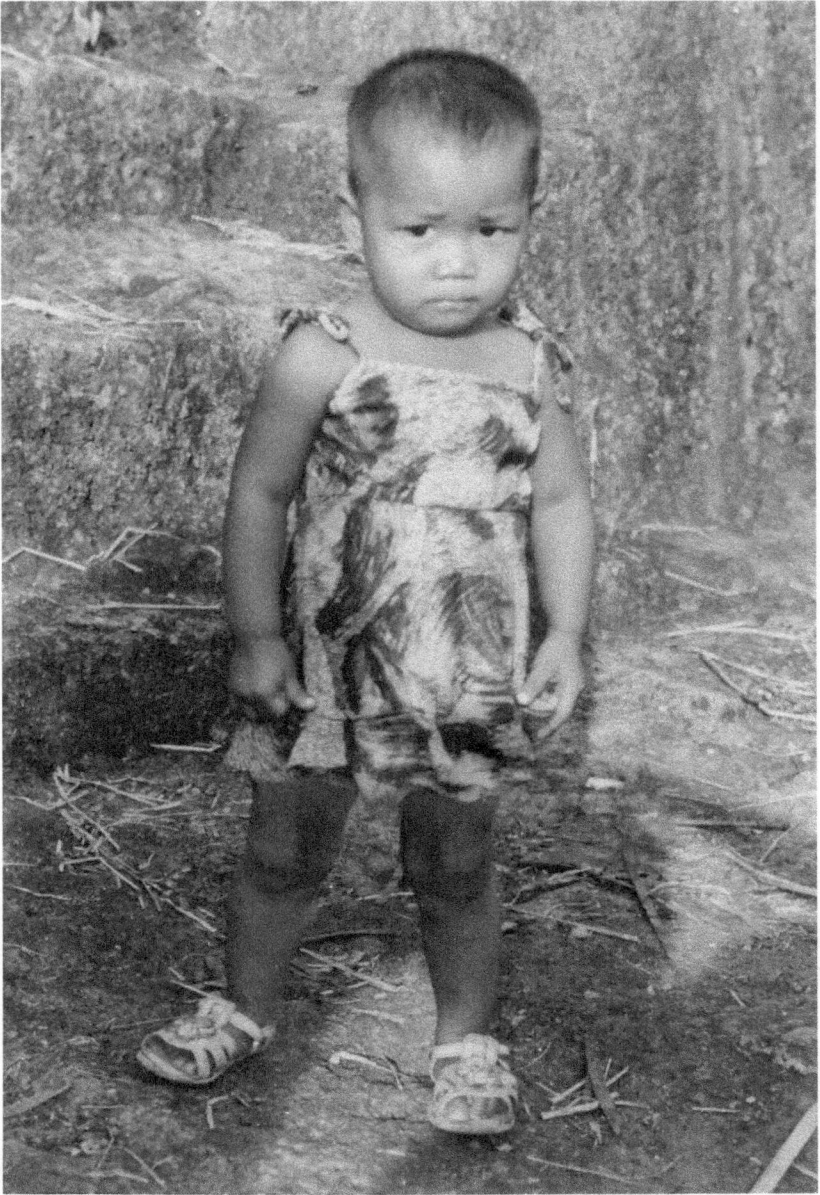

Sister Neneng, shortly after she took a stroll

Back row, left to right: Father, Uncle Ellio, Uncle Pablo,
Unknown Uncle, Grandfather, Aunt Li, Uncle Eddie, Mother,
Unknown Aunt. Front row: Brother Di in front of Cousin
Violet, Sister Bebeng in front of Xulli

Aunt Li pinning
honorary ribbon
on Xulli

Aunt Li pinning a ribbon on Di

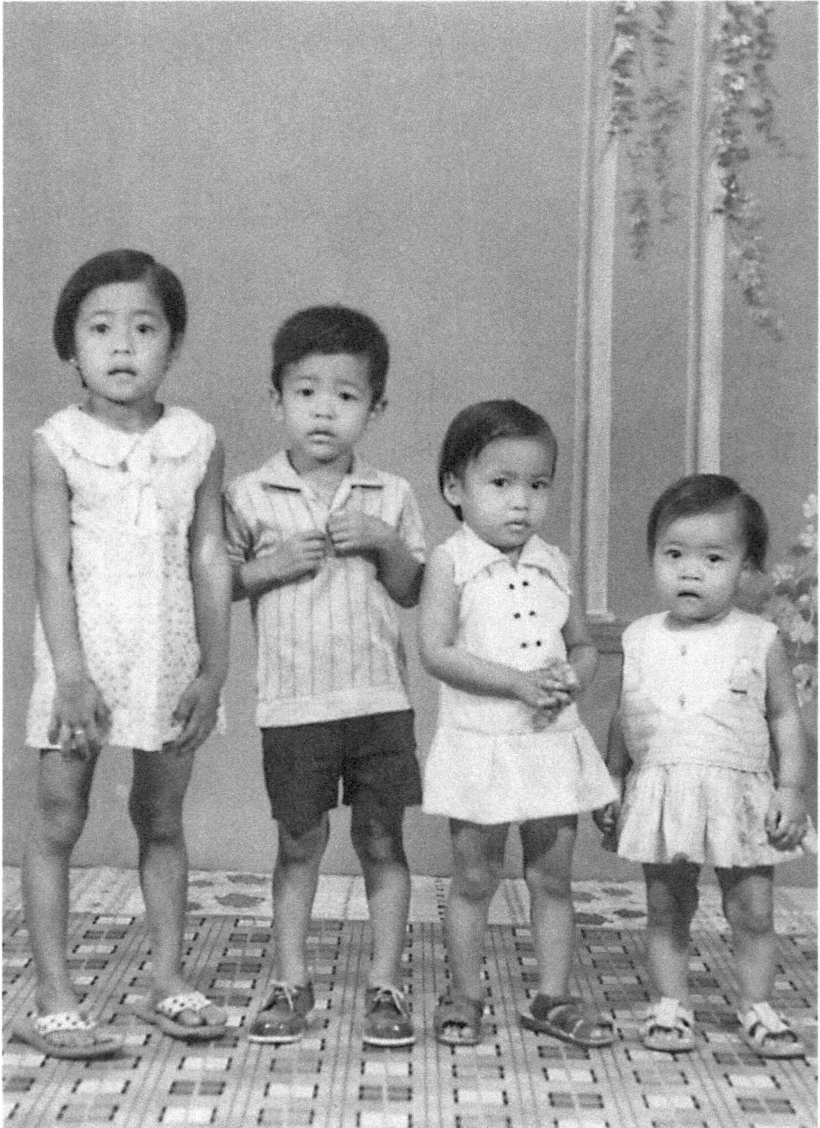

Left to right: Xulli, 5; Di, 4; Bebeng, 3; Moon-ay, almost 2

At St. Christopher Church, left to right: Cousin Violet, Bebeng,
Di, Xulli, and Mother overlooking Sister Moon-ay

St. Christopher Church. Everyone watched the
front stairs, waiting for the four men to carry their
mother's casket down.

Pamboy came running from his house down the
street, waving his hands in the air, saying, "Stop! Wait! Just
a moment!" He ran up the stairs, panting.

I wanted to see what he was going to do,
so I followed.

"I want the letter back," he demanded, huffing and
puffing on his way up the stairs. He darted into the living
room, looking more sober.

Dad and the three uncles had to put the coffin back
on its stand and open it. Pamboy desperately searched for
the letter he had tucked in there the night before. Dad
joined in the search, while his three younger brothers
and I looked on. He groped around by Grandmother's
feet, up her sides, feeling for his paper. He looked like
he was molesting grandmother's corpse.

Pamboy started to look anxious, desperate, scared to
his sober senses. They could not find the note, and Dad
suggested Pamboy must have removed it the night before.

"I swear to the Almighty, I don't have the note," he
cried nervously. They tried lifting Grandmother's body
from side to side. Nothing. No note.

"Are you sure you left the note here?" Dad
asked, frustrated.

"Yes! I'm positively, one hundred percent sure!" he
snapped. "I don't have it. I want that note back!" Beads
of sweats showed on Pamboy's forehead as he continued
to search. "I was pretty sure I placed it on her right side,"
he kept saying.

Aunt Ud, Aunt Li, and Aunt C joined us upstairs,
asking what was going on, what was taking the men so
long. "Now that you're sober, have you come to your
senses?" Aunt C asked. "Last night you were spouting
crazy talk." She chided him in front of everyone.

"I found it!" screamed Pamboy, waving the note with
relief on his face.

Dad asked him where he had found it.

"On her chest, under one hand," Pamboy answered.

Dad and his brothers again closed the casket.
The three women hurried down the stairs and started
wailing in a singsong pattern to encourage others to
join into their depressed mood. In their mourning,
they also apologized to their dead mother for the
ridiculous drunken men.

The trumpet blared a call to the Angels of Heaven.
It startled the white horse and gave a frantic rise of
his front legs. A thunder of drums reverberated deep
through all the living souls present while the four men
descended the stairs with the departed. Everyone in the
street watched as they appeared at the top of the stairs
and then starting down. Dad lost his footing. He plopped
down on his rear end, still holding onto the coffin
with one hand, red in the face. This time he was sober,
albeit hung over.

Everyone gasped. Luckily his three brothers were
able to keep balanced and held onto the coffin. Jolted
by his fall, Dad jumped up and took up his position,
standing straighter.

"Why do bad things keep happening?" murmured
Aunt C, loud enough for all close by to hear.

"You better watch your step, boy!" shouted Pamboy
from the bottom of the stairs. "Or you'll be in that coffin
yourself!" He laughed wildly. All heads turned to him,
some with disgust. Dad heard him and grinned.

"I don't think that's funny," Aunt Li
whispered to Aunt C.

"The way they continue their drinking, they will be
buried next!" Aunt C answered.

The casket was placed in the horse drawn carriage
led by a coach driver on its way to St. Christopher Church.
The three aunts followed, while the rest of us trailed
behind. The wailing continued. Neighbors of all ages
stood in front of their houses and shops to pay respect for
the passing funeral. It did not matter whether they knew
the deceased or not. They offered a minute of their time
to show reverence for the dead, as fixed by tradition.

We were near St. Christopher Church, ready to cross
the highway, when the horse decided to do its business.
It stopped in the middle of the road and took a dump
while we all waited. The horse owner could not leave
his horse's crap in the middle of the highway. Hurriedly,
he jumped out of the carriage and shoveled the horse's
droppings and placed it in a small bucket hanging on
the side of the coach, as if it was purposely kept there for
emergencies such as this one. The band, the prayers, and
the crying continued. Pamboy, Andres, and Dad called
the traffic to a halt in opposite directions.

As soon as the horse finished and was ready to move,
we proceeded to the church. The horse and carriage
stayed outside the church, and we walked right in and
up to the altar. The priest, who had been waiting for our
arrival, gave his special prayers. We took our seats and

listened to his blessings and ceremony, which seemed to go on forever, speaking to a decaying body and immortal souls destined for all eternity. My mind went blank, my ass numb. As soon as he finished, we all stood, gathered around the coffin, took photos, and proceeded to the cemetery. Grandmother's coffin was placed in a vault. For the first time, I saw Grandfather wipe tears off his cheeks. As soon as we said our last prayers, we walked back home.

THE AFTERMATH

Back at home, Grandmother's house felt eerily quiet and empty. I kept expecting to see her in the kitchen, blowing on a pile of sticks to make fire under the stove or walking from her bedroom to the living room with a gas lantern in one hand, talking to herself, tipsy. I could not stay another minute in her house and went outside. I walked up the street to see our old house. Still there, it, too, chilled my bones. Overgrown with weeds all around, it looked uninviting. I dared not go near. Clearly no one had lived there since my family left three years before.

Aunt C decided we should stay a couple more days in La Union to get things in order. She told Grandfather he could go stay in Manila at her house, if he wanted, to help him get over his grief. Aunt Li suggested that Bebeng stay with her still. She would be well taken care of, like her own child, she said. Mom missed Bebeng

and wanted her to be close to her during our visit, but
Bebeng was distant. She was reminded that Aunt Li was
not her real mother. That she should show affection to
our real mother. She tried.

Mom hesitated about leaving her again, but Dad
said it was an excellent idea. "She can go to school with
Violet, and be well fed and cared for," Dad pitched for it.

On the day we were to leave La Union, Mom was
in tears as the jeepney pulled away from Aunt Li's house.
She could not take her wet eyes off Bebeng, who stood
in front of the house, waving good-bye to us. She kept
waving until we could no longer see her. I, too, felt sad
that she would not be with us, but I envied the good food,
the nice clothes, and comforts. I worried again about
how Violet might treat her, knowing how she treated
me. Bebeng was always quiet as a mouse, never one to
complain or cry. She never talked to me about how she
had been treated.

BACK TO MANILA

Grandfather and the uncles followed us to Manila the
following week. They took the shuttle bus. Uncle Ellio
and Uncle Cardo stayed at our house, while Grandfather
and Uncle Toy stayed at Aunt C's. Dad built two
bamboo beds, for Uncle Ellio and Cardo, downstairs.

With two more people to live with us, the house was packed like sardines.

Uncle Eddie had already started teaching Social Studies at one of the prominent universities in Manila and was living elsewhere. The arrangement seemed to work just fine, except Uncle Ellio and Uncle Cardo were unemployed, had no money, and hardly any clothes. They also had voracious appetites. Mom would have to cook extra meals to feed them. After eating a big meal at our house, they went to Aunt C's to get more. Dad was out of work and Mom started going out to work as a laundry person again. She came home late in the evening, due to heavy traffic. She was descaling fresh fish she had brought home from the market. Dad got upset with her and accused her of being unfaithful. Mom just stayed quiet, trying to ignore him, hurrying to get supper ready. Finally, she decided to speak up, explained her reason for being late, but her reasoning fell on deaf ears. Dissatisfied, he smacked her across the mouth. She was shocked and covered her mouth, telling him again that she was not meeting anyone and she had never been unfaithful. It was the traffic.

"Blame it on the traffic!" she shouted at him.

"You always say you're caught in traffic. I think you're lying!" Dad accused, threatening with his voice. Now they had a shouting match. We children watched from the corner, dreading what Dad might do next.

"What is it that you are doing with your boss?" he asked her.

"Nothing!" she screamed back. "I'm not doing anything with anybody! I go to work all day, slave away with hard work, and come home. I'm tired, and you treat me this way!" The more she tried to reason with him, the angrier he became. He slapped her again.

"Please stop!" I cried. "Please stop fighting!" I yelled at the top of my lungs, staying at a distance.

He ignored me.

"I'm very tired," Mom pleaded. "I've been working all day. Please, let's not argue." She tried to stay calm, as if ready to forgive him and move on with our lives. She stopped cleaning the fish and placed it in the bowl, setting it aside in the corner. I looked at Di next to me. He was trembling and sobbing quietly.

Mom usually bought food already cooked and brought it home, still hot, when she worked late, but she couldn't afford to buy a lot. Sometimes we were already asleep, having gone to bed without supper. Too sleepy to wait longer to eat, even when mom brought dinner already cooked. But they were too costly and given in meager size. Mom preferred to cook to save more money. Unfortunately, whenever she arrived at past nine or ten in the evening, we had already fallen asleep.

By the time she arrived with her groceries in plastic bags, Dad was at boiling point. He didn't seem to give a second thought that his wife might have been hit by a bus, robbed, or raped in the dark streets while walking home alone. It never seemed to cross his mind that she was exhausted, after scrubbing mountains of dirty clothes all day, then battling traffic, walking home from the bus stop, only to have to cook dinner for us. He had made up his mind. His wife was unfaithful, having a great time all day in bed with her boss, a lover or with whoever, eating bonbons, drinking champagne, indulging in sexcapades.

But if that were true, why not just stay there? Why come back home to be a punching bag? What a life!

"From now on you do not go back to work," Dad commanded, pointing his index finger into her face.

"Fine," Mom replied. "If that's what you want. You better bring home enough money to feed all of us then!" That was all she said. Clearly she didn't want to provoke another rage.

A brief silence fell on the room and Dad walked out. Quickly, I got up from the corner to help Mom with plates, spreading them out on the floor in a circle for us to eat before Dad returned. It tore me apart to see tears in her eyes. I wanted to hug her and tell her, "You work so hard. You're a good mom, no matter what Dad says." But we had never talked that way. I couldn't add more emotions to an already dramatic state.

Mom chopped onions occasionally sobbing, wiping her tears away with her blouse or her arm. The onions didn't help. They burned her delicate, watery eyes. It was getting very late. Dad would be back any minute. We gathered in circle, sat down, and ate in silence.

Weeks later, Dad found a job at a lumber mill, in walking distance from our house. Mom got up at 6 AM to prepare breakfast and lunch boxes. Dad got up at 7 AM, ate breakfast, dressed, and went out the door.

When we got home from school, the house was immaculately clean, clothes washed, and food ready, because Mom was staying home and not going out to work. Dad gave her his week's salary, which she budgeted like before. Dad kept a few pesos for cigarettes, he said. But when his money ran out, he asked Mom for a few more pesos. Mom hesitated, afraid he would spend it on gin even though he said he was quitting.

"What's the point of handing me over your salary when you ask for money every hour?" she asked him.

"Just one more peso and that's all," he kept repeating. Apparently he had collected enough pesos in three days to buy him and his buddies a couple bottles of gin.

On payday, Mom sent me to Dad's work, to make sure he came straight home. I had to make sure he didn't stop off for gin. So I waited by the gate outside his work. When employees started leaving, I stood up and watched for him in a crowd of men, carrying their lunch boxes. Not seeing him, I went inside the compound, and I asked one of his coworkers if he knew my dad. I told him his name and described him.

"You must be his daughter," the man said.

"Yes, I am," I answered.

He told me Dad was still working and offered to take me inside. I didn't trust him. He looked devious. So I told him no, I would wait outside a while longer. It was closing time and no one else was coming out. I snuck in and kept walking until I found Dad feeding a four-by-four into an electric saw. He was surprised to see me.

"What are you doing here?" he asked sharply. "What do you want?" He turned red, as if he had been caught.

"Mom told me to look for you, and make sure you came straight home from work with the paycheck," I told him loudly, competing with the noise of the blade.

He stopped working and told me I'd better get back home, pointing his finger to the exit. "Get!" he shouted, dismissing me with a wave of his hand.

I went home thinking I might have embarrassed him. I had better get ready for a lashing. But I didn't get one that time. Mom didn't send me after that.

CHRISTMAS

Christmas was always celebrated with so much spirit in the community. Vibrant and colorful decorations flashed in every household. Loud holiday music blared as if there were a competition for who had the loudest stereo.

Holiday music started as early as October to motivate consumers to start planning ahead for their spending. Christmas lanterns and multicolored tree lights flickered inside and out of every household, school, church, and shopping mall. Even jeepneys, tricycles, and buses had Christmas songs blaring alongside each other.

Every house in town had Filipino Capiz *Parols*—a star-shaped lantern that emitted bright, beautiful lights. They flickered brilliantly all night long, giving the entire cluster the holiday spirit. *Parols* in various designs, giant and small, hung outside anyone's home, as long as they had electricity.

Everyone got into the festive mood, but not us. For one thing, we had no electricity to plug in Christmas lights, and my family barely could afford our meals, let alone buy a stereo. My brother and I made our own paper star lanterns to decorate our windows. We used sticks we found outside and used leftover cooked rice for glue. Di had plenty of rubber bands, which we used to tie the ends of sticks together. To design our *Parols,* we collected old newspapers and colored pages of magazines from neighbors because we didn't have proper materials. We entered our finished projects in a school *Parol* contest, like we did every year. We never won, but our *Parols* hung proudly in our classrooms for everyone to see. That was good enough for us.

They didn't have flickering lights, fancy *capiz,* rice paper, foil, or colored glass, but we felt like winners when we looked at them hanging there with their long, spiral patterns and streamer tails dancing in the wind.

As I looked at all of them, I noticed two other *Parols* that were not very fancy. I asked other students who had made them. They pointed to a couple of students who looked rather unkempt and were probably just as poor as us, if not poorer. They didn't seem to mind that their *Parols* looked scruffy compared with the rest of students'. They had used old, worn newspapers to cover bamboo sticks, giving their *Parol* a dull appearance. But what mattered to them was that they had something to show off, something they had made with their own hands. They, too, were proud of their creations.

In the middle of December, Di and I searched for a small tree with lots of branches. We removed the leaves and set it in a small tin bucket. We filled it with rocks to keep the tree balanced and erect. We put it in the living room, and then we collected silver foil papers from cigarette packs, cut the foil into spaghetti size strips, and used it as tinsel to decorate our tree. Di hung G.I. Joes on the branches while I chained together rubber bands of different colors and strung them in the branches. The G.I. Joes looked like they had committed suicide because Di had wrapped the threads around their necks to hang them on the tree.

The silver foil papers, brother's plastic soldiers, and colorful rubber bands gave our tree a Christmas glow. As soon as we finished decorating, we placed the tree by the window for everyone to see.

On Christmas Eve, we went to Aunt C's for a family gathering. Aunt C never missed her obligatory prayers, so she announced we would join her at church for the Christmas Eve mass. No one said anything then, but there was some grumbling as everybody started to leave later that evening.

But Dad said he had already celebrated the child's birthday with his friends with a bottle of gin and raw calamari squids. He said that there was no need to go to church.

Aunt C insisted that, with all his drinking, going to church to get baptized by baby Jesus would be a good idea, so he could free his evil soul from all his sins in the past and present. She added that, this way, his spirit might reach heaven when he died.

"That's a bunch of bull crap!" Dad exclaimed to his older sister. "Those Catholic priests talk to you that way to make you feel guilty so you keep going to church to give them money."

"Please do not speak with evil tongue, or you will surely burn in hell!" replied Aunt C, now clearly irritated.

"What rubbish. I'm already in hell!" Dad countered, as if to invite more argument.

But Aunt C, who would rather spend her time and energy with Baby Jesus than with a drunk, decided to head off for church. Dad blew a puff of cigarette smoke her way as she crossed the porch. She turned and told him she would pray for him, for the remainder of his soul, to reach the high heavens.

"Then you had better pray twice as hard. And maybe give that money to me instead of the church," Dad barked, a grin on his face.

"I feel like I'm talking to the devil himself!" Aunt C muttered. "Who do you think I am? Do you think I'm stupid? You'd just spend the money on gin! The church will put it to better use." Aunt C walked away, dismissing the argument with a wave of her hand.

Aunt Ud, who was staying with Aunt C, decided to stay to keep an eye on the house and serve the kids their meals.

Uncle Fred had started his cooking preparations two days before Christmas Eve. He got up very early and started cooking sweet rice cakes, spaghetti with hotdogs and cheese, chow mein noodles, pork and beef stew, steamed buns stuffed with chicken filling, and hard boiled eggs. He bought special fruit cakes from one of the finest bakeries in town, mounds of mangoes, and a bucket of purple yam ice cream. There was no way Di and I would pass up a chance of eating delicious meals like these. Thanks be to baby Jesus!

We ate as if we had not been fed for a week, devouring so much that our bellies ached, and came back for more the next day.

ANOTHER ONE?

A year passed, and Mom was pregnant again.

"Why do you have to keep bringing more babies?" I screamed at her.

"Shut your mouth or I'll make it bleed," she warned me.

I could not bear looking at her protruding belly. I pouted every time she was near me.

"Come over here and let me look at your head," she commanded one day. She wanted to check for lice. I pretended not to hear. "Get over here when I call you!" she said, voice raised.

"There's nothing wrong with my head. It's your head that needs checking!" I yelled back, thoroughly fed up with her and her babies that I had to care for.

"Don't you dare talk to me that way. Don't you make me get up to drag you over here." Her voice had a menacing tone.

I walked begrudgingly to her and sat in front of her, facing away. She grabbed my shoulder. "Get closer!" She pulled me to her. I purposely bumped into her stomach with my full weight, hitting her belly with my head and back. *You wanted my head, here it is.*

"Ouch!" she yelped and gave me a hard slap on the shoulder. "That hurts me. Don't you ever do that to me again. Do you hear me?"

"I just hate having to babysit all the time," I cried.

"You do not talk to me that way. Do you understand?" She waved her finger at me.

By this time I'd turned to her, and we met eye to eye, both glaring. "But why do you have to have another baby?" I asked.

"The baby is here now. There's nothing I can do about it."

I had no choice but to keep quiet about it as she pulled me close and began searching for lice in my hair. I made no more comments about having too many kids. Perhaps this was her way of expressing affection. But at that point, I didn't want it.

UNCLE EDDIE AND HIS PROFESSOR WIFE BRING TEMPTATION

Uncle Eddie came to visit with his new wife, who was also a professor. We were to address her as Aunt Besse. She was a very thin, dark-skinned woman in her mid-thirties. Mom and Dad were in a state of disbelief to find that Uncle Eddie had decided to marry a woman. He and his wife seemed very happy about their union and wanted to celebrate at our house. They brought with them roasted pig and chickens as well as sweet rice cakes for dessert and two pitchers of coca cola. Mom cooked the rice.

Over supper, they announced that they would live at
our house. The house would be divided in half, one half
their living quarters. The two other uncles could live with
them downstairs.

The following week, they moved in, with modern
furniture, an electric fan, a small television, a brand new
stereo with disco lights on both sides above the speakers,
and large suitcases full of their nice clothing. My eyes
lit up when I saw their television. Di and I would be
able to watch movies. I assumed they would have the
entire house wired. I was excited. The atmosphere was
electric enough.

Our house now seemed crowded. There was hardly
a bare space. Mom and Dad seemed to have no say who
stayed and who went, because legally the house was under
Grandfather's name and the materials used to build it
were paid for by Aunt C.

Now that the newlyweds lived with us, the house had
electricity. Because they were both professors, they could
afford it. Uncle Eddie listened to his disco collections
with the strobe lights going, dancing in the living room,
and shaking his booty joyously. Wilma and I joined in
with the dancing. Disco music blaring, strobe lights
blinking in different colors, late in the afternoon, early
in the evening.

On weekdays, before going off to work, they
warned us children not to touch their personal property,
especially their stereo. We were not allowed to use their
electric fan without their permission, or to turn on their
television. The television was secured in a wooden frame
with double doors secured and a lock.

When they came home, they brought back with them fried chicken, spaghetti, barbecued pork or beef for dinner, served with steamed rice, but it was not for us. We just watched them eat it. On Friday nights, Aunt Besse would bring home fresh chicken meat, which she chopped into small pieces. From upstairs or outside, we could hear the sizzling as she threw pieces of chicken into hot oil. The smell of the food she cooked filled the air and tortured us. We wished they would share a little bit with us. But there were too many of us to feed, which would mean leaving them unsatisfied.

Mom warned us not to go to their living quarters for fear we would get blamed for stealing something they had, in fact, just misplaced, or accuse us of tinkering and hurting their belongings. So we stayed in our confined little space. But on weekends, when they were away, I snuck in to their place to watch television. I used the pointed tip of a plastic comb handle to unlock the television doors and watched with the sound turned way down. When I was finished watching a show, I would lock the doors back and made sure I had not left traces to be questioned later.

MAYBE NOT SO HETERO

As months passed, Uncle Eddie started to come home much later in the evening than his wife. The foods Aunt

Besse had prepared grew cold as she herself started to worry and wonder why her husband was coming home later and later at night. She asked me if I would meet her at the bus stop and walk home with her. I did not mind going out with her at night, but I hated standing on the street corner with her watching for Uncle Eddie to step out of a bus or jeepney. Passersby, especially old men, gave us long stares, thinking we were prostitutes looking for customers.

Some of them had the nerve to stop, stand in front of us, puffing cigarette smoke in our faces while they looked us over, head to toe, then turned and walked away when we ignored them.

Some nights, Aunt Besse brought me to the bus depot where she waited patiently, as late as 11 PM, hoping and praying that her husband would step out of a crowded bus. Each time a jeepney or a bus stopped in front of us, Aunt Besse craned her long, thin neck, eagerly searching for her husband.

One evening, Aunt Besse came to our living quarters upstairs and asked my dad permission to let me go with her. Dad approved, but I told her I hated standing on the street corner, being eaten alive by giant mosquitos. Besides, I had to be up early in the morning for school. She said she was very worried that something had happened to Uncle Eddie. She could not bear the thought of him walking home alone in the dark, maybe mugged by hoodlums, a gun pointed at his head. She elaborated on these terrible scenarios of what might happen to her husband if she did not go out and fetch him, looking frightened and teary-eyed. A pang of guilt pierced me. I felt sorry for her and reluctantly gave in. I told her I would go with her this one last time.

So again we stood and waited. I was irritated and she was worried sick. I was sleepy and tired of standing and slapping mosquitoes all over my arms, legs, and neck for what seemed like an eternity. Surely her legs must have felt rubbery as well, but she persevered, mumbling a prayer, never losing hope, heart filled with her love for Uncle Eddie.

"It's time to go home, Aunt Besse. It's late." I reminded her sympathetically.

"One more minute, please. I am sure he will be on the next bus," she said convincingly.

I finally told her there were no more buses or jeepneys coming, and it was getting very late. We had to go home now. Her face looked empty as she accepted the truth, and we walked back home in the dark with our flashlight. The streets were quite empty and abandoned. A few kept a yellow bulb softly glowing on their front porches, their shops, or in their kitchens. Only hungry dogs and stray cats searched for food in the streets. The humid air was more breathable at this late hour.

As soon as we got home, I crawled into bed, looking for a spot to lie. Aunt Besse's room was as quiet as the moon in the sky. She left the door unlocked, in case her husband walked in, hoping any minute that might become a reality. She, too, was exhausted, maybe more spiritually than physically. She had been waiting many nights for her husband, barely enduring.

Maybe I should have reassured her that he would come home soon, to lighten her spirit, I thought, as I drifted to sleep. Our living areas were divided only by plywood, and I could hear her sobbing below.

WEEKENDS IN THE FULL HOUSE

Over the weekend, my duty first thing in the morning was to fetch water. I took large buckets with me and lined them up along with neighbors' buckets and pails by the water collection station to hold my place. I made several round trips to the station until I filled the two home tanks.

Whenever Aunt Besse did her laundry, she asked me to fetch water for her. I told her to pay me a quarter each time. She asked me to buy her Tide laundry soap. When she asked how much it cost, I told her twenty centavos. But I was lying. I was charging her an extra ten centavos for making me walk to the store and back. She asked me to find out how much one cigarette costs. I came back with the Tide and told her the price for one cigarette. I lied again, so she could give me more extra money for the trip. I had to make money to buy special treats since they never shared theirs and just made me jealous. She was the perfect customer. She had the money.

As I poured water into the tank, she began separating the whites from colors. She noticed spots of blood on the crotch of all of Uncle Eddie's underwear, pants, shorts, and pajamas. With a quizzical look, she examined the garments.

"Why is he bleeding?" she pondered. "He's not a girl, to have a period." She poured the Tide into the water, allowing it to froth, then started scrubbing the blood stains out, trying to protect her long, painted nails with long, yellow gloves. As soon as she finished the laundry, I collected what she owed, not saying a word about what I suspected.

DISCOVERY

Rarely did I hear Aunt Besse and Uncle Eddie argue. But when they did, it was always about the same subject.

Why he was always coming home late.

"What have you been doing after class hours? Where do you go?" Normal, inquisitive questions any wife has the right to ask, but prying questions to put any cheating husband in a defensive mood.

He always gave her the same answer, that he was tied up at work, inundated with term papers to correct, or there was a staff meeting. Having said his piece, he walked away from the argument to avoid heated debate and grilling. But she followed after him, unsatisfied. She offered to help correct test papers at home. After all, she, too, was an instructor and quite used to correcting papers.

He said, "Okay."

For days, Uncle Eddie brought home test papers
for her to correct, and piles of essays for her to read. He
made sure there was truly piles of work to be done, and
he dumped them all on his wife at home. It would stop
her from interrogating him about his whereabouts.

Aunt Besse stayed up late on weekdays and
continued her work on the weekends. Whenever I
stopped in to say hello, she complained of back and neck
pain. I gave her short massages. I even offered to lessen
the load of test papers. All I had to do was compare the
student's multiple choice answers with the list of correct
answers that Uncle Eddie had written down. I made sure
I checked the answers correctly. Aunt Besse was relieved.
She thanked me and went back to work. On lighter days,
when finals were over, and not as much paperwork came
home, she tried to get closer to her husband, rubbing
his back lovingly. But I noticed he pulled away from
her, irritated.

One day he called me, yelling so I could hear from
across the house. I walked in to their quarters and asked
what they wanted. There was Aunt Besse, rubbing his back
so lovingly, as he asked me, "Can you go to the bakery
and buy fresh-baked steam buns with pork or chicken
filling?" he asked nicely. "First, go see if they have any.
Then come back and I'll give you the money."

Excitedly I agreed, thinking they would share with
us if I went and fetched them. I ran to the bakery, my
mouth watering with the thought of sinking my teeth into
those hot, soft, steaming buns. My stomach growled, and
I could hardly wait to eat them.

Mr. and Mrs. Pang had a bakery on the first floor
of their house. Behind the glass shelves, towards the

kitchen, were giant, stainless steel ovens where fresh, hot buns and breads come out. How I envied their children, always having fresh baked bread and buns every day. They looked healthy and well fed. The Pangs sold cakes, cookies, and pastries and had a booming business, always busy. Sometimes the line seemed a mile long. All their items sold out fast, and they always ran out of customers' favorites. Orders had to be placed in advance. No credits allowed.

This, time it was not so bad, and I got right up to the front. They still had pork buns in stock. I rushed home, hoping they didn't sell out of them in the meantime. I found Uncle Eddie and Aunt Besse lying on the bed entwined, a sheet wrapped around them. Embarrassed, I turned around quickly. I pretended not to notice that they were in bed at an odd hour, in the middle of afternoon. I started to walk away, out of the house, but I wanted a steam bun.

Uncle Eddie caught sight of me. "What did you find out?" he asked. It looked like he was trying to put on his underwear under the sheet. I avoided looking in that direction. His wife turned and looked at me, still lying next to Uncle Eddie.

I told him they had what he wanted. As soon as he had his shorts back on, he pushed back the sheet and got out of bed with urgency, leaving his wife there. He got his wallet from his pants hanging from a nail on the wall and gave me the money. He told me the number of buns to buy for him and his wife and said to buy extra for me, my sisters and brother.

My eyes turned big and round and a great big smile was plastered on my face as I ran back to the bakery.

I bought all our favorites with what he gave me and brought them home to share with my brother and sisters. We ate slowly, savoring every bite. Our two unemployed uncles were not around, so we had them all to ourselves.

STILL THE MYSTERY CONTINUES

For several more months Aunt Besse met Uncle Eddie late at the bus depot. Most nights she braved going out alone with her flashlight. She made sure she lit up her path on her way home because the streets got pretty dark around 11 PM. Most houses have turned off their electricity to save energy and only very few streetlights were turned on.

On rainy days, she brought along with her a big umbrella so they could be sheltered together under it. She held the umbrella over their heads while keeping pace with uncle's fast walk. As soon as they reached home, clothes soaked from the rain, she ran for a big towel and dried him before warming his dinner. She had already prepared him mango or orange drinks. While he ate his dinner, she gathered his wet clothes and hung them to dry. When he finished his dinner, she gathered and washed the dishes. Her inner beauty sparked and shone like the sun when she served him. To me, her true beauty was revealed through her loving and caring ways.

Despite her skeleton thin figure, flat chest and
bottom, and unremarkable complexion—darker than
was admired in Filipino society—I thought her inner
beauty glowed with her love. Uncle Eddie was obviously
her first true amour. She would do anything for him,
even wipe his ass, probably. She loved him madly,
insanely, beyond reason.

But I could tell that he did not love her the way
she loved him. Everybody in our family knew that Aunt
Besse was loving a man who was loving another man. And
that hurt. She must not know his past, not have been
aware that he loved other men before she married him.
Did she suspect he loved someone else? All the nights
of heartache, tears, eating alone were going to drive
her mad. But not Aunt Besse, whose unconditional love
could not be bought or replaced with the finest rubies
and gold in all the world. She just seemed to show him
all the more love. She wanted a child, just one, from
Uncle Eddie, she told me, even though she continued to
notice more spots of blood on Uncle Eddie's underwear
or trousers. I heard her talking to Mother, who felt her
concern, and advised her to take him to a doctor.

I tried to make Aunt Besse feel better by curling
or braiding her hair, applying makeup to make her look
beautiful for her husband. She loved the attention I gave
her before her husband came home.

Dad was aware of what was going on with his
brother and brother's wife. He, too, had heard their,
arguments and the discussion about them among family
members. He thought he had better have a talk with
Uncle Eddie. He just needed to find the right moment to
meddle in their affairs. That was Dad. I knew he would

have to have a drink first before having the courage to confront his brother.

When Uncle Eddie came home early, for once, Dad, who had been drinking all afternoon and evening, decided to confront him. He asked Uncle Eddie what was going on. He said he heard his wife crying at night and what was all this stuff about him not coming home sometimes. Uncle Eddie said he did not want to talk to a drunk, and told my father to stay out of his business. Dad kept at him until Uncle Eddie decided to leave the house. Aunt Besse followed him outside.

Dad came back to our quarters, tipsy, and dropped to the floor, face down. We all left him where he was, reeking of alcohol. Mosquitoes turning into vampires, having a banquet with dad's body and soul.

"Where is everybody!" he yelled, still face down. "Where's Xulli!"

"I'm down here, Dad," I called up to the ceiling.

"Where's Di!" he yelled.

"He's down here, too," I answered promptly for my brother. "Everybody's downstairs, Dad."

He became quiet. Passed out.

CHANGES

Uncle Eddie went to Aunt C's house to talk about our living situation. He could not continue living in a

crowded house with four men, two women, and soon
to be five children even if the living quarters were
partitioned off. The house was just too crowded with all
of us. Uncles Ellio and Cardo had been shuffling back
and forth, from our house to Aunt C's. Eating our food
and theirs, he pointed out.

It was decided that my family would move to another
place. Since Uncle Eddie's name was also on the deed to
the house in Tatalon, Quezon City, he had the right to
stay and live with whomever he chose. Dad would have to
take his family someplace else. Aunt C agreed and waited
for an opportune moment to speak to Dad, ideally when
he was sober and in his senses.

Mom was disappointed and worried when she
heard the news. Her family would soon be homeless,
with nowhere to go, despite the work they had put into
the house. She resented Uncle Eddie's decision and
called him a traitor for talking to Aunt C behind her
back. Uncle Eddie lashed back and told Mother it was
his house, that she had no right to it and should live
someplace else.

Aunt C told Dad there was a vacant lot in Fairview,
Quezon City, about half an hour's trip by bus. She told
him the local government was thinking of giving the land
to displaced, homeless families and she thought Dad
should claim a piece. Uncle Toy, another brother of
Father's liked the idea as well, and wanted a small piece
of property for himself. He and Dad found that several
families had already built temporary housing and had
been living there for almost a year. Dad and Uncle Toy
went there and chose a spot.

Dad and Uncle Toy borrowed money from Aunt C for building materials and Dad built a shanty house for us, another box. Uncle Toy built himself two shanty houses, away from ours and brought a new wife, Nattie, to live there. Nattie was Aunt C's maid who had decided not to work for Aunt C's family anymore. According to her, she was fed up with Aunt C's nasty ways and her unruly, unsympathetic children.

In her early fifties, Nattie had fallen in love with Uncle Toy—twenty years her senior—and dreamed of marrying him. She wanted to join him at his new house, where she would no longer serve, others but instead serve her husband-to-be breakfast, lunch, and dinner, like a traditional housewife. She liked the idea of serving a loving husband who gave her his salary when he came home. Because she had no children of her own, she had ample time for makeovers. She visited beauty parlors to have her hair colored and nails manicured, using his money.

Our temporary house was small, about ten feet wide by twelve feet long. We all fit in, though like a pack of sardines in a small can. At least it was now just us—Mom, Dad, me, Di, Wilma, Neneng, and Weng. Bebeng was still in the province, living with Aunt Li and Violet.

Our new house had no windows, just one door which we left open at night for fresh air. We picked a corner where we put our pots and pans and called that the kitchen. We, again, cooked with our small, portable gas stove. After we finished cooking and eating, we put away the dishes and small stove and spread the mat, on the same floor, for sleeping, as always, under our big, green mosquito net.

WATER IN FAIRVIEW

About a dozen other settler families joined us across this large acreage of undeveloped land, all having decided to build temporary housing. Nearby was a six-story office building, adjacent to a freeway. As neglected, government-owned property, it was overgrown with shrubs and tall weeds, dotted with a few scrawny trees. In the middle of this vacant land was a well, fed by a distant spring.

There was no electricity nor sanitation provided to the area. The residents had to dig holes in the ground to bury both excrement and garbage far away from their house and the well.

The newly-established residents washed their clothes and dirty dishes on the concrete block, covered in a carpet of moss beside the well. No public water system was yet available to provide fresh, drinking water to the residents who had chosen to live there. Everyone fetched drinking water from the nearby office building, not trusting the well. Every day, each resident snuck in and out, or waited until after business hours, when all the employees had left the building. The security guard got bribed regularly by one of the neighbors to keep quiet. He understood our living situation and dire need for clean drinking water.

Di and I climbed up the seven-foot-high concrete wall on a make-shift wooden ladder that had been placed

there. Another ladder leaned against the other side, next
to a faucet behind the building. I told Di to climb first
and check the area to see if the right guard was there—
the young, skinny one. If not, he was to come back down,
but if he were, he was to give me a nod that it was safe
to proceed. At the top of the wall, Di signaled for me to
climb up with the buckets and jugs and hand them over
to him. I climbed the ladder, gave him the containers
and he took them down the other side. He had to climb
the ladder with a full bucket, careful not to slip or spill.
No room for mistakes allowed as we tried to hurry out of
there before the guard caught us.

My brother and I knew we were stealing fresh
drinking water. He filled the jugs while I waited at the top.
One at a time, he climbed with filled bucket. I climbed
down with it, and returned for the next. When he'd filled
the last one and I carried it down, we headed home.

On occasion, the friendly guard, patrolling the
area, saw us. "Hurry up, you two!" he whispered. "If my
boss finds out about this, I'll lose my job! No trespassers
allowed. The signs are everywhere."

We tried to hurry. Every day we repeated the process,
or we had no water to drink. Some days, a different guard
showed up. He would likely chase us away, yelling at us to
never come back or he'll report us to the boss.

"Trespassers will be prosecuted, serve time in jail
and pay fines. Don't you see the signs everywhere?"
he'd shout at our retreating backs. "It's in big letters.
Can't you read?"

We waited until he left, and then went back. Those
signs couldn't keep us away. We needed water to drink.
Di was on the lookout for the guard by the corner of the

building. I could see him while I filled the jug. He turned his head occasionally to let me know we're safe.

One day when we arrived, we discovered the guard had taken the inside ladder down. So we ran home and got our own. After that, everybody borrowed each other's ladders and played a cat-and-mouse game with the less kind guards. Di and I decided that if one of the guards caught us, we'd beat him up. It'd be two against one.

"Screw his gun. He just wears it for decoration, to intimidate us," we'd said. "He won't shoot."

"I bet you it's not loaded," Di said. "He probably doesn't even know how to use it."

"Well, what if it is loaded? He'll shoot us both," I worried.

LIFE MOVES ON IN FAIRVIEW

Dad worked as a security officer and Mom returned to her old job doing laundry for the rich family in the city. Dad's salary was not enough to feed all of us. My brother and I stayed home to babysit our sisters. Wilma was now five. Neneng was one and a half, and Weng was 8 months. There were two other children in the neighborhood, one my age (I was now 11) and another was Wilma's age with whom we could play.

One day I told Di, who was ten, to watch our sisters while I took the dishes to wash at the well. As soon as I returned with clean dishes, I looked for my sisters, but saw Weng by herself. The two little ones usually play next to each other. I asked Di where she was. He gave me a scared look. Wasting no more time, we knocked on every neighbor's door, asking if they'd seen Neneng.

"She has no hair, has slanted eyes and brown skin, and is wearing a blue dress and yellow sandals," we described. No one had seen her. Nervously, we searched. I carried Weng, and Di carried Wilma on his back. We looked everywhere, especially around the well. She wasn't anywhere. Fear ran through me. I started to cry, not just for our sister, but for our lives if our parents found out. I could tell Di's heart was pounding like mine. We were dead meat.

We kept walking and walking, out on the busy streets, searching and asking strangers if they'd seen her. We shuddered, watching the cars racing back and forth. We walked further and further, calling her name, hoping she would hear and recognize our voices. But with all that noise from cars and busses speeding by, it seemed impossible she would hear us.

Wilma got heavy for my brother. I told him to put her down and hold her hand, and to follow me as I carried the baby on my side. Wilma was not wearing sandals. She walked barefooted. We walked along the side of the highway, searched between buildings, and in shops. We must have walked for four hours. It was late in the afternoon, and we were exhausted, emotionally and physically. We were thirsty, and we were also desperate to find Neneng. I decided we had better go back before we got lost or picked up by strangers.

Perspiration dripped into my brother's eyes, or perhaps they were tears.

We both anticipated a terrible beating. My brother felt responsible because I had told him to keep an eye on her. I felt sorry for brother and imagined that dad was going to hurt him badly. I was prepared to take the fall. Tell dad it was all my fault.

"I'll tell Dad she just wandered off and it wasn't your fault," I assured him, fearing Dad's beating of my brother worse than my own. "I won't tell him you lost sight of her." We walked back home, afraid, hopeless. Wilma was starting to limp after too much walking for her little feet. Di picked her up and put her on his back again. Gray clouds were gathering, covering the darkening sky. The sun was no longer visible as we approached our house.

A woman wearing a yellow t-shirt and orange pants stood in front of our house, talking to Nattie and holding Neneng! She found her and brought her home! Nattie explained that she was a street sweeper, but somehow seemed sarcastic. I was too relieved to care. I could not stop crying. The street sweeper had found Neneng walking by herself, passing right by on her way toward the highway. The woman had stopped sweeping and followed her to make sure she was alone, and then picked her up before she crossed the busy road, was run over, or picked up by a stranger. The lady explained that she remembered striking up a conversation with my mother a day or so earlier where she was assigned to sweep. She remembered admiring my sister's bald head, her sweet slanted eyes, and tanned skin. The lady knew where my mother lived and thus brought my sister back.

After she left, Nattie chided us, "There you go, abandoning your sister. You're lucky this lady found her. What if she was picked up by someone else and not returned? What then, huh?" She went on and on. "You had better do a better job at keeping an eye on your sisters!"

In our house, I put Weng down and held Neneng close to me for the longest time. I was in a state of shock. I turned to Di, and we shared the biggest smile. Neither one of us could stop crying. She had taken an adventure stroll alone and luckily a street sweeper noticed her. I was so thankful to have her back, I could not have cared less about the punishment I anticipated getting in the evening when our parents found out what had happened. All I cared about was that my precious sister was back home with us, unscathed. When Mom found out the news from Nattie, she did not get mad at us. She just lectured us to keep a good eye on my younger sisters while she was at work. She reminded us she had to work so we would have food to eat. We promised we would. We did not want to repeat that scare.

DAD S WORK

A security guard, Dad had to wear a uniform. He only had two so I had to wash one outfit early in the morning to be dry and ready by the next day. I would instruct Di and Wilma, now old enough to help, to keep an eye on the little ones while I took Dad's dirty uniform, along with our family's other dirty clothes, to the well to wash. I cleaned them with my bare hands, stomping our pants, especially jeans, with my feet. I sat next to old ladies from the neighborhood and listened to them gossip about who smelled bad, who had the clap or other sexually transmitted disease. They said whores had a fishy odor and discharge leaking out of their vaginas that produce a bad smell. So, they knew if they were sitting next to one.

I dipped out water from the well and rinsed the clothes while I listened to them talk and laugh. When I finished, I carried the heavy wet clothes back home to hang on the clothesline in front of our house. We didn't have hangers like Nattie did to hang them up, so I used old and worn clothespins to keep the clothes from being blown by the wind. When I finished hanging all the clothes, I went inside our little house. Closed the front door. Turned away from little sisters and removed my panties. I held the crotch area close to my nose to smell any fishy odor and looked for some type of discharge that the old ladies were talking about. I found none and hurriedly put back on my panties before brother or Dad opened the front door.

In the late afternoon, I boiled water for the baby's milk for that evening and the next day, keeping the reconstituted milk in a thermos. Just as I did the days when Mother had been missing back in the Province.

I sat by the only door to our house and watched other kids play. I dared not leave for fear one of my sisters might go missing, or Dad might come home unexpectedly and not find me there. It was clear I was in charge of the household while he and Mom were at work.

"If I ever find out you've wandered off playing while your sisters are left unattended, you will answer to me," he warned. "Do you hear me?"

"Yes, Dad, I hear you loud and clear," I answered dutifully.

Then he was off.

I did not want to be punished, so I played inside the house or sat by the front door. I could play with Carolina, the girl my age, but she liked to flirt with the older boys in our small community. I watched her talking and laughing with a boy five years older than us. They seemed to like each other's company. They played a hand slapping game quite a few times. She'd hold out her hands, then pull them away before he could slap them. I heard giggling from her whenever he missed her hands. I was also keeping my eyes on Wilma playing with children her age in front of our house. I let her know sternly not to go out of my sight. Neneng stood next to me, holding onto my shirt, while Weng crawled around our one room.

I sat by the door, engrossed in Carolina's flirtations, wishing I could join them. I envied all of the other kids because they did not have any younger sisters or brothers to take care of. Carolina was the younger of two children. Her older brother was a professional pickpocket and was away a lot. On a mission. He brought back expensive watches, bracelets, gold and silver necklaces. He tried to sell them door-to-door. He bragged about how easily he snatched watches without the victim ever knowing.

His mother was worried sick about him. She imagined the day he got caught and thrown in jail, or killed! But he seemed beyond rehabilitation and now entering into drugs.

Watching Carolina and how she lived, already so aware of her body and its allures, intimidated me. She had plenty of time on her hands to do as she pleased. She could stay out all day and night, as long as she wanted, whenever she wanted, and with whomever she wanted. I wanted to play slap the hands with her and her friends, not just be a spectator. I wanted to laugh like them.

I watched them longingly when Weng cried out. I ran to her. I found her standing and holding onto the end of a table to keep her balance. The hot thermos that had been cooling on it had toppled over, and the hot liquid had splashed on her arm. I had just poured it in there to let it cool a bit. Her arm was turning strawberry red. She cried louder and louder. I picked her up, righted the thermos, and put the lid on it. I held her and cradled her, rocking her gently. She would not stop crying, and I started to panic. I threw cold water on her arm and dabbed it gently with a wet cloth, but she screamed louder and louder. I found cardboard and fanned her arm, thinking the cool air might help. Her big mouth opened wide, screaming in pain, tears wetting her tiny face. Blisters formed on her skin. I did not know what else to do, so I just carried her until she calmed down.

"Oh, please, Sister, don't be badly burned," was all I could say to my nine-month-old sister. I was beginning to worry about the consequences of my carelessness. At the same time I had to think what to tell Mom, and especially Dad, who would definitely kill me when he got home. I could not stop blaming myself for my stupidity. I should have been watching her, not Carolina. How would I explain it to my parents when they saw her burned arm? How could I have left an open thermos full of hot water on the table, knowing a crawling baby might tip it over? I was not thinking. I was busy envying my friend. I hated my stupid self.

Di heard the crying and came in. He saw the baby's arm. The bubble, filled with air and water, covered half her little arm. It looked bigger than the last time I looked. Di checked the rest of her body and told me there were more blisters, one on her chest and another on the left side of her body! I stared at the fluid filled blisters on her delicate skin. I knew I was dead. I began crying myself. I was scared for her but also scared for myself. Our crying was in sync.

I prepared myself to be smashed into pieces by my dad. Oh, how I wished I had been showered with scalding water, not her. I wanted to turn time back. I deserved to be punished.

I got Di to play with Weng while I prepared her a milk bottle. I used the point of a sharp knife to open a can of condensed milk. I dripped an ounce into the bottle, watching the line, and then filled it halfway with some hot water, some tepid. I shook the milk bottle to mix it. I tested the temperature on my arm, so it did not burn her throat. I had known how to do this since I was four.

The milk felt hot on my skin. Weng still cried. Quickly, I added just a little bit more cold water into the bottle, squirted some in my mouth to make sure it was sweet and ready, and then put the nipple in my sister's mouth. She stopped crying and sucked her bottle hungrily, holding it with her tiny hands. Tears rolling down the corners of her eyes. She appeared at ease now, and I laid her down in the corner with her bottle. Her eyes grew heavy. I sang her a lullaby:

Hush, hush, little Sister
Little Sister, please don't you cry
Big Sister is so sorry
So very sorry for her sweet little sister.
Hush, Hush little Sister
I see you are now sleepy
Please dream sweetly . . . and I hope you forgive me.

Mother arrived home early in the evening, and I ran to her, meeting her as she approached the house. I told her exactly what had happened earlier in the day to Weng. I thought I'd confess the truth, the whole truth and nothing but the truth. She rushed into the house, dropped the grocery bags on the floor, and checked Weng, who was sleeping on the mat with the bottle still at her mouth. She lovingly patted her head and kissed her cheeks. The baby gave a sigh, as if to respond to our mother's touch and love. Mom undressed her and examined her body, as I continued to explain what happened. Neneng and Wilma were lying down next to her but still awake, waiting for supper. Di sat quietly in, another corner. I told Mother how sorry I was. She just busied herself preparing dinner before dad got home. I held my breath, but nothing happened.

Every day I helped Mom dress the baby's wounds. She came home with white, powdery talc and applied it to the affected areas to keep the skin dry. She left the blisters open to the air to let them heal.

When Dad found out about the incident, he just remarked how fortunate that Weng's face was spared from the hot water. I stared, waiting for the other shoe to drop, but it never did. Mom just told me to keep a close eye on Weng every second while she was away at work.

"Yes! I will. I promise!" I assured her. I had somehow escaped punishment from them, yet I punished myself.

TROUBLE AGAIN

Mother started coming home late, as before, due to heavy traffic in downtown Manila. She prepared dinner as soon as she arrived home. Our stomachs growled as my siblings and I struggled to keep our eyes open. We were already in bed, but Mom got us up to eat. Dad came home drunk one night and told Mother to follow him.

He calmly said he wanted to talk to her in private. Neneng started throwing a tantrum. She wanted Mom to carry her. Mom picked her up and told Dad she was busy, that we needed to be fed.

"Forget the cooking. Come with me," he demanded, raising his tone a bit but looking calm.

She turned off the stove, put lid on the pots, and picked up Neneng, who was crying for her attention. Dad said to leave Neneng with me, but she refused to be put down, screaming as soon as she was placed on the floor. Mom picked her back up and went with Dad. My eyes followed the three of them as they disappeared into the dark shadows of the evening.

Everything was peaceful in the neighborhood at this time of the night. Wick lamps still flickered in a few households while others were extinguished already. Eyelids heavy, my brother and sisters went right back to sleep. My eyelids were heavy, too, but I forced them open, waiting for their return. We had not eaten supper. Our stomachs were still growling, but we would rather go to sleep at this point. Letting the hunger pass, I dozed off.

The crowing of roosters and the clattering of pots and pans from a neighbor's kitchen woke me. Morning sunlight shone through the edges of our front door, showing lint dust particles floating in different directions. Everyone was still asleep under the mosquito net, including my father lying on his stomach in the corner. I had not heard him come in during the night.

I looked around quickly, puzzled. Where was Mom? I thought she might have left early for work. Everybody was there except Mother and Neneng.

Quietly I crawled out from under the net and stepped outside into the fresh morning air. I closed the door behind me without a sound. It was still, morning but almost noon. I could tell by the sun.

Thoughts of the events of the night before filled my mind, and I could not help but feel dread. I hoped with all my might that what I feared had not happened.

Carolina stepped out her front door and motioned to me to follow her. She put her finger to her lips for me to keep quiet. I followed, saying nothing. We passed all the houses in our small community and approached the freeway. She whispered that she had been waiting all morning for me to come outside our front door. She said she'd gone to the store early in the morning and came across my mother.

"Your Mom said to tell you to get your sisters and brother ready tonight."

"Ready for what?" I asked.

"Your mom said she wants to take all of you away from here tonight. She's hiding at Mrs. Daniko's house. Meet her there tonight. But don't tell your dad!"

I nodded, bowing my head. I wanted to cry. I was crying inside. I knew my fears had been real the night before.

"Your dad tried to kill your mom last night," Carolina explained. "She managed to run away, barefooted." She thought Mom not having flip-flops on might have helped her to get away.

I nodded, feeling frozen. "I had better go back home before Dad wakes up," I said nervously.

"Wait until your dad's not around, then all of you sneak out," she urged.

"Okay. I have to tell brother. But can you go back and tell my mother to wait for us until it's safe to leave?"

"Okay. I'll tell her I talked to you. You had better go before your dad sees us talking."

I thanked Carolina and walked home with a knot in my stomach. In a way, I was glad she had not come home last night, so that the cycle wouldn't start again. I was glad she had managed to get away from him. Maybe he did not hurt her that much this time. Maybe he did not have the chance to hurt her at all.

When I reached home, Dad was trying to boil water for coffee. Di went outside, into the bushes, to relieve himself, while Wilma and Weng sat waiting for breakfast.

As soon as his water came to a boil, Dad made rice porridge. He instructed me to keep stirring the pot and help him serve the little ones. Meekly, I did as I was told. I took over stirring the pot while Dad stepped outside. My mind was spinning with the porridge, thinking about escaping tonight with my brother and sisters. How would I do it? Where would dad be when we all tried to walk away? I had yet to talk to my brother about it.

"Where's Mama?" Wilma asked.

"She'll be back," I assured her as I added a spoonful of sugar into the porridge. I turned off the burner, scooped porridge into small bowls and placed them in front of my sisters. With small cardboard scrap, Wilma fanned their porridge to cool it. Di came back in and sat with us. I gave him his portion and fed myself and my sisters intermittently. We sat and ate, quietly blowing and chewing. The air was filled with chewing and blowing noises.

Dad arrived with a steaming bowl of *dinugu-an*, or 'chocolate soup'. It was one of his favorite dishes, and it was made of pork and intestines, simmered with pork's blood, giving it the black color it is known for.

He added green chilies to make it spicy, and then he asked me if there was any cooked rice left over. I showed him some in a covered pot. It was expected that I would serve him the rice. I dished it out onto a plate and served it to him. I thought he must have more cash than usual in his pockets to be able to afford *dinugu-an* from the corner store for breakfast.

He went out and washed his hands in a pail of water by the door, then sat with us, pouring a small portion of soup over his cold rice and eating it with his bare hands.

No one spoke. Someone burped. No one laughed like they usually did. Who did it? Nobody cared. Everyone eyed each other.

My sisters needed to relieve themselves. I took them outside near the well and waited while they did what they needed to do, and then I buried whatever needed burying. I led them to the well to wash their bottoms, then took them back into the house, and put on clean clothes.

Dad saved some of his chocolate soup for lunch and an early supper for everyone. I covered it with a plate and placed in the middle of a bigger plate filled with water so ants could not get into it. I also placed the can of condensed milk on top of the covered bowl, so the ants would not get it either. I asked my brother to help me collect the dirty dishes to take to the well and wash while I swept the floor. Wilma sat in the corner by herself, watching me sweep. She and Weng were playmates now while Neneng was with mother. Dad relaxed by the front door, one leg stretched out, the other bent, with his hand resting on it as he held a lit cigarette. Deep in thought, he intermittently picked his teeth with a toothpick.

I continued sweeping. I told my sisters to move to another corner, and they crawled away, looking back, mesmerized by the movement of the broom. They had no toys or dolls. Their big eyes followed the broom. I felt sorry for them. They seemed confused. I stopped sweeping and gave them a clean plastic plate to play with. I showed them how to spin it on its side. Then I set two plates spinning. They clapped and shrieked, entertained. I let them try to do the spinning while I continued my sweeping and planning.

I told Dad I needed to go outside to relieve myself. I said that to indicate that he should make use of his time by watching the little ones. He curled up his legs and let me pass through the door, as if he had been guarding us. I found Di by the well and helped him finish cleaning the dishes. As we placed them in a clean bucket, I told him in a hush voice that we would be meeting Mother later in the evening. I explained what Carolina had told me.

Di nodded that he understood, but anger showed on his face as we walked back to the house. Angry at Dad, perhaps at our whole situation. I did not ask him. I did not know where we would go, and I wondered where we would live next.

I paid attention to Dad's whereabouts all day, keeping my eyes and ears open at all times. We would have to meet Mom as we were, wearing the same clothes. Maybe I could pack a few clean clothes in grocery bags, and prepare the baby's milk bottle before we would walk away quietly. It seemed like an easy enough plan. When I couldn't keep track of him, my brother would, and he kept me informed of where Dad was at every moment.

A profound sadness came over me, thinking of his family leaving him. He was our father, and we loved him, despite his abusive and violent behavior, which caused all of us anxiety. His drinking had cast a pall over our household and brought terror into our hearts. We had to leave him, and I had to stop loving him.

While Dad was still outside, I gathered some clothes, put them into a couple of grocery bags, and covered them over with a pile of pillows in the corner to hide until we were ready to leave.

At lunchtime, we all gathered in the middle of the
floor. Dad ate with us. The five of us slathered *dinugu-an*
over our rice. The baby ate very little, and Dad fed her
bites of rice. After lunch, I went to the well and, being
careful not to fall in, leaned over and looked at my
reflection. I could see my face on its stillness, my image
staring back at me. Behind my head, I saw scattered
white clouds. *No one would hear me if I fell in*, I thought.
Then I noticed a solitary black fish swimming about
quickly. I lowered the tin bucket with a long rope, waiting
for it to swim over so I could pull it up. I caught it and
brought it back to the house. My little sisters were afraid
of it, but mesmerized. They could not take their eyes
off it and reached for the little strange swimming black
creature. They watched and giggled to each other. We
decided not to eat it.

Soon after, Di came in with a small green frog he'd
caught. He allowed it to jump around the floor in front
of our sisters to entertain them. Weng laughed and
crawled after the frog, trying to pick it up with one hand,
then two. My brother picked it up for her and helped her
hold it. She squeezed the frog and tried to stuff it into
her mouth. The creature took a flying leap to get away.
Startled, Weng screamed and retreated to the corner of
the room, safe but her chest still heaving from her fright.
We laughed. She looked ready to cry.

It was starting to get dark outside. I lost track
of dad's whereabouts; he snuck out without my
knowing. Dad came back home with uncooked rice in
a small pouch and a couple of live catfish. He told me
to start cooking the rice while he went to the well to
clean the fish and get it ready for frying. He asked for

a big bowl and the butcher knife. I grabbed them and gave them to him as he waited outside the door, holding onto the wiggling fish by strings that were stitched through their mouths.

I was thinking this might be the opportune moment to run. Dad walked away with the catfish, his figure disappearing beyond the bushes. Di was in front of the house, and I called him to come in, quickly.

"Grab Wilma and go," I told him. "I will carry Weng, the bags of clothes, and the baby's bottle. You and I will have to run fast! As fast as we can."

He looked in the direction dad had gone, then back at me, and gave me a nod. "We better hurry," he said.

I grabbed the clothes and milk bottles, put my flip-flops on, and we ran.

"Hey, where are you going?" Nattie asked. She happened to be sitting by her window. I turned around and placed my finger over my lips to silence her as we continued running. Two male neighbors standing in front of their houses watched us, silent but quizzical. I didn't have time to worry. Weng was getting heavy. I lifted her tighter into my arms as I continued running quickly. Di, with Wilma on his back, was already far ahead of us. I ran faster, thinking Dad would be busy chopping up the catfish. We kept running as fast as we could, panting, out of breath with our heavy loads, until we arrived at Mrs. Daniko's. Di and Wilma waited for me to arrive with Weng before knocking on the door.

"Hurry, get in. All of you!" Mrs. Daniko said as she pulled us gently into her house. She peeked her head outside, looked left and right, and then closed and locked the door. "Be quiet, all of you. Not a sound," she warned. She didn't want her neighbors to hear anything for fear they would gossip and word would get back to Dad on our location. She also didn't want Dad to hear if he happened to be outside looking for us.

ESCAPE

Di, Wilma, and I were panting hard as we tried to explain our escape, but our exhaustion disappeared when we saw our mother. At first glance, I did not recognize her. She had a huge black and blue circle around one eye, and the other was swollen shut. There was purple, black, and blue discoloration and swelling all over her face. I started to cry quietly as Di lowered Wilma to the floor. He was clearly, shocked but said nothing. He did not, cry but was suffused with an angry color. There were bruises and scratches on both of Mom's legs, maybe from running through bushes. And her feet were muddy.

"Come sit with your mother," instructed Mrs. Daniko as she walked back to the kitchen. I handed Weng to my brother, who then handed her over to Mom. I gave Weng her milk bottle, and I saw Neneng nibbling on a cookie to keep her quiet. We all sat together on the couch, and Mother began to cry. She looked unkempt, her skirt dirty and torn, her blouse stained with dried blood. I felt ashamed for her, looking this way, and I felt ashamed about our situation and about my family. Grandmother

Estella, Mother's mom, appeared in the living room. We all stared. Surprised.

"Your father picked up a rock and hit your mother in the head and face with it several times," Grandmother told us, "while she was carrying your sister, Neneng. Your sister was dropped onto the ground." Her voice held anger and disbelief.

Apparently, Dad had been dragging her by the hair at one point, and she managed to pull away from Dad's grip, pick up Neneng, and run as fast and far as she could. Dad chased her as blood gushed from her head. She hid behind a house, waiting, somehow keeping Neneng silent, until she was sure it was safe to emerge. She was feeling, faint but kept walking until she had found a hospital emergency room. Neneng had fallen asleep on her shoulder, wearing only a t-shirt and no underwear.

The on-call doctor who examined her told the nurse to clean the wounds on her head and face, and said she might need stitches. Mother told the doctor what had happened and that she had no money to pay for medical care or to stay in the hospital, so the nurse just cleaned the wounds and let her use the restroom to clean herself and Neneng up. The nurses could not bear seeing a child leave the hospital naked. Diapers were too expensive and a waste for just one use, so they gave Mother a towel to wrap around our sister's waist.

After leaving the ER, mom walked barefoot through the rest of the night, searching for a quiet sidewalk between houses, away from noise of streetcars and passersby. As Neneng slept on her lap, she stayed awake thinking of a plan. Before daylight, she wrapped Neneng's bottom with the same towel the nurse had given her, got up, and started walking back nearby where we lived, but she was careful to not be seen by Father.

Mrs. Daniko was opening her store when Mother approached her and asked if she had a telephone she could use to call grandmother. She had not slept at all. When Grandmother came, they went to Mrs. Daniko's house to fetch the rest of us.

"Be very quiet, all of you," Grandmother said. "We don't live here. It was kind of Mrs. Daniko to hide your mother. We will be leaving soon. That demon father of yours can go to hell."

Mom held the baby in her lap. My brother and I sat, tired and sleepy, yet excited that we were leaving to go somewhere unknown. It seemed like an adventure to a new place we had never been before. Scruffy vagrants but at least we were together.

TO A NEW PLACE

Grandma Estella had been living with Mother's younger sister Carmen. She had dressed and rushed out of the house as soon as she heard my mom needed her help. It took two bus rides and a jeepney to get to Mrs. Daniko's house, in order to help us get away. Mom surely needed help to take all five children somewhere, and her mother was the only one available to help us at this crucial moment.

It was only my second time meeting Grandma
Estella. The first time was when she visited us in La Union
province for three weeks. She was about four feet tall
with long, silvery hair, and slanted brown eyes. Grandma
Estella was very strict. She always sounded upset when she
talked to any of us. She kept busy around the house with
cooking and cleaning, even washing our bottoms every
night with soap and a pail of water. Facing away from her,
we had to squat while she washed our private parts.

"You should always make your private's clean before
you go to bed!" She said in the middle of this thorough
cleaning. One at a time, she lathered us and then rinsed.
"Go dry yourself!" she'd say, as if we'd irritated her. She
made sure we brushed our teeth and changed into clean
bedclothes. "Xulli, scrub the soles of your feet! You could
grow potatoes in the dirt on them! You are all filthy! Go!"

We would go dry ourselves with clean, fresh towels
she had washed and hung to dry. We put on clean clothes
whenever she told us. That's how I remembered her. I was
glad she was with us to help mother, but I was leery about
staying with her too. I did not know where we would go
from here or how we would hide from Dad, but I did
not want him to get a hold of Mom again. I heard Mom,
Grandma, and Mrs. Daniko talking.

"We'll figure it out," I heard Grandmother muttering.

I wondered what was going on in Dad's head, when
he returned home with his cleaned catfish, and found the
house empty, his children gone. Did he go out looking
for us like a madman? The thought scared me. I tried to
stay quiet for fear he might be lurking outside, searching
with his sharpened machete.

"Be polite and go clean your hands before dinner!" Grandmother snapped in a low voice as she led all of us to the bathroom. One at a time, she helped us lather and rinse our hands. "Now sit down and be quiet." She had a way of letting us feel that she was some kind of enemy to be revered, taken seriously. Although she was always angry at us, she loved each one of us. Her unconditional love was apparent through her care and devotion. She was a very confusing, sour old lady. We had not said a word since we'd first seen her.

For dinner, Mrs. Daniko served us hot beef soup with cabbage and potatoes along with steamed rice. My siblings and I were in heaven with this bountiful meal. Our eyes grew big at the sight of the steaming soup. We had not had beef for dinner in a very long time. The beef was chopped in delicious cubes. We had been eating fish for breakfast, lunch, and dinner for months. Fish and rice at every meal for too long became sickening. I was so grateful for her kindness and wondered if there were many more Mrs. Danikos out there. I knew she felt sorry for us. I just had to swallow my pride and learn to accept our situation for what it was.

While Mrs. Daniko served us dinner, I listened to her talk to Grandmother and Mom about her family and her business, and how she had managed to send all three of her children to college. Her firstborn, a registered nurse, lived in another town with the other two children who were still in college. Mrs. Daniko's husband helped her financially and with cooking and cleaning. I sank further into my own depression, losing my appetite. It became harder to swallow. Grandmother then criticized Dad for being a lazy son of a bitch and wished he was like Mrs. Daniko's husband, who never drank or beat up his wife.

I bowed my head almost down to my plate with embarrassment, picturing Mother walking in her door with bruises on her face, arms and legs from my father, bare feet and all, begging Mrs. Daniko to take her and sister in her home. Just to add insult to injury, Grandmother talked about Dad's drinking, with the evidence for all to see right next to her. It was embarrassing enough to know that Mrs. Daniko was not really a friend of Mom's, that it was their first time meeting. The thought of Mom fleeing to her house, looking battered like this, made me feel miserable for all of us. Here we were, eating her delicious meal, Mother looking helpless and stripped of human dignity, with her five hungry children.

But I was very hungry. Di, and Wilma and Neneng, enjoyed their dinner, while Weng sucked on her bottle on Mom's lap. I had to swallow my pride, with the beef tasting so good. I had to force the food down. I knew it would be a long while before we could have another taste of delicious, homemade cooking.

We ate like we hadn't eaten for days, except Mom, who had no appetite. I can not ever recall seeing Grandma Estella eat in front of us. She always said she was not hungry. I guess she was just being polite to Mrs. Daniko while trying to think of Plan B.

THE NEXT ESCAPE

We waited until it was dark, safe for all of us to leave
Mrs. Daniko's house and head to Aunt Zenia's house.
Grandmother had suggested we hide at her daughter-
in-law's place. Aunt Zenia was keeping house for some
rich folks. The owners of the property were outside
the country and had an empty guesthouse we could
stay at temporarily, at least until the owners of the
property returned.

Grandmother forbade us from wandering around
the property, even though it was unknown territory and
intrigued us. Still, I liked the place a lot because Di and
I did not have to fetch water. There was a small faucet in
the kitchen sink, and one in the bathroom. We collected
water in a bucket and poured it over our heads to shower.
There was even a ten inch black and white television in
the kitchen! The place was heaven with amenities we'd
never had before! But we couldn't touch them without
grandmother's approval.

"Don't touch that television!" Grandmother
cautioned. "The owners will wonder why the electricity
bill is so high, and your Aunt Zenia will get in trouble.
Just stay away from it!"

I liked staying in our temporary housing and wished
we didn't have to leave when the owners returned.

"Can't you ask the owners if we can live here, and work here in exchange for rent, Grandmother?" I asked. "Maybe there's work we could do here."

"Your Aunt Zenia and her baby are already living and working here. There are too many of you to be staying here," she snapped, sounding angry as usual. "Go find your brother! Make sure he does not wander into the main house, or I'll twist his ears."

It was impossible to talk to Grandma Estella. I never knew what mood she would be in, and mostly it was bad.

FLIGHT AGAIN

The property had a high wall of concrete blocks around it for privacy and to keep out trespassers and thievery. The iron gate squeaked as I push it open. I stepped out, walked a few steps away and walked in a sea of tall grass, above my waist. The vast, light brown sea of grass swayed in the breeze, under the bright sun. I ran my hands over it and the fronds tickled my palms. I wanted to just stay in the tranquil scene a little while longer. I made up an intimate prayer and let it glide away on the gentle spirit of the wind, to carry to the high heavens. "If there is a place called Heaven out there, where God lives, may He get my message, have mercy on this wretched family, and help us find a place."

Our last night at Aunt Zenia's, we lay on the floor, at peace for the moment, as we tried to get some sleep. There was no drunk, wife-beating father around to terrify us. Only calmness and silence. I savored the sweet taste of freedom, however brief.

The adults decided that we needed to be divided up. No one could manage all of us, so I was the one to be separated once again. Mom was to take my brother and three sisters to live with her at Mrs. Vienna's, another of Grandmother's longtime, well-to-do friends. Her husband was a successful attorney in the city. I was to go live with Grandmother Estella and Aunt Carmen. Aunt Carmen had five children, all younger than me. I could help out with the household, Grandmother said.

Living with cousins I'd never met sounded exciting, but at the same time I had reservations. I had heard how perfect Aunt Carmen's children were, with their perfect light skin and flawless teeth. I was to be torn from my family. I knew how that felt from when they first went to Manila. But it was not my decision. I had to do what Grandmother and Mother decided was best for us.

"You behave and do what Aunt Carmen tells you," Mother said, with a worried look on her face. "Your Uncle Conrad has a quiet demeanor and he's rather aloof," she forewarned, "but you will get used to him. All will go well as long as you behave. Don't cause trouble."

Aunt Carmen's husband, Uncle Conrad, worked as a manager at Country Bank. And I tried to imagine what Aunt Carmen's house looked like since her husband made a lot of money. At the same time, images of my mom, brother, and sisters crept through me. I have heard from one of the talks that Mrs. Vienna had a big modern house in Manila, complete with latest amenities. Two maids lived with her. Her husband was an attorney who had earned his degree in America and had returned to the Philippines to practice law. Only English was spoken in the house. My mom would go to Mrs. Vienna's house and ask if she and her children could stay at her house while grandmother took me to Aunt Carmen's to live. It would be impossible to take all six of us to live at Aunt Carmen's house. We said our goodbyes and parted ways.

"You're going to help your aunt with whatever she asks you to do, understand?" Grandmother reminded me again as we hopped in the bus.

"Yes, Grandmother. I understand," I assured her as I sat on our chosen seat and looked out of the window. Through it, I watched vendors crowding the sides of the streets for miles as I struggled with the knowledge that I was separated from my brother and sisters. I was comforted that they would be with Mother and well cared for, but I hung onto my curiosity about living with cousins I had yet to meet.

Would they be nice to me, or would they treat me like Cousin Violet did? Would Aunt Carmen take care of me the same way as her own children or order me about as if I were a servant?

AUNT CARMEN S

The white tile floor was immaculately clean and led into a dining area with a long, rectangular glass table and eight chairs. There was running water inside the apartment, and the bathroom had a flushing toilet. Aunt Carmen did not allow her children to go outside to play or talk to neighbors. They were to remain indoors at all times and could not associate with anyone in the neighborhood. Five children, all inside an apartment, all the time! The two boys were eight and nine years old, and the three girls were five, six, and seven. My duty was to entertain them by reading to them and playing with them. I was also to help them with their schoolwork while Aunt Carmen and Grandmother Estella busied themselves with cooking, cleaning, and washing clothes. This was not as bad as hauling water!

During supper the first night, Aunt Carmen explained to the family the reason I was living with them for the time being. The children sat on designated seats. With me being extra, Grandmother added another chair, and I sat with the girls, on one side of the table. Uncle Conrad sat at the head, with Aunt Carmen at the other end. "I would never let a man lay a hand on me," Aunt Carmen blurted out. "I'm not like your mother, weak and timid. I'd fight back. Your mom needs to learn to stand up for herself!" Aunt Carmen went on as if to explain to her husband they have to let me stay with them on account that my family was all screwed up at the moment. Her husband ate quietly at the other end of the table.

I started to lose my appetite as she continued berating the evil of my father and my mother's weakness in not being able to protect herself.

She got so mad and worked up as she talked that she choked on rice and had to sip water. As soon as she had her voice again she continued, "If your Uncle ever laid hands on me, I'd kick his nuts all the way to kingdom come."

Uncle Conrad heard her loud and clear. A grin on his face showed and went back to eating. Her children giggled into their napkins. They might have figured their mother was stronger than their dad anyway. Grandmother busied herself in the background, refilling our plates with rice and filling up empty glasses with cold water. She mumbled as she served us, agreeing with Aunt Carmen. But then again, Aunt Carmen was with a mild-mannered man.

The way she kept on talking, getting excited and all, seemed like she'd like to find my father at that very moment and kick his ass. "One time, your uncle came home late, drunk," she recounted, her spoon full of rice poised midway to her mouth. "I locked him out! 'You want to be out?' I said. 'Then you stay out!' He pounded on the door, pleading to be let in. But no way. I don't tolerate that drunken stuff." Uncle Conrad sobered up at a friend's house and returned the following afternoon. I looked at Uncle Conrad. His eyes looked at his plate, but he was grinning.

"You can stay here for as long as you like," Aunt Carmen told me, and my stomach settled a little. Still her husband didn't say a word. He just listened. I felt, grateful but homesick for my sisters and brother. Tears started down my cheek. I couldn't say anything. After supper, I helped Grandmother collect the dishes while my cousins rushed upstairs to spend time with their dad. Not one offered to help clean up. Their only jobs were to do their schoolwork and play.

As the days passed, my cousins and I got along very well, except when one threw a tantrum. Then everyone got time out and the blame fell on me since I was the oldest. I bore the brunt for the consequences of their actions. They had a scapegoat. If one cousin hurt another or misbehaved in any way, I was called in and scolded on immaturity and lack of social skills.

If I told my aunt that one of the boys punched one of their siblings, she spanked her son on the bottom and put him in time out. Then my cousins would gang up on me and would stop talking to me, so I lost either way. When we were on good terms again, they asked me to play hide and seek. Sometimes I buried one of the cousins with a stack of pillows, neatly piled up around her, meticulously covered. They searched the whole house. Finally she burst out of her hiding place, gasping for breath and looking pale, covered in perspiration. She'd nearly passed out. I guess I loaded too many pillows on. She said she felt faint and thought she was about to die. We rushed to her and put an electric fan near her until she was better. This incident was reported to their parents, and I was again reprimanded. No more hide and seek. We were confined to reading, dancing, singing, or just telling stories. I told stories I made up. Sometimes they told their parents about them, and I retold them at dinner.

After playing with the cousins, I helped Grandmother iron pillowcases while the girls watched. One time the oldest came closer as I was testing the temperature by touching the steel base with my finger. I decided it was not yet hot.

"Test it on my arm," my cousin said, lifting it to me.

I placed the bottom of the iron to her right arm. She gave a great yelp and yanked her arm away. It had a three-inch burn on it. I seized the iron and turned it off, feeling stupid for having done what she said. She ran from the room, screaming for her mother. Perhaps her parents were right. I was immature. I knew I was in serious trouble. I had made a terrible mistake. Everyone was stunned.

Aunt Carmen came to me. She did not raise her voice, or strike me, but asked, "What in the world did you just do? What possessed you to do this? How could you be so thoughtless? Can you explain?" She was exasperated.

I waited for her to slap me, but she didn't. I felt terrible. I had ruined her child's perfect, smooth arm.

Later on that evening, the burn turned into a big blister and my cousin was in a lot of pain. She kept crying and crying. The minute Uncle Conrad arrived home, my aunt greeted him at the door and told him to follow her upstairs. He did. She talked and explained to him. I was sure she was telling him what had happened, what I had done. After that, Uncle Conrad scolded and lectured me every day until he stopped talking to me altogether and instructed his children to stay away from me.

I knew I was no longer welcome to stay in his house. Testing a hot iron on my cousin's arm was not exemplary behavior. At bedtime, I could hear them whispering about me from the room where Grandmother Estella and I slept on the floor.

"You should have known better than to test the iron on your cousin's arm even if you thought it wasn't hot yet. But never mind. It's done now. Just ask your uncle to forgive you," Grandmother suggested in a whisper.

"I have, many times," I whispered back.

One morning I got up early and waited at the bottom of the stairs for Uncle Conrad to come down. "I'm so very sorry for what I did to your daughter's arm," I confessed, my voice shaking.

"Why did you do such a thing?" Uncle asked. I bowed my head, looking at my feet, finding no way to explain. "You have disfigured her arm," he said, disappointment rich in his voice.

"Yes, Uncle. I'm terribly sorry. I didn't know it was hot, but I still shouldn't have done it," I said, my head still bowed.

"I don't allow such harmful behavior in my household," he scolded. He was a loving, protective father, unlike mine who actually caused harm. I understood, and I respected him. I did not blame him for being angry.

Having said his peace, he walked away without another word. For the next few days, none of my cousins wanted to be near me. I thought they feared what I might do next, that I might come up with other means of harming them. They gave me the silent treatment, and no doubt, they were following their parents' instruction.

Aunt Carmen, too, was not talking to me. I thought she might be regretting the length of my stay. I only spoke to grandmother and busied myself helping her around the house

ANOTHER ERA ENDS

One day, Mother came to pick me up. She announced that Mrs. Vienna could not take all of us to her house, so Mom had decided to go back to Tatalon, Quezon City. Since Dad no longer lived there, having moved back to the Province of La Union with his two other brothers. She had found out that only Uncle Eddie and Aunt Besse lived in our old house, and we could return. Mom and my siblings had already gone back. Mom had asked Aunt Besse to keep an eye on my brother and sisters while she came to fetch me. Aunt Carmen told Mom I had been a good girl, except on the day I burned her child's arm with a hot iron.

Mom looked at me, shocked, and asked what possessed me to do such a thing. I had no answer. I turned and went up to pack my few possessions in a plastic bag, apologized profusely to my cousin again, and we left.

BACK IN QUEZON CITY

Staying inside for a month at Aunt Carmen's had made my skin lighter. I had also gained weight and was about the cleanest and healthiest I'd ever been. There wasn't even a trace of cracks or dryness on the heels of my feet. I'd been fed by Grandmother's cooking every day. Compared to me, my brother and little sisters looked skinny, brown, malnourished, and unkempt.

The first day back, Mother told me to keep an eye on my brother and sisters while she worked. She had run into an old friend who told her about a job selling the national airline's luggage and travel bags door-to-door. So she walked along streets and alleys for miles to look for prospective buyers. She knocked on gates and rang the doorbells of rich folks with mansions. The maids usually answered and decided whether the owners would be interested or not. No doubt those wealthy folks already owned travel bags, ordered from abroad, or purchased on their travels in Europe and America. They probably owned fashionable, expensive luggage and did not need what Mother sold.

Mother travelled by foot through the crowded markets, offering her goods. Any money she gained from the sales, she spent on food for us. She used every penny to us to buy rice and also milk for the babies. She gave cash to Di and me to run the household for the week while she was gone. But most days, she sold nothing. She had to borrow money to feed all of us.

I wanted to help Mom earn money. One of the neighbors, Mrs. Morita started a home-based business, connecting plastic flowers onto artificial pine tree branches. All I had to do was attach coin-sized, pink plastic flowers onto each branch. Heaped up in the corner of her living room floor were piles of plastic, pink flowers and trees. It looked like she could use an extra worker to help her finish the task. Furthermore, old folks around our cluster area had been talking about Mrs. Morita having had a contract dealing in some factory's import and export business, and she was not telling anyone or revealing such a company name for fear of prospective competitors and job-seekers who might slow down her business. Slow business to her meant less money for her family.

That's a piece of cake, I thought when she described it. I asked her if she would let me do some for pay. I had noticed her three children already working. I told her I wanted to help Mother bring in money for our household. I tried to convince her that I would work fast, and she would do better business.

"I'm sorry, but we really do not need any more help. Thank you, though," she said kindly.

"Why don't you just give me a chance," I persisted, not wanting to give up. "Give me one day, and I'll prove to you I'm worth it."

One of her older daughters suggested that her mother go ahead and give me a try. Maybe she was tired of listening to me beg. Or maybe she wanted to do a bit less, or felt sorry for me and my family. Her family was better off financially compared to mine. In fact it was Mrs. Morita who referred mother to rich folks needing a laundry person.

"Okay," her mother said at least, counting out a pile of tree branches and pink flowers and placing them in a plastic bag for me to take home. She would pay me a penny per branch.

"Deal," I said enthusiastically. I could do it while babysitting at home. Better than no pay at all. As soon as I got home, I went to work attaching five flowers to each tree branch. I worked all day and late into the night. When mom came home, I explained what I was doing. She was glad I was doing something constructive instead of just playing and getting dirty. I worked through the night until I was very sleepy, determined to finish by daylight to collect the money. The following day, I returned the finish product and Mrs. Morita paid me two pesos for the work.

I was the happiest kid on the block! "Can I do more?" I asked. I really wanted to keep earning money, and it was such an easy job.

"Sorry, that's all we can do this time. You are taking away work we can do, and some of our profit." She said. Three of her children were busily adorning each plastic tree as I looked on with envy.

THE RETURN

After we lived in Tatalon for three months, Dad showed up. He just walked in the door, sober. From the way he looked at us, it appeared he was surprised we were back in the house.

"So you decided to return," he said snidely to Mother, who was washing clothes.

"We had no place else to go!" she said defensively. "We would not be here at all if we could afford our own place!"

He had the right to live in Tatalon, Quezon City because he was Grandfather's oldest son. He could come and go as he pleased. This also meant that his children had to be made welcome there. He had also built the house with his own hands, although his older sister, Aunt C, had financed it.

The first week of his return, I refused to speak to him or be near him. My blood still boiled from his mistreatment of my mother. I had not forgiven him, but for some reason I was no longer afraid of him. Still, I wished we had not returned and lived somewhere else. I wish we had a place to call our own without father around. It was the beginning of a deep-seated hatred for my father. I no longer felt sorry for him. I did not wish to acknowledge him as my father. He had caused so much pain, so much humiliation, and so much heartache to all of us. Truth be told, I wished him dead. To save our sanity.

I noticed Di also trying to avoid him. As soon as he saw Dad walk in the house, he slipped out of sight. I sensed that he, too, had built up an unquenchable anger for Dad. Living under the same roof with him felt like waiting for a volcano to burst. Any moment the boiling steam and molten lava might build to its pressure limit and scald us all. A sudden outburst was always eminent. We just waited for the day to come when Dad would start punching us, beating us with whatever he could get his hands on. I was grateful that he never laid his hands on the babies and prayed it would not happen.

Maybe before he lost his temper and beat up one of us again, I thought maybe I should do something to him, to protect us. Maybe I should kill him before he killed one of us. It would sure get rid of our biggest problem. Killing him would end our miseries, embarrassments, and homelessness. Though, getting rid of him was not going to be easy. So, I tried to think how I would do it. I told my brother my thoughts. He was already thinking the same thing. He wanted him dead as well.

"But how?" I asked.

He suggested we collect poisonous powder from inside of a fluorescent bulb. Then, pulverize the bulb into powder and mix it in his food, or else use rat poison.

"We will let him suffer. Let him feel the pain and beg us for mercy."

"Then I'll get the butcher knife and chop him up into pieces," I added.

"I'll dig a hole and bury his body in the backyard," brother said.

Thoughts of murder sounded easy. We thought we had a good plan. We separated, each carrying those criminal thoughts.

In the evening, as we were gathered around the floor having dinner, Dad walked in, drunk. "Ahhh, what have we here?" he said in a loud voice. "Something smells delicious!" The smell of liquor wafted to me where I sat between Neneng and Weng. He gave them a scary look, frightening Neneng most. Mom was downstairs.

Dad tried to play with my sisters, pretending his fingers were walking on the floor towards them, ready to pinch my sister's inner thighs, like he wanted to play. Whoever was closest to the fingers got the first pinching. The babies crawled away from the walking fingers that approached their thighs. The drunken fingers stumbled, got up and started chasing Neneng because she moved backwards slower. I watched with disgust. Neneng started to cry, nervously. She did not want to be pinched in the inner thighs. She crossed her legs together.

"Here it comes!" The fingers crawled on her thigh and then pinched.

I was terrified. I had to protect her. Neneng yelled out loud. The pinch hurt her. She screamed, rubbing her thighs with her tiny hands to smother the pain. I grabbed Neneng away from him. I picked her up. I did not want him to continue hurting Neneng.

He looked at me and sneered. Then turned his head towards another sister. Dad warned Weng, "It's your turn now."

Weng crawled away on her hands and knees. She giggled, thinking it must be a fun game. Dad was on his hands and knees, his fingers running on the floor, chasing her. She stopped occasionally to giggle and then crawled again, waited for Dad to chase her. She did not seem bothered, like Neneng. What did she know? She was just one year old. I carried Neneng who was sobbing.

"Ahhh, you sissy!" Dad chided her.

"It's okay, Sister," I comforted, rocking her in my arms. "Dad was only playing. He's stopped now, see? Please don't cry." I carried her away from everyone.

Mom arrived back upstairs and gave Dad his dinner plate. He did not even wash his hands, just took a bite, and then pushed the food away. He must have eaten somewhere else. He collapsed in the corner. We took his plate of food and ate quietly so as to not waken the devil.

After we finished, we gathered the dishes, and Mother took them to wash downstairs while Di and I played with our little sisters. We spread the mat on the floor and put out the mosquito net, leaving Dad to be feasted on by mosquitoes since we dared not wake him and detested touching him. The gin vapor seeped in and out of his nostrils. His breath was nauseating. It reeked from him, as though he'd bathed in gin. But over the years, our nostrils had adapted themselves to the offensive stench of alcohol.

Around dawn, he awakened and crawled inside the net with us. It was then I thought of a plan to get rid of him, with little or no pain. It would have to be done when no one else was in the house. Only me and him.

THE PLAN

A week passed. Thoughts of murder wouldn't leave my head. The more I thought about it, the more I stayed away from him. We were back in our old school, and I was on my way home from school one day in the scorching afternoon heat. Big flies swarmed on ripe mangoes at food stalls outside a neighbor's home-store. The ripe fruit gave off a sweet sticky smell. The exorbitant price was more than the little change I had saved in my pocket.

I went inside our house to look for something to eat. The pots were empty. The house seemed deserted, but when I climbed the stairs, I found Dad asleep on the floor. As I took the last step, I stood quietly studying his intoxicated form. He was face down, snoring, with no worries in the world. He had no concern that his children had nothing to eat.

Suddenly he turned. I tiptoed past him. I had better hurry before he finds me standing near him, I thought as the devil in me whispered, "This is the opportune moment to chop off his head. Go on. Do it now before he wakes up!"

I descended the stairs again and grabbed the butcher knife that he kept meticulously sharpened. I stared at its edge and then I went back up the stairs.

What do I need to do first? Chop off his arms and legs so he will never use them to hit or kick us again. But, if he lived through me cutting off his arms and legs, Mother will have to take care of an invalid with a nasty mouth and nasty temper. She'd have to feed him, clean him, and dress him. She'd have to wipe his ass.

He moved again, shifting position, flopping so he laid on his back now. I moved quietly above his head and froze. The butcher knife was in my right hand, held above him as I watched his stomach rise and fall. His skinny ribs protruded. He stunk. He looked vulnerable, innocent even, as he ground his teeth loudly like a cow chewing its cud. I hated that sound.

He kept grinding them as he turned onto his side. *I better get going*, I thought. With a firm grip on the machete handle, I raised the knife, ready to chop his neck off first. My heart was racing. I froze momentarily, staring at his pathetic figure. My hands and chin began to tremble.

"I love you, Dad." I whispered, and I tried to remember if there were any days he ever did anything good to any one of us while growing up. Did he ever show affection and love? None that I could think of at that moment. He had absolute power over anyone of us. He could do as he pleased. To him, he was our superior. Drunk or not. Some days he was sober, and those were the days when he was quiet. Days when we feared being near him. We did not want to give him a bad impression that could be brought up later on when he was drunk. I remembered some days when he cooked meals for us, when he chose to be sober for the day.

No. Stop a moment. Slow down. I had to think what I was about to do. An image of the devil in red suit, exactly the ones printed on every label of gin he made me buy, went through my head. A pitchfork wielding devil

in a red suit about to strike a helpless and defeated angel
who was wearing a long white gown and was lying on
his back on the ground. The angel's palms were raised,
blocking the devil's strike. I was the devil in charge. My
father, on the floor, was my helpless angel. Like the
picture on the gin bottle, I was ready to kill my sleeping,
innocent-looking angel. That's right. My father's real
name was Angel. Short for Angelito, a name he was given
when baptized as an infant. But he was nothing like any
angel I have heard of nor seen in any movies.

In fact, there was no angel in his blood at all. He
was quite the opposite. At the age of fifteen, he had his
first taste of gin. And since then, instead of drinking
milk, Angelito had been drinking the blood of the devil
straight from the bottles of gin until he was hooked. He
could drink gin as early as six in the morning and all
through the night, occasionally taking breaks to take a
piss, defecate, eat, and sleep - work a few hours of the
day, if he had a job. He became the devil on the label
and I pictured myself as his offspring. A product about
to defeat Angel, my father. *I had better get going*, I thought.
With both hands on the handle of the machete, I raised
it above my head. I was ready to cut off his head, staring
at the pulsating of his carotid where the sharp end of the
machete would land, but I couldn't move. My arms froze.

My head balancing good against evil. Then, I began
to remember what the priests and nuns taught in our
school. "Thou shalt not kill." Those words echoed in my
ears, non-stop. "That's what Jesus wanted us to remember
always," the priests said numerous times. "Do you want to
be a murderer?" something inside my head asked me.

I realized at that moment I still loved him. I still loved Angel, my father. I could not hurt him. He was my own flesh and blood—despite what he had done to all of us. My bottom dropped on the floor, weakened by the thought of murdering my own father. The sharp tip of my weapon dug into the wooden floor, my hands rested on the handle. I bowed my head and sobbed, feeling defeated.

Besides, I did not want to be locked up in a prison for juveniles like I'd seen in movies, where people were put in straight jackets screaming and begging to be released. I did not want my soul to burn in hell like the Catholic priests said. But father's soul would.

I was weak. Instead I crouched in the corner and prayed to the Higher Power, if there was one, to soften my father's heart. I prayed with all my heart that he would never lay his hands on any of us again, that he would stop drinking. That he should choke on his saliva and die that moment. It would be a miracle come true.

The priests and nuns who visited our school and community told us there was a God who heard our plight and prayers. "God is watching you," they told us. "He knows what you are doing. He is everywhere." So, if God was everywhere, then He must have seen me and have heard of my desperate call for help.

I stood up and walked away on tiptoes, deeply sad, leaving Dad sprawled on the floor, high on gin. I put back the butcher knife, hanging it in its place on the kitchen wall. I went outside, closing the front door behind me and leaving it to God. I wondered where the rest of my family was.

SAVING MONEY

Dad had made a box the size of a shoebox, sealing the
corners with molten metal. It had a slit two inches long in
the top for dropping coins and paper money in. He said
he and Mom were going to put money in it to save for the
future and that we children had better keep our hands
off. No matter how desperate our situation got, no one
was to open this box and take money from it.

"Do you all hear me?"

"Yes, father. We hear you," we said.

Every week, Mom and Dad put one or two pesos into
the box until it started to get very heavy.

When Dad came home from work, especially on
payday, he would drop money in it and then put the box
on a high shelf so we could not reach it. No intruder
would ever notice it. Every morning before he left for
work, he felt the weight of the box and smiled, looking
like he was reaching his ambition.

"For the future," he'd say.

But whose future? I wondered. We were miserable
with hunger now and maybe dead by the time his
future came. My stomach growled and that box
looked really good.

One day, I climbed up to the shelf and got the box
down. I thought I would just get one coin, a peso, to buy
us some bread to eat. The weight of the box wouldn't

change so much if I took only one peso out. Dad wouldn't know the difference. He couldn't know exactly how much was in the box. He didn't count it each day. Then I wouldn't do it again, I promised myself. I turned the box upside down, with the hole facing down toward my face and squinted inside. None dropped out.

I got a butter knife and held it upside down again, inserting the tip of the knife into the hole. I wiggled it back and forth until it was slightly wider. It was easy! And not a mark showed on the box. A coin slipped out. I slid the box back in its place and climbed down. I returned the butter knife back to the kitchen. I told Wilma to keep an eye on the little ones. "I'll be right back," I said and ran to the store. There I bought five hot buns called Pandesal.

I raced home with them, and we devoured them while they were still warm. I watched my younger sisters eating slowly, making the most of each bite, like they'd never taste another one. They vanished so quickly. We were still hungry, and now we were thirsty, too. I could not stand it. I climbed back up and got one more peso from the tin box. Then I returned to the bakery and bought five more hot buns. We ate them all. Di was selling newspapers and could take care of himself that day.

It wasn't long before Dad noticed that the hole on the piggy bank appeared wider, as if bent at the corners slightly. And it felt lighter.

"Di!" he yelled loud for my brother to come upstairs.

My knees were trembling and heart pounding fast, pressure on my ears, fearful of what Dad might do to my brother. Di responded as soon as he heard his name and climbed the stairs.

"Tell me the truth," Dad said, holding the box and pointing at Di. "Did you steal money from this box?"

"No. I did not," he said, tears building in his eyes.

"Do I have to ask you again? Did you take money from this box?"

There was a long pause, and then Di finally admitted taking some money from the box. I was shocked! I thought I was the only one taking any. I never thought he would do it, too. Dad smacked my brother's face with the tin box.

Di yelped. He started screaming. I had stayed downstairs and started crying, hearing the *thunks* as my brother was hit hard. Footsteps thumped everywhere, and the floorboards creaked. I heard my brother yelling that he was sorry, that he would never do it again.

"Please stop!" I heard him pleading, but the beating didn't stop..

I was so sorry for my brother. I just whimpered in a corner downstairs. I wanted to scream, to tell my dad that I, too, was a thief. That I did it because we were hungry. I wanted to yell this out to Dad so that brother did not have to bear all the beatings. I imagined the pain he was going through. He got my portion of the beatings. I was a chicken, whimpering in a corner. I should have been beaten, too. I felt sick with guilt, crouching in the corner, knees to my chin, both hands covering my ears so I did not hear Di's screams. I hated myself for not speaking up. I hated myself for not defending brother. I should have taken his place.

It seemed to go on forever. When Dad was satisfied, he stopped. I could hear Di sobbing, alone, as Dad descended the stairs. Our eyes met briefly as he passed. He was fuming like a bull, like steam might come from his nostrils. He stormed out of the house, slamming the door.

Di slowly came down the stairs and sat in a chair. His eyes were red, and his face was wet and swollen. His lips were cut. I saw red patches on the backs of his legs. He must have known that I had been taking money, too. Maybe he hadn't taken any. Maybe he just admitted it to keep Dad from beating me nearly to death again. I had never seen Di take the box down.

Two hours later, Dad returned, climbed the stairs and came down with the tin box. He went to the kitchen, and I heard him pounding the box, prying it open. As soon as the box was open, he put the remaining coins in his pockets and left the house. Our little sisters were quiet. Their eyes followed Dad as he passed us.

I got up and went to my brother. He turned his back to me, refusing to look at me or let me see him tearful. I walked to the kitchen and found the tin box turned upside down, empty. I returned to the living room, trying to think what I could do to make Di feel better. No doubt Dad would buy himself and his friends many bottles of gin with the heavy load of coins in his pockets while his children starved. He treated his drinking buddies with far more decency than his own family. He served them pork, beef, or barbecued chicken appetizers whenever he had extra cash, and drank with them all day and night. We watched them feasting and telling stories, having a merry time with their gin. I hated him more than ever now.

"I pray he chokes on his food and dies," I said.

"Stay away from me!" Di responded, angrily.

"Fine! Be that way, if you like!" I snapped at him, moving away, angry, too.

Wilma had been crying. The toddlers still did not know what was happening around them. I feared for what would happen when Dad came back drunk, and I wondered if he would bring up the tin box again. I worried for my mother when she would get home tired later that evening.

As soon as she arrived home, she started unloading groceries to prepare supper, already tired from her hard job all day, and now she had to feed us. I told her what dad had done to brother. She stopped unloading and approached brother, waiting for her in the corner of the room. She tried to touch him on the shoulder to show him how sorry she was for what had happened, her way of expressing her love to him. Angrily, he pushed her hand away. He did not want to be touched. His blood was still boiling. She left him be and went back to preparing our meal.

After supper, I helped clean up. I put all dirty dishes in a corner for me to wash when I had time. It was too late to be washing the dishes.

She was first to fall asleep. The minute she laid down, she was dead to the world and was snoring loudly.

A RESPITE

In a few days, Aunt Zenia came to visit with her two
year old son, Hugo Jr. Her visit calmed the disorder and
distress in our dysfunctional family. Her presence served
as a temporary distraction. He came home sober, just
to impress Aunt Zenia. He wanted to show her that
he was not really the irresponsible drunken husband
Grandmother Estella said he was. He showed himself
as helpful with household chores, fetching water and
cooking dinner before Mom came home from work. He
polished and sharpened his knives, which was his favorite
chore by far, and swept the dirt floor. He woke early
to prepare breakfast, helped Mother put lunch boxes
together, and even ironed Di's shirt and shorts.

Seeing him as a changed man made me
uncomfortable, confused, and suspicious. But I tried
to remind myself that miracles do happen. Perhaps my
prayers came true. That the Supreme Being out there
had heard of my prayer. Then again, I suspected it was
a temporary display, but maybe, just maybe, he felt
remorseful and wanted to atone. I watched and waited for
the moment his true self would reemerge. Probably the
minute Aunt Zenia's visit ended.

However, Zenia extended her stay for another six
months. She seemed comfortable living with us while
her husband, Hugo Senior, was away at sea. She must

have been tired of being lonely. Luckily, she received her husband's salary every month and contributed to the household, but she refused to help around the house. She did not like to cook nor help wash dishes and her dirty laundry piled up. She crocheted all day as she watched her toddler crawling, playing by himself, and pissing on the floor near her.

In the afternoon, she took him out and didn't let any of us go with her. If Wilma asked to go with them, Aunt Zenia flatly refused. One day I decided to follow them. I stayed out of sight and watched them stop at a bakery for hot buns, which they sat and ate, drinking coke. The next time I followed, Wilma did too. She walked right up to them, and Aunt Zenia spanked her bottom for following. She did not offer any of the hot bun or coke to Wilma, who stood next to them and watched.

On the way back, Aunt Zenia told Wilma to stop swinging from a tree branch and gave her another smack on the bottom. She gave her a twisting pinch on the side of her leg and then motioned to her son that it was time to go. She looked angrily at my sister, picked up little Hugo Jr., and carried him away, leaving Wilma alone.

I hated the way my aunt treated my sister. All the time she and her son lived with us, Di and I fetched water for her to shower and wash her laundry. I walked to the store to buy her soap and put up with sleeping next to her son, who peed in the bed because she was too lazy to get up and take him out to pee. I had to get out of the mosquito net and clean off. Then I changed to dry bedclothes. I'd put a dry towel between us, wipe off the urine on the mat, and try to get back to sleep while

Aunt Zenia snored away, blissfully unaware. If I told her in the morning about him peeing in the night, she just said, "Oh, dear, I'm sorry." She never bothered to wash the mat afterward.

I wanted to slap him. I hated them both and wished they would leave our house so I wouldn't have to be her slave anymore. Aunt Zenia let Junior walk around the house naked because she was too lazy to wash his clothes.

WORMS AGAIN

One day I came home from school to find Aunt Zenia crocheting away as usual. I noticed they had had what looked like spaghetti for lunch. I thought the sauce had spilled on the floor. It turned out I was wrong.

Her son had diarrhea on the floor while she was crocheting, and she had been oblivious for hours. It was not, spaghetti but intestinal worms crawling about the feces.

But, in fact she did know. "I'm waiting for the worms to die before cleaning the floor," she told me while she continued crocheting.

The air in the room smelled of diarrhea. Her son lay on the floor in the corner, with an Ascaris parasite hanging halfway out of his anus. I wanted to scream at Aunt Zenia to put her crocheting down and get her stupid, lazy ass out of the chair and help her son! But

I feared she might slap me. She was taller than I and a lot stronger.

This time I was not going to clean up her mess. I decided to get out of there fast before she told me to. The little boy tried to get up. I turned around and descended the stairs.

"Xulli, will you help me take care of these worms?" Aunt Zenia asked, disgusted by the sight.

I felt utter contempt and anger towards her. I could not believe it! I pretended not to hear her, but then I paused and thought if I didn't help her now, how much longer will she sit there crocheting and let the crap be sprawled on the floor?

"Xulli, Please help me. I would be forever grateful," she called out again.

I had no choice. I had to obey any elder. I climbed back up the stairs. She called him to come closer to her. There were no gloves in our house. For poor people, gloves would be a luxury. I looked for newspapers downstairs, the kitchen, and more papers from my school bag to use to pick up Junior's shit on the floor. The rest of the paper I saved to pull the white worm dangling halfway out of his anus.

I wrapped the white worm around with an old newspaper with my hand. Holding it firmly, I pulled it out slowly.

Then I showed Aunt Zenia the length of it, still wiggling weakly. "Yak! That's a long one!" she exclaimed looking disgusted. I wrapped the rest with the newspaper and disposed of it outside in the trash.

I carried a pail of water, a brush, and soap upstairs. I scrubbed the floor.

"We let the floor air dry," I told Aunt Zenia who was already downstairs giving her son a good scrubbing. She thanked me, and I stormed out of the house.

That evening when Mom and Dad came home, they noticed a stale, offensive odor in the air.

"What is that smell?" Dad asked loudly for anyone who cared to respond.

Aunt Zenia told them what had happened, that it had taken about six or seven hours for the intestinal worms to stop moving and die. She announced excitedly, as if telling my parents the news would enlighten them both, that she was afraid to get close to the creepy crawling things and waited for me to come home to help her with them. She halfway told the truth. I didn't bother to say any more. Mom and Dad knew she could not have done the work all by herself.

BACK TO HIS OLD WAYS

During this, time dad slowly regressed to his old habits, coming home later and later at night, drunk and talking loud. Annoyed by his foul habits, Aunt Zenia decided to take the money she received from her fisherman-sailor husband and looked for another place to live. It did not take long for her to find a one-bedroom. She announced that her husband would be coming home and they needed a place of their own. When I heard the news, I was elated. I would no longer have to put up with my cousin peeing in bed next to me, and I would not have to do extra work around the house for her.

When Aunt Zenia's husband arrived home after having been working out at sea for six months as a fisherman/sailor, he looked darker from being out under the sun every day on the ships. He was about the same height as Aunt Zenia, but average looking, muscular, with a pug nose.

Our grandmother and other relatives called them "coffee and cream." He was dark skinned, and she was very light. They did not seem to care. Opposites do attract sometimes, I guess. He came home with a lot of money. He had saved up while at sea, plus he brought lots of shark meat, which he divided up and distributed between his brother and sisters, including my mother. He handed over his salary to his wife, and let her budget it after paying the rent and credits she'd built up at shops while he was away.

One day, after a week Uncle Hugo came home, Aunt Zenia invited me to go to the movie theater with her, leaving Uncle Hugo to babysit Little Hugo. I was excited. I hadn't been to a movie since that disastrous time with Aunt C's family. I rushed home and asked Dad for permission because Mom was at work, doing laundry for rich folks. Dad said yes, so I quickly changed into my best clothes. I ran back to Aunt Zenia's and waited for her outside.

We caught a jeepney to go downtown to Metro Manila, to one of the most popular cinemas. Everywhere, men stared at Aunt Zenia, even while we were still riding inside the jeepney. When we got out, men smiled. In the theater, one particularly handsome young man noticed us and followed.

"Ignore him," Aunt Zenia said.

We continued inside the theater, holding our popcorn, and found good seats. The young man sat right behind Aunt Zenia. During the movie, I noticed once in a while he leaned over Aunt Zenia's shoulder and whispered something to her. Being friendly, Aunt Zenia responded to his questions and, once in a while, nodded. After the movie, as we were leaving our seats, he was still talking to her and followed us out. He and Aunt Zenia were actually holding a conversation now. I waited nearby, outside the theater. Finally we rode the jeepney home.

Uncle Hugo had prepared dinner and tidied up the place. "How was the movie, Xulli?" he asked.

"It was good," I replied.

"What did you see?"

"Oh, just some drama, but a guy followed us and sat behind us. It was hard to concentrate with them talking." I walked home then.

A couple of hours later, Aunt Zenia came to our house looking for me, her eyes red and swollen. As I approached her, she punched me in the mouth.

"I'm going to make that mouth of yours bleed!" she said angrily and hit me three more times. We were out on the street, and a lot of people were passing by and witnessed the spectacle. "You need to learn to keep your mouth shut!"

I tried to get away, covering my mouth with my hands. My lips burned. A few neighbors outside saw her hitting me and looked like they wondered what was going on. Some even stopped close to us.

"What did I do?" I asked her, in shock.

"You told your uncle some story about me meeting a guy at the theater!" she yelled.

"No, I did not!" I cried. "I told him there was a guy who followed us and kept talking to you! That's all I told uncle!"

"Well, your uncle thinks I went out to meet a guy!"

"I'm sorry. I don't know anything!" I told her and ran back into our house.

Dad was in the kitchen preparing dinner as I entered. He took the large towel he had wrapped around his neck, twisted it, and hit me on my already sore mouth. It stung like crazy.

"What have you done now?" he asked as he kept hitting me with the towel.

"Nothing!" I told him, covering my aching mouth.

"Your uncle wants to talk to you. He's been looking for you. Go meet him by the public bathrooms."

I ran to the public restrooms. Uncle Hugo was there waiting for me.

With my head bowed, sobbing, I approached him. He raised my chin while I continued to sob. My mouth was on fire. It was red and swollen after being pounded by Aunt Zenia's fist and then Dad's towel whipping. Uncle asked me what really happened at the theater. I told him again that a stranger followed us inside the theater and sat behind Aunt Zenia's seat, that he kept whispering to her.

"That's all I know," I said. "I did not hear what they were talking about. That's the truth, Uncle."

He was sympathetic then and said he was sorry. He remained silent, thinking, while I ran. I wasn't going home because dad might hit me some more. I sat on a curb, sobbing. People passed by, looking at me while I tried to get over my shock.

How could Aunt Zenia hit me the way she did? It took me by such utter surprise, coming out of nowhere. Maybe I deserved it, I finally thought. I should have kept my mouth shut, and if I don't get back home, Dad would hit me for being late.

On my way home, I wiped my tears with my shirt, thinking how I caused a rift in my aunt and uncle's nice marriage. That was the last I saw of Aunt Zenia, her husband, and Little Pisser all together.

D≡≡D≡≡

It was after school, and most students lived nearby. They were just a short walk from their home. Others were picked up by their parents with tricycles, but it was a long hot walk home from Tatalon Elementary School for me and Di.

Exhausted and sweating, I headed to the kitchen for a glass of water. To my surprise, I found a new girl there who looked very young and chubby. Half of her head was bald. She was washing dishes. I walked into the living room and found Aunt Besse telling Mother that she, Uncle Eddie, and the little girl would be living with us. Half the house would be partitioned as their living quarters.

"That's Deedee in the kitchen. She will be living with us for a while," Aunt Besse said, as she introduced me to her. Aunt Besse explained that Deedee's mother was a prostitute in Olongapo, a place popular with sailors and soldiers from around the world. Ships full of navy men stationed in Olongapo frequented the bars and bought themselves 'pleasure women' while stationed at the Naval Base there. She said that the girl's mother found the girl a burden and could not support her nor take care of her. Having her around obstructed her work, so she set Deedee on fire, trying to get rid of her when she was just a toddler.

Deedee had burns on her arm and legs. The flame had spread up her scalp, burning half her hair and head, sparing her face. The mother had two more children, fathered by different men. Deedee was left at home to care for them while the mother worked. When she got home one day, she had beaten Deedee with a stick. The mother's excuse was that she was punishing Deedee for not doing her chores. Deedee's family live only a walking distance from Aunt Besse's relatives. When she had heard that Aunt Besse was childless, had a good career, and a husband who worked, she decided Besse would be the best candidate to take Deedee.

Aunt Besse had given the woman ten pesos (less than one dollar) to help her out by taking the girl off her hands. Deedee's, younger siblings, were distributed among distant relatives. Aunt Besse said she would take Deedee for a year. But the year had passed, and her mother had never came back for her.

For a seven year old, Deedee was small for her age. She had light skin and light brown hair. She was very helpful and energetic. She had perfect white teeth and laughed a lot. Every day at five in the morning, she got up and fetched water with me. She provided the water for Aunt Besse and Uncle Eddie to take showers before they went to work. Together, Deedee and I woke up early to be at the head of the line. We alternated going back and forth to the water collection site, to fill up the two big drums at home. Afterwards, Deedee fried eggs and cooked rice for breakfast for Aunt and Uncle's breakfast while I went back to bed.

While I was at school, she cleaned dishes and took a short nap, waking before Aunt Besse got home, so she could get things started for dinner. On Saturdays, she gathered all the dirty clothes and washed them by hand.

Deedee refused to go to school, ashamed of the burn scars all over her. She feared the children would make fun of her as they did in Tondo. She was not only bullied for her half bald head but also for being the daughter of a prostitute. Children at her old school followed her outside and teased her, calling her and her mother insulting, degrading names until she would get home crying. She had engaged in many fights, defending her innocence and her mother whom she loved, despite how ugly her reputation was. But it was such a daily struggle that she stopped going to school all together.

She pleaded to Aunt Besse never to take her back to school. On many occasions, Aunt tried to persuade her to go, but she would throw a tantrum until Aunt Besse gave up altogether. It appeared to me that Aunt Besse had bought herself a slave for ten pesos, but Aunt

Besse brought some books and school supplies for her to use at home.

Deedee was also not allowed to play outside for too long, as she might get distracted from her responsibilities at home. She slept downstairs by the kitchen while Aunt Besse and Uncle Eddie slept in another room.

At five o'clock early morning, I got out of bed and went to wake Deedee. "Come on, get up!" I jiggled her. She was too sleepy. She just moaned about how she ached. She sounded like an eighty year old as opposed to a seven year old. "You have to get up or you'll get spanked later for being lazy," I reminded her. "Come on!" I tried to get her into a sitting position. Finally she sat up, sleepily, and forced herself to stand.

"Hurry up!" I said. "The line is probably getting long and it'll take forever to get water.

"Okay," she said as she struggled to wake up, scratching her arms, walking very slowly. We gathered our buckets and headed to the water line. It took nearly two hours to fill up our drums, but we always made it.

When we finished, I crawled back in bed, but Deedee stayed up and ironed Aunt's uniform for the day. Then she cooked them breakfast, including coffee. At last, when Aunt and Uncle had left, she went back to bed.

Aunt Besse left money for Deedee to buy food. She was learning to budget for their household. She walked to the market to buy fresh fish or meat for supper, and she'd buy herself lunch. She always turned the receipts over to Aunt Besse, who examined them and calculated the amounts to be sure Deedee did not get cheated by the vendors.

When Deedee had a little time, she played with the neighborhood children. Some were older than her. It bothered Deedee when brother Di teased her, calling her 'granny' because she dressed like an old lady and sometimes talked like one. She lectured, giving us orders. She had had to grow up too fast.

"Hey, Granny, what are you cooking today?" he teased, maybe trying to get her to rebel. I told Di to leave her alone but he was stubborn.

"You call me Granny one more time and I'll kick your ass!" Deedee threatened. She had lived a tough life and could stand up to bullies. She would pick up a stick, a small rock, or anything she could find on the ground next to her, and she would throw it in my brother's direction. Di giggling as he tried to run away before getting hit, but he just got a kick out of her defensiveness and laughed all the more. Sometimes Deedee ran after Di and kicked him in the behind. Di yelped, but he found that amusing as well.

"That didn't even hurt." He taunted her, sticking out his rear end for her to give him some more. Deedee picked up a stick and tried to hit him but missed.

Di leapt out of the way and called her *peklat* (Scarhead) to describe the big, bald scar on her head.

"Stop it!" I yelled at my brother. It angered me that he would act like such a stupid bully.

"Oh, you're going her side now, eh?" He asked.

"You don't need to be so mean to her," I defended. "She has no mother or father. We should be good to her."

He looked dumbfounded, like he'd never thought of it the way I was saying it. I knew my message woke him up. Deedee's mind must have been full of miserable memories—abandonment by her own mother, teasing, suffering from burns, going without, bullies, and more. She sat in the corner, knees folded to her chest, crying so forlornly, like she longed for a mother who would protect her in moments of despair. Cruel as her mother had been, it probably hurt even more that she never came back for her. Deedee cried her heart out.

I felt so sorry for her and gave Di another mean look. "See what you've done?" I yelled at him.

A guilty look crossed his face as he turned and left. After that, he just avoided her, but he also stopped bullying her.

Aunt Besse came home tired, and hungry and there was no food prepared, the house in disarray. She yelled for Deedee.

I heard Deedee's trembling voice, "What is it, Ma?" Then I heard her yelp and started crying. I heard smacking sounds. "I'm sorry, I'm sorry."

"How many times do I have to tell you to behave?" I heard Aunt Besse say. I felt sick to my stomach and ran to their side of the house. There was Aunt Besse, red faced and angry. Deedee cried in front of her, covering her cheek with her hand.

"Deedee didn't feel well," I told my aunt. "Our buckets were at the end of the line. There were too many people at the water collection, and we spent the entire day watching our buckets. We had no time to cook and clean house." I tried to convince her.

Deedee pulled away from Aunt Besse and stood in the corner, sobbing, one hand pressed to her cheek.

"Get out of my sight!" Aunt Besse said, with spite.

Deedee and I descended the stairs together. She sat on the edge of her bed sobbing. I did not know what to do to help her. She began neatly folding clothes. I thought about her awful mother. Where was she? Did she even miss her child? And here was my aunt, treating her like a slave. My stomach churned as I returned to our side of the house, depressed. That night, I lay next to Deedee's bed. We had sort of a sleep over, whispering about her past. She said she missed her mother, and her brothers and sisters. She had vowed to search for them and find them someday.

PUSH CART

Dad made a wooden pushcart for transporting water. We could now bring five–to–seven containers at a time (each container held five gallons of water), making it quicker to fill the two drums of rain barrels at home. Dad had seen other families using them. Some kids used theirs to do business, delivering water for other families and charging them.

Di and I just used it to collect our own water. We took turns and even left it in line full of empty buckets. Grownups without carts resented the hours they spent collecting water, carrying buckets by hand, and made nasty comments to us, but we ignored them. They thought it was a great idea having push carts and tried to manipulate us kids into lending it to them for a while. A while could mean anywhere from a few hours to a few days. If we lent it out, we may never see it again. But Di and I knew better than being suckered and deceived by grownups. If we lent it to one person and never got it back, Dad would have whipped us badly. Back and forth we went, six or seven times a day, every day, whether it was a school day or the weekend. At least we no longer had to carry heavy loads by hand. We even had to fill Uncle Eddie's metal drums as well.

During the rainy, seasons we got breaks because our barrels were placed alongside the rainspout to collect fresh rainwater. But during typhoons, the water overflowed, flooding our downstairs, turning the cluster into a giant lake. At least then we had ample water to wash clothes and use for showers. For drinking, we just boiled it. We'd park our pushcart, our lifesaver, indoors.

MORE VISITORS

One hot summer afternoon, as I was pushing the wooden pushcart that father had built for me and brother to the water station, a yellow taxi cab pulled up and stopped. I watched, amazed. Rarely did visitors have the money for a taxi! Then I saw Aunt Li and Cousin Violet step out, along with a little girl. It was Bebeng! It had been so long, I hadn't even recognized her at first!

I dropped the cart handles. It rolled and created disarray, spilling collected water. I did not care. All I knew was I had to get closer to my relatives and my sister.

I left angry neighbors swearing, figuring out whose buckets were first in line.

"Aunt Li!" I screamed as I ran toward them. Bebeng looked healthy and clean in a pretty red dress and shiny, black shoes. As I rushed up, I did not know what to do. I paused momentarily to catch my breath, trying to decide whether to hug and kiss her or just pat her on the shoulder. I had not seen her in two years. She had grown taller. Her light brown hair was even lighter. Her natural beauty glowed like a bright star. I realized how much I'd missed her quiet, uncomplaining ways. I could not take my eyes off her and grinned down at her. I was all smiles.

But she did not recognize me. She did not know who I was and stayed close to Violet and clung to the only mother she remembered knowing—Aunt Li. She glanced at me shyly, quizzical. We were strangers as far as she knew. Their visit was an utter surprise. I had no idea they were coming, and already I did not want them to leave.

"How long are you staying?" I asked Aunt Li.

"What? We just got here, and you already ask when we're leaving?" Aunt Li remarked as she was paying the cab driver.

"I didn't mean it that way. I want you to stay for a very long time," I explained.

I looked at Violet. She was dressed up nicely for travel, as elegant as I remembered. Bebeng and Violet were both dressed so neatly. I glanced down at my own dirty t-shirt, with holes in it, dirty skirt, and my worn out flip-flops. I compared my outfit with their dresses and

sequined, beaded slippers that looked brand new. I felt
ashamed of my appearance. Aunt Li remarked on the
chaos I had made with my cart and told me to go get it
and straighten the situation out.

"Okay, I'll meet you at Aunt C's house!" I yelled as
I rushed back to the line. When I'd put my cart back in
line, I hurried to follow our guests as they paraded up the
street to Aunt C's.

As we approached, I already heard someone
shouting, "Xulli, you are not to come inside this house
with those dirty feet of yours!" My nice entrance
came to a halt.

"Go clean your feet first," Aunt C commanded.

It would take too long to clean my feet properly,
and I didn't want to take my eyes off my sister. From the
doorway, I asked Cousin Violet if she happened to have
brought along the latest *Liwayway* with a Kling Kling
story. "Yes, I have," she said politely, demonstrating her
cultivated manners.

I was euphoric thinking about it. I nearly fainted
from too much excitement. First, seeing Bebeng and
Aunt Li made me deliriously happy. To find out Violet
had brought the latest issue of my favorite magazine was a
dream come true.

"Can I borrow it?" I asked her.

"Yeah, after you clean your feet."

"Okay." That's fair enough. I had to get home
and cook rice for lunch anyway. I ran back to the water
line, waited my turn to fill my buckets, went home, and
poured the water into the drums. I placed the empty
buckets back into the cart, scooped up three cups of
grains of rice, added and measured the water into the

pot (up to the middle knuckle line of my middle finger) to cook perfect white rice. I had to cook extra rice just in case the new visitors come by to eat with us at our house.

To cook it, I made sawdust stove with two Coca-Cola bottles and an empty paint can with a hole cut out on the side just above the base of the pan. I placed one of the bottles upright at the bottom of the paint can and the other bottle was inserted sideway into the side hole, touching the standing bottle. I then put sawdust around the bottles and compressed it. Once fully packed, I removed the bottles to create an air chamber to fuel the fire. I ignited a match from a matchbox. The dry saw dust burned very quickly. I blew the fire until it gave a soft, steady flame. Then I placed the pot on the burner. With speed, excitement, and carelessness all blended together, I neglected to balance the pot and it toppled to the ground floor, spilling the water and uncooked rice. Meticulously, I scooped the rice from the ground with my bare hands, cupping every scoop back into the pot. We couldn't afford to waste it. I picked any tiny stones out of it, rinsed it and added fresh water. All the while, I could think of nothing else but the magazine and reading Kling Kling again. It had been more than two years since I last read it.

While the rice cooked, I scrubbed the bottom of my feet with a rough rock, soaping and rubbing off layers of callouses and corns. As soon as the rice started boiling, I loosened the lid cover. Dad walked in carrying a burlap sack of sawdust, which he dropped to the floor. More sawdust for a week's worth of cooking.

"Bebeng is here, Dad, with Aunt Li and Violet," I announced while rinsing off my feet and slipping on my old flip-flops.

He told me to invite them to our house for lunch. "Just let it be known that Aunt Li has to provide something to eat with our rice."

At last, I finally got to be close to my sister and read the magazine. I ran back to Aunt C's and announced, "My feet are clean now. I'm coming in. Oh," I remembered, "and Dad said to come and eat at our house."

Aunt Li usually refused to visit our house. Even when we'd lived only a couple of minutes away by foot, she had rarely ever come to visit us. But that day she bought dishes made of roasted pig, deep-fried fish, and beef stew at a corner store, and brought them to our house. She also brought along a potful of already steamed rice to share in addition to what I had already made.

"Where is it?" I asked Violet."

"Uncle Fred has it," she said. "He wanted to read it first."

"What?" I was heartbroken. "Well, can I have it next?"

"You'll get it. Just be patient!" Aunt Li scolded me as we walked to our house as the aroma of roasted pork and steamed rice rose from the containers.

As we gathered around our wooden table, I was sweating, worrying that someone might taste the dirt in the rice I'd made. "This rice is a little overdone, but it tastes good, Xulli," Aunt Li commented while everybody was busy taking big bites. I gave a sigh of relief. With my head bowed, I stayed quiet. The meal was delicious. I wished we had meals like that every day.

After lunch, I cleaned the table and washed the dishes all by myself. As soon as I finished, I headed to Aunt C's house where everybody was talking in the living room. I searched for Kling Kling around the house.

I knew Mom would be very happy to find Bebeng home. She was now nine, almost ten years old. My parents had left her in the province when she was barely seven and had not had the money to visit except for during Grandmother's funeral.

Bebeng remained quiet, never separating from Aunt Li who had been her mother since she was seven years old. Whenever Aunt Li came to Manila, our family enjoyed lavish meals. Now she owned and managed hectares of rice and sugar cane and had even more money than before. She employed farmers to work the fields, and owned livestock—goats and cows. Every time she came to Manila, she brought burlap sacks of rice, bundles of fresh fish, and meat, and usually brought along one or two maids.

My eyes wandered around Aunt C's living room and dining area for *Liwayway*. It had to be someplace. I was not welcome to go upstairs for fear of being reprimanded in front of the guests, especially in front of Bebeng. I decided to go home and planned to return later.

Mom came home, and we greeted her with good news. Her face lit up, tears welling in her eyes. We all went with her, rushing to Aunt C's, where Bebeng, Aunt Li, and Violet were staying. I was sure she wanted to hold Bebeng in her arms, cradle her, and smother her with hugs and kisses. As soon as we arrived, she called to Bebeng.

Everyone called to her, "Come greet your mother!"

But Bebeng refused to come close to her biological mother.

"Go on, Bebeng, this is your mother," Aunt Li said tenderly. "Go on now, give your mom a hug." She

gave her a light push towards Mother, but Bebeng
clung to Aunt Li.

Mom coaxed her, arms extended, "Come here
Bebeng, give me a hug. Let me see you up close." Still
Bebeng refused. Bright tears glistened in Mother's eyes,
rejected, forgotten.

"Just wait awhile. She'll come around," Aunt
Li reassured her.

I watched from the balcony, through the glass sliding
door, thinking she was no longer my sister. She was now
Violet's sister. We were once her family, but now we're
strangers. I headed home with Neneng and Weng while
Wilma and Di stayed at Aunt C's house.

The next day, I invited Bebeng to come to our house
and play with us. She had on a neat dress again, no doubt
Violet had outgrown it. As she walked along with me, I
discovered she also had hundreds of pesos in her pocket.
I was shocked. A little girl of nine, almost ten, having
hundreds of pesos was beyond my comprehension. There
we were, her own brother and sisters with not a penny
and always hungry while she has bundles of cash in her
pocket and perhaps somewhere else.

I wasted no time convincing her to go to the
store to buy us coke and snacks. I lead her to the mom
and pop bakery and asked her if she could buy us
something to eat.

Without hesitation, she pulled money out of her
pocket and said, "Get whatever you want."

I picked up goodies I only usually dreamed of
buying. I bought hot buns with chicken and pork fillings,
five bottles of coke, and a dozen rice cakes for all of us at

home. She paid the cashier without protest. Excited, we hurried back home with our goodies.

Every day, I invited her to the house to play with Sisters Wilma, Neneng, and Weng, until she was comfortable again to be around us. And every day, we bought treats at the store, paying with her money. Three days before their departure, I went to Aunt C's house to pick up Bebeng.

On the day they were getting ready to go back to La Union, Bebeng gave me one hundred and fifty pesos. She told me to keep it and to be quiet about it.

"Okay," I said, as I happily tucked the money in my pocket.

An hour later, Aunt Li gave me five hundred pesos to spend on the household and the little ones' needs, but she instructed me to keep it from Father. She knew that he would just ask me to share the money with him and then spend it on liquor. Aunt Li was always thinking of our situation and helped whenever she could, as she had since before I was born. That day, Bebeng finally gave Mother a hug and kissed both her cheeks, as Aunt Li instructed. Deeply touched, tears glittered in Mother's eyes as she held on to her second oldest daughter.

"You be a good girl to Auntie," she said. "Do as she tells you." Mother held onto her, pressing her small frame to her and rubbing her back. Bebeng struggled to get away, and Mother released her grip. Immediately Bebeng went back to Aunt Li.

Mom's eyes followed her. Composed and calm, Mother promised to bring her back home soon.

In the late afternoon, Dad came over to me and asked, "How much did your auntie give you?"

Remembering what Aunt Li had said, I told him, "She gave me very little."

"Will you give me twenty to buy cigarettes," he asked, quite politely, for him.

I said it did not cost twenty pesos for a pack of cigarettes. I already sensed he would be using the rest of the money to buy bottles of gin for him and his drinking buddies.

"Don't be a smart ass," he said. "I want to keep the rest for later. Come on, just twenty."

If I refused, he might beat me so I gave him ten pesos. He refused to accept it though, insisting on twenty with a scowl. I reminded him that Di and I needed money for school supplies. He was like a giant fly buzzing around my head and would not stop demanding it. I handed him the money and left the house.

Secretly, Aunt Li gave Mother cash, too, before she left, for us to get by for a few months. She understood poverty. She had tasted it growing up in Bangar. She knew the struggles and had suffered the physical abuses from her father, but she lived far from us now and couldn't help us nearly as often as she had when we lived in La Union. It was Aunt Li who paid for sister Moon-ay's hospitalization and burial. It was always she to whom we turned in hours of desperation.

Lying in bed that night, I thought about Kling Kling and the other stories in *Liwayway* that had brought into my childhood stories of adventure, moral lessons, and human goodness. Kling Kling had brought to countless readers ideas of kindness and true compassion, the value and meaning of unconditional love, in her captivating adventures.

One of the great inspirations for me and many others was *Darna,* a supergirl hero who wiped out bad guys with her Kung Fu. This woman warrior of flawless beauty, dexterity, and quick thinking, defeated her opponents, preventing them from taking over the world, and restoring peace. Like Superman, she had two personalities, one living as a normal human being, poor and humble, the other flying and using magical superpowers for a good cause. I wanted to be like her, become her. If I were *Darna,* I could stop husbands like my father from beating their wives.

PEACE COULDN T LAST

Mom came home later and later. Dad became suspicious again of her whereabouts. She returned tired, only to encounter his accusations that she had a lover somewhere with whom she had been meeting secretly after work. No matter how many times she explained the traffic situation, the loads of laundry she had to do, or how exhausted and uninterested in having an affair she was, her reasoning never deterred him from believing her an adulterer.

One night we'd finished eating and had gone to bed. Mom already passed out on the floor, and Dad took notice of her being fast asleep. He was still awake, shouting and complaining, while the neighborhood was silent. Annoyed to have no audience and be ignored, he kicked Mother in the stomach with deliberate intent to wake her and make her listen. Awakened by the sharp pain, she tried to get up, still half asleep.

I heard the commotion. It was as if an earthquake rattled the house. Once again, Dad was slapping and hitting Mother with his fist, while she tried to protect herself and cover her face with her hands.

"How many times do I have to tell you I don't like not being taken seriously," he repeated, thumping her as she tried to crawl away.

"Stop it!" I screamed. "Stop hitting Mother!" I'm sure I yelled loud enough to wake the entire neighborhood. My sisters cried hysterically. Di tried to pull Dad away but got shoved across the room. Mom stood. I grabbed Dad's leg, hanging my whole weight on him. I wanted to buy Mom time to get away. He kicked me in the ribs, and I flew across the room. I shouted, "Kick him mom!" I wanted her to fight back, but she wouldn't dare to do it. I was surprised. She was as big as him and not weak, after all her physical work, but she dared not hit back.

"Shut your mouth, you little bastard!" Dad yelled at me, attacking me with his fist. I tumbled onto Neneng, not knowing she'd gotten behind me. I pulled her to me, and we huddled in the corner. Di rushed downstairs. Mom tried to reach the stairs. Dad did not want her to get away this time and blocked her. Di came back with a long knife. "Stop it or I *will kill* you this time!" He pointed the knife at Dad.

Dad looked at his eleven-year-old with the knife. Mom took the moment to run downstairs while Dad grabbed my brother's arm that held the knife. "Please don't hurt Di!" I yelled.

"Stop that, brother," a voice called out from one of the male neighbors outside, asking father to stop whatever he was doing and calm down.

"Oh, I see, so you want to kill me, do you?" Dad mocked my brother. "Give me that!" He grabbed the knife. "Give it to me before I use it on you!" He swung the hand with the knife so the fist hit my brother. "I'm not done with you yet," he said as he headed after my mother.

Di, eyes red, showed no fear this time. He was only angry. He looked grown up, all too fast and was ready to face up to Dad, whatever the consequences. He was building a rebellious spirit, based on long oppression that had driven our lives to a chaotic mess.

We were both sick of it. We waited to see who returned, knowing Dad was out chasing Mom, a knife in his hand. When will this domestic violence end? This was a never-ending cycle of abominable humiliation, being unable to stop our father from his hideous treatment of our mother, and of us. All I could hope was that he never caught Mother. What if he stabbed her? Perhaps Di should never have gotten the knife. Dad might not have obtained it. What would he do to my brother when he came back? The more I imagined what might happen, the more nervous and angry I became. Anger and hatred seemed easier than fear to deal with. Anger gave us courage, roaring to fight back. Fear only brought worry and hopelessness.

I was surprised to see the change in my brother. No doubt, like me, he had been imagining a day when he could defend himself and the people he loved. Uncle Eddie and his wife, still living in the other half of our house, despite no longer having Deedee, were of course awakened by the commotion, but they didn't dare intervene. After all, this was no different from their father all those years growing up. I heard them talking. I even heard people outside, talking in low voices, awakened by my father yet again and mightily annoyed.

"We've had about enough!"

"This has to stop." I wondered how far Mom got, if she'd thought of a friend to take refuge with. I pressed her dress against my face, smelling her scent, imagining her with her arms around me. Would I ever see her again?

It must have been four o'clock in the morning. Roosters crowed in the distance. Di and I still waited, wide eyed, but our little sisters had gone back to sleep. What was taking Dad so long to return? I had a feeling Mom would never return. Still I had a tiny hope that she might find her way to help like last time. I was already imagining life with me taking care of the household, meeting my mother secretly for her to give me money for our food.

Soon I would have to get ready for school. Mom and Dad had been alternating their work schedules so that someone was home with the girls. On weekends, Dad worked at his old job, shaving and polishing four-by-fours. He liked that job because it was good pay and walking distance from home. He also got free wood chips and sawdust for cooking. I was starting to feel lightheaded from no sleep. The rays of the sun shone through cracks in the walls, starting to warm up the house. I looked around. Di had fallen asleep at last.

I would have to forget about going to school. The
little ones would have no one to care for them. I got up
and walked downstairs. Dad was on the bench, facing
away from me, curled up, dirty feet hanging off. I tiptoed
into the kitchen, afraid to wake the devil. How I despised
him. How I wish I were *Darna*. I would have beaten
him up long ago. Put him in the corner instead of him
throwing me in the corner to whimper like a wounded
puppy. Mom would not be running away like she did
so many times, if I were as powerful as the Supergirl. I
would save this family from going deeper into hell.

I had no idea what had come of Mother. I sat down
at the table and rested my head on my arms. I noticed
the long knife my dad had been brandishing. There was
no blood on it, and it was back on the kitchen wall. That's
a good sign, he did not use it on mother. But he could
have cleaned it. I wished I had the guts to butcher him,
with it but brushed those grim thoughts aside. I knew
I could never kill anyone. I had already tested myself. I
thought I had not slept at all. How did I not hear him
come home? I proceeded down the stairs, ready to care
for my siblings. I would have to forge a note for my
excused absence when I returned to school. If I ever did.

I could hear Uncle Eddie and Aunt Besse getting
ready for work. I heard Dad grinding his teeth in his
sleep. Outside, I heard kids on their way to school,
shouting and laughing. I sat, back to the wall, pondering
whether to get Di and Wilma up for school. I resented
the fact that I had to stay home with Father—the man I
hated—to babysit, taking Mother's place because he had
chased her out and possibly killed her. Making up my
mind, I headed back down to the kitchen and looked

for something to feed my little siblings. I did not mind preparing it, as long as there was something to fill their bellies. I found last night's leftovers and heated them. Then I got everyone up, except Father, keeping them quiet so as not to wake him.

I prepared Di and Wilma's lunches and then sent them off to school.

After they left, I would be taking care of Sisters Neneng and Weng, figuring out what to feed all of us for supper. The money Aunt Li had left me had long run out. I'd be washing their school uniforms and fetching water instead of learning in school. I'd be falling behind in my classes. I could only excuse myself for one day. I could only hope Mom would be back after that. Someone had to keep an eye on the little ones so I could go back to school without being dropped.

The next day, Aunt Besse came up to me while I was washing dishes and motioned me to be quiet. She had met with my mother who had given her money for the household. "Don't tell your father that I talked to her," she said. "She told me to give you money every day before you go to school so you had better come to me before you leave for school."

"How will I go to school? Who will watch my younger sisters?" I whispered.

We spoke in hushed voices even though Dad was not around. Supposedly he was in charge of the household. I would be able to go back to school. He was supposed to cook our meals, get our lunches ready, and give us pocket money.

The next day, he woke up sober, took a pee, cleaned himself up, and looked for something to eat. Finding nothing, he told me to keep an eye on the children and was out the door. I did not know what he was planning. Maybe he went to look for work. Very rarely did he communicate with me, and I asked him nothing.

I was just a kid. I hated being the eldest. It always fell on me to be responsible. Why did I suddenly have to be a wife with small children? I knew if I expressed my disgust for him I'd be smacked in the mouth. But I wanted desperately to be back at school and had to know whether he'd be back to watch the girls.

He did not come back that day, and I stayed home again. The next morning I reminded him that I needed to not miss any more school or they'd drop me out.

"Did I not I tell you?" he said angrily. "You need to stay home while I look for a job."

I wanted to say, "If you hadn't stupidly chased mom away again, everything would be fine." But I stayed silent.

Di and I figured we should alternate missing school. I would get too behind in my schoolwork and needed to catch up. He agreed. I think secretly he liked missing school. He would rather play than study. Not me.

Every other day, we switched between babysitting and going to school. He started liking it so much, he offered every day for two weeks to be the one to stay home, while I got all caught up. I told him if Dad figured out how much school he was missing, he'd get lashings. But he said he didn't care. Alternating babysitting and going to school with Di became cumbersome. Missing some days of school was so difficult to manage that I finally got up the courage to talk to dad about the importance of graduating school. I convinced him that I was doing well in school, and it would be a great waste to stop my studying now. After explaining and begging, he agreed to stay at home to look after the little ones while Di and I to went school.

Aunt Besse only gave us fifty cents a day and only when we asked for it. If neither Di nor I asked for money, she didn't give it. She'd happily go to work leaving us without a penny, so I made sure to catch her before she left.

This routine went on for three months. Aunt Besse was frugal with the money Mother had given her for us. In fact she kept it all for herself, never even telling us what the total was or letting us budget what we really needed.

It became a struggle for me to catch up with my studies, with all my other responsibilities at home. My brother, on the other hand, happily neglected his studies altogether, cutting school, pretending to be dressed for school in the morning, but turning a different direction and selling newspapers instead, or collecting bottles from garbage cans and empty lots to sell. That way he fed himself better than we could eat at home with the meager money Aunt Besse was passing out to us. He walked miles, far away from school and fought his way through the congested city. Sometimes he had to cover his mouth and nose with a handkerchief to keep from inhaling the exhaust fumes thick in the air in some areas.

I knew this because when he got home, he smelled of exhaust and was filthy. His t-shirt, which had started out white, was now brown. He washed it and hung it to dry, and sewed a rip in his shorts, which I knew he didn't get at school. Besides, I hadn't seen him there. I tried to pull the needle from his hand, to talk to him, but he just yelled, "Get the hell away from me!" The thread came out the other end.

"You have to knot the end, you fool!" I laughed. He hadn't learned to sew and was hoping to fix his pants in secret. He got irritated, embarrassed. He owned only two pairs of shorts and two t-shirts. When one got damaged, it had to be fixed while he wore the other.

MOM

Before school one day, I went to Aunt Besse for our money. She handed over one peso for me and one for my brother. Walking to and from school under the scorching sun was torture. It was almost an hour walk each way. So we used half a peso sometimes, on the worst hot days, to pay for jeepney rides. We saved the other half to get home. This left us nothing for lunch or snacks and if there wasn't much at home to bring. Di and I were always hungry. There was often nothing to eat for breakfast and nothing to pack for a lunch. We watched other children opening their lunch boxes, smelling the stews their parents had packed for them. My stomach growled painfully, and it felt like it was pressed to my back. I looked around me. It seemed like Di and I were the only kids in the cafeteria with nothing to eat and no money for food.

My stomach ached as I returned to class after lunch, having filled my stomach with water from a fountain. Sometimes I hid behind the school building waiting to go back to class, so as not to have to see and smell the food and be seen with nothing.

Some days school recess took more than two hours. I got a ride home with a classmate. Then I could have a snack at her house and even save some money for food. Each day, I asked a different person so no one would get tired of me eating at her house. Tradition dictated that they must serve a guest. Putting aside my pride, I stuffed food in then, unable to help myself. There was no place for shame. This was survival.

I heard whispers behind my back, but I devoured food every time I got a chance, knowing there probably wouldn't be any at home. Some classmates had cooks to serve them meals any time they wanted. For months, I alternated classmates with whom I could go home and eat. Whatever they could feed me, I ate without a second thought, wishing I had my sisters and brother with me. I wished they could enjoy the meals I was served. I managed to live this way, sometimes going home at lunch with a friend and even taking an hour nap before we went back for the second half of the school day. As I lay on their soft, clean beds, thoughts of our living situation filled my heart with great sadness. It seemed like no matter how many times I had prayed, on my knees, begging for some kind of relief from our life of poverty and chaos, we were denied mercy and grace.

There were days when I had no choice but to use the remaining half peso for food. I debated having food in my stomach temporarily versus having to walk

the whole way home in the heat. Half a peso, about
equivalent to less than ten cents, did not buy much
food, maybe a small orange juice or two slices of white
bread. A vendor outside the school sold hot fish balls with
sweet and sour sauce, four for fifty cents. The smell was
hard to resist.

If I managed to get two slices of white bread with a
smear of peanut butter on it, I savored the flavors and
chewed slowly to make it last longer, to last all the time
that other kids were eating, as jealousy swirled inside me
like a monster living in there that needed feeding.

If I went without food for too long, I became weak
and shaky. I might not be able to walk all the way home.
As much as I hated walking long distances, I surrendered
to food. And when I got home, I still I had to fulfill my
obligations, whether I was too tired to do anything or not
I had to finish my chores or get a beating.

Once a week, Mom showed up outside the school
gate. She was waiting out there for us during our break.
She asked one of the kids to look for us, told them what
classrooms we'd be coming from. She would tell her or
him she was outside waiting. We should meet her at a
designated spot. Whenever I found out from a student
that mother was visiting, I was elated. It reassured me that
she was still alive.

I was filled with joy! She asked how we were. We
knew she could not come to the house. If she did, she
would risk being killed. She told us to take good care
of our sisters, keep them clean and fed. She asked if
Aunt Besse had been giving us the money she gave
her, every day.

I told her, "Yes. She gives us one peso each everyday."

"What! That's all?" she exclaimed, furious. "That Besse has not been giving you what we agreed on," she fumed.

I told her that I asked Aunt Besse every morning to give us school money before she left for work.

"Sometimes I feel like she's avoiding us," I said. "We have to chase after her down the street, like she slipped out before we saw her. If we don't ask, she doesn't bother to give us any, even when we have no food in the house. One day, I had to ask her four times before she handed me any."

Mother's nostrils flared with anger. "I give her forty pesos every week for you!" she exclaimed. "She's kept thirty pesos for herself, the witch! Wait 'til I see her again!" Mother had thought Aunt Besse would be the perfect reliable person to deliver the money in secret since she lived right there. She asked if Aunt Besse had delivered the powdered milk that she'd given her for the babies.

I told her, "Yes, I got the tins of powdered milk."

She said she would speak to her about the money. Then she handed me forty pesos, her day's salary, and instructed me to be frugal with it, spend it wisely, only on food and drinks for all of us.

It was time for us to go back to class. She said goodbye. No hugs or kisses. It was just something we never did. We never showed affection. Our eyes spoke the loving messages from our hearts. There was no need for display of affection, especially in public. Her eyes glistened as I turned and walked away.

"Take good care of your little sisters!" She called as I neared the gate.

"I will. I promise!" I called back. Every week after that she came and did the same—told a student to find us and where to meet her. After that, Mom gave me forty pesos a week, more than enough for all of us to live on, including Dad. He was fed by the woman he repeatedly tried to kill. He was fed with mother's hard earned money. I kept it a secret and hid the money. I also made sure Di got an allowance for spending money.

NO MORE SCHOOL

Dad came home from work one day, late, and woke me. "I want to talk to you," he said as I struggled to wake up.

"What do you want to talk about, Dad?" I asked sleepily.

"It's better you don't go to school anymore," he said. In an instant, I was wide awake.

"Whahh? Why?" I asked nervously.

"You have to stay home and take care of your sisters while I make a living," he told me.

"No! I can't do that!" I protested. "I want to finish school. I want to graduate high school and go to college. I don't want to be poor all my life."

"No one is here to take care of your sisters while I'm at work. Your brother will go to school. It's more important for a boy to get an education."

With that, he left, leaving my world crumbling. Inside I was crying.

There I was, forlorn, stripped of the right to an education, reduced to nothing. I couldn't believe he didn't care if I was educated, that I would be illiterate like him. Oh, how I hated him all the more. Why do people like him and Mother have to make too many children in the first place, leaving the older ones to take care of what they've created? I'd seen so many poor families whose oldest daughter had to take the place of the wife, the caregiver, and the parent of the parents. It was so very unfair. Why do people choose to make many babies when they could not take care of them, when they leave them hungry because they had no jobs, no money, and no education?

Amazingly, I didn't for one minute consider running away. Where would I go? Where would I live? I could not possibly leave my younger sisters to fend for themselves. They were just babies. Di could take care of himself. But I was thinking deeply about our living situation. I could not counter Father's decision. I did not sleep that night.

In the morning, I helped Di and Wilma get ready for school. I prepared their breakfast as usual and went to the mini-store to buy hot steam buns, rice and stew, and bottles of coke for their lunches. When they were off to school, I fed Neneng and Weng, helped them go potty, cleaned them, and changed their clothes. Then I took them for walks and played with them.

I was just a kid myself. *I should be in school with kids my age*, I thought. But no, I had to stay home because my father had terrorized our mother. I did not want to be my father's wife. I did not feel good about any of it. I felt sick thinking about him chasing after his wife with a knife and then demanding that his twelve year old take her place.

But I had no control over the situation. I thought of my classmates getting ahead in school and graduating, while I was at home, learning nothing to prepare myself for a better life.

By the weekend, all the adults—Dad, Uncle Eddie, and Aunt Besse - woke up late, but I couldn't. I had little sisters who needed to go potty. They needed to be cleaned and fed. As soon as I got up, early in the morning, I started cooking, feeding my sisters, cleaning, and fetching water.

By late morning, I gathered all the dirty clothes, the bed sheets and towels. Usually Aunt Besse joined me, washing her uniforms and her husband's while I washed the clothes for the family. She expected me to collect enough water for her as well.

As soon as she got out of bed and relieved herself, Aunt Besse fixed their breakfast of white rice and fried eggs as I was starting to soak the laundry. Scrubbing Dad's and Di's shirts first, squeezing and wringing them with my bare hands, using a paddle with the jeans, shorts and skirts of heavier fabric. I used a four-by-four to flatten them, on occasion stomping them on the concrete floor with my bare feet. Another chance for my feet to get cleaned besides scrubbing them on hard concrete.

Then she quietly eats alone, saving a plate for her husband. Aunt Besse was in the middle of eating breakfast, chewing the rice and egg in her mouth. She looked way too content and deep in thought. I wasn't too happy with her over the money, so I thought I'd play a trick on her. Besides, I also wanted to take her mind off her husband's problems and make her feel better. As she filled her mouth with more rice and eggs, I took some fresh yellow poo from one of the diapers, and held it out to her, "Look at my hand, Aunt Besse! Want some yellow, hard shit on your eggs?"

She took one whiff and threw up all the breakfast she'd been happily chewing. Watching her throw up again and again made me laugh all the more. I almost peed my pants.

CIRCUMCISION

Di was eleven years old and about to get circumcised. Mom and Dad had not taken care of it shortly after he was born, and Aunt C said it was time. Her son, Zac, was the same age and was having his done. Aunt C thought that it would lessen her son's fear if my brother were getting it done as well. Aunt C had a talk with my brother and explained to him that he would be better off having it done, but Di was strongly against it.

Rumor spread around the cluster about the circumcisions and who was having them done. The boys in the neighborhood teased Di, that his pecker might get chopped off by accident and he would come out of the hospital a girl.

Uncle Eddie, who was an adult and should have known better, only heightened Di's fear by telling him it was going to hurt like hell. He was still his old cruel, teasing self, I thought. Even the girls—my cousins included—giggled about it. Pressure mounted until my brother packed his clothes to run away.

Since Aunt C was paying for the procedure, she thought Di should appreciate the offer. He might never get another chance. When it was two days away, Di took refuge at a friend's house. But the friend's mother went directly to Aunt C and told on him. Aunt C rushed to fetch my brother who burst into tears.

"Stop crying. This is for your own good," Aunt C lectured. "It's not going to hurt because you will be numb!" she tried to appease him. "The doctor is only going to remove the extra skin. You're not the only one having it done! Look, you don't see your cousin Zac crying." She brought him home. I remained quiet.

Dad knew about the procedure and said nothing, agreeing with Aunt C's decision. After all, it was not going to cost him a penny. In the afternoon following the procedure, I went to Aunt C's house to wait for the boys to come home. Cousin Zac walked in first with his dad. He strutted around as if nothing had happened.

"Is it over?" I asked.

He did not say a word, climbed the stairs to his bedroom.

"Where's Di?" I asked Uncle Eddie.

"He's walking slow."

They left him alone? I ran out the door and looked for Di. I found him, still a half mile from home, eyes red, hand pulling out the front of his shorts, taking baby steps.

I looked him over, checking to see how he was. He sobbed, still in a lot of pain. I trailed behind him, trying to look normal so as not to attract public attention. As soon as we reached our house, he crawled up the stairs very slowly. I followed and laid the mat and a pillow for him. He looked pale and fragile lying on the floor. I left him upstairs to rest.

As soon as I got downstairs, Aunt C came to inquire about him. She gave me money to buy him a soft drink and a treat. I was happy she was showing him care. She told me to take care of my brother. "I will!" I promised.

Di laid in bed for three days, only getting up to pee in a tin can I placed by the bedside. When it got full, I emptied it.

By the seventh night, he was moaning in his sleep. At dawn, he was shivering, burning up with fever. I awakened to his groaning, and tossing and turning. I did not know what to do, but I kept him covered with a sheet and offered him water. He shook his head. He kept holding his shorts away from his penis.

Wide awake and panicking, I ran downstairs, woke Dad, and told him Di was feverish. He got up in an instant, climbed the stairs, and pulled down Di's pants. I dared not look both for fear of what I might see and out of respect for Di's privacy, so I went downstairs and waited.

Dad came down stairs and told me he would talk to Aunt C first thing in the morning. "Go back to sleep," he said.

I climbed the stairs with a heavy heart, worried for my brother. I could not sleep. I noticed brother had not urinated in a long while. I was puzzled why Di's wound was taking longer than Zac's to heal. They said he was back to his normal self, and I'd seen him walked right after the procedure as if he felt fine.

I had to wonder if he received better care in the hospital. Why was Di suffering so? I could not go back to sleep. I watched my three sisters lying close to Di, sound asleep, without any worry in the world, while I lay worrying. There was calmness outside the cluster at this hour. No dogs barking, no cricket's rhythmical sound, only brief hums of passing vehicles. It must be four o'clock in the morning. Dad's removal of Di's shorts must have helped because he was quiet for a while. I dozed off.

Early in the morning, I went downstairs and noticed Dad was not home. It was unusual that he got up so early and left. I thought, he must have gone by to Aunt C's because she came over the minute I walked in the kitchen.

She told me to take my brother to see a doctor and find out what was going on with his circumcision, why it wasn't healing, and gave me fifty pesos to cover the round trip by jeepney and the doctor's fees. "When you two get back, come see me," she said, and left.

I helped him to get out of bed and told him to get dressed. He moved gingerly, taking all the time in the world. I told him he must hurry or the clinic would close by the time we get there. When he told me to go out for him to put his shorts on, I giggled. He scowled. I could see he was still burning up, and dizzy, unable to maintain his equilibrium, and felt bad for laughing.

I waited for him downstairs, not even bothering to change the clothes I'd slept in. I did borrow flip-flops from Uncle Eddie and Aunt Besse since mine were worn

out. Dad came home, and I told him I was taking Di
to the doctor.

"Yes, you go with him. That's a very good
idea," he told me.

I figured he did not feel comfortable talking to the
doctor. He probably did not know what to say. He never
went to doctors and had always tried to do all our healing
himself, no matter what it was. I asked him to watch my
sisters. Let him figure out what to feed them. I was fired
up about getting out of the house, taking a little trip
to see a doctor. Di descended the stairs slowly, sideways,
holding his shorts away from his privates.

"Do you want to wear looser clothing?" I suggest.
"Why don't you put on my skirt?" I wasn't teasing this time.
He ignored me as he took his time to get down the stairs.
He did not answer still.

Dad said, "He'll be fine. Leave him."

We had to walk half a mile to the depot. It was an
agony, seeing Di walk. His fever was increasing, and he
was growing pale. A street he normally walked in less
than five minutes took him an hour. I wasn't sure if we
had enough money. We did not bother taking a tricycle.
We didn't want to spend the money, opting to save it
for medicine and to pay the doctor. He could make it, I
thought. He stopped often and pulled his shorts away,
taking deep breaths before proceeding.

I knew the name of the hospital. I've seen it more
than a dozen times whenever I rode in a jeepney to travel
far away places and back. I knew exactly how to get there.
We waited for the right jeepney, waving it down to stop in
front of us. The other passengers watched as my brother
slowly climbed in. My brother's face, previously pale, now

turned red. Given his condition, he probably did not care
about all eyes on him. I told the driver the hospital and
paid the fare, telling him to stop his jeepney in front
of the hospital. Every time the jeepney hit bumps and
potholes, I looked at Di, who was still pulling his shorts
away from his crotch.

It took less than half an hour to get there. The
driver had to wait patiently as, again, my brother
slowly climbed out.

"Hurry up," I snapped impatiently. We still had a long
walk to get inside the hospital from the street corner, and
he was moving like a decrepit old man.

The doctor took one look and said, "Your brother
has an infection. His penis and scrotum are swelled
twice their normal size." I could not picture it because
I had never really seen a penis or scrotum except brief
glances and not since my brother was a baby. But I knew
that much swelling couldn't be good, and cringed at the
thought of private parts swelling. He wrote a prescription
for antibiotics and told me exactly when to administer
them. He also wrote the instructions and made me repeat
them. Then he asked, "Where is your mother?"

I looked him in the eye, his spectacles resting on
the bridge of his nose, and told him she had run away
because my father tried to kill her. He lowered his
head and shook it.

"Where is your father, then?"

"At home with our three little sisters."

"Well, I'm very sorry to hear about your situation," he
said and asked, "How old are you?"

"I'm twelve," I said, and pointed to my brother,
curled up on a chair. "He's eleven."

The doctor looked sympathetic as he handed me the prescription. I wished he would not charge me for the visit, as we needed the rest of the money to buy the medicine and maybe colas to drink on the way home.

"Make sure you do not miss a time giving the medicine or something bad will happen to your brother. Do you understand?"

"Yes, doctor, I promise, I will not miss."

"Okay then, out you go to the pharmacy next door and get the medicine." He added, "You do not have to pay me."

I stared at him. At last a wish of mine had come true! I thought. I beamed and thanked him.

"You're welcome," he said as I helped Di up from his seat. We started walking. I grabbed his arm. He shoved me away, not wanting any touch.

"You don't have to hold me," Di said.

I looked behind me. The doctor's eyes followed us all the way down the hall.

As soon as we arrived home, I told Di to lie down and keep an eye on our sisters. I gave him his first dose of medicine and then rushed to Aunt C's to tell her what had happened. "Go home and boil all your brother's shorts," she instructed. "You don't want them to re-infect him."

I ran back home, Di looked passed out. Wilma playing with the little ones downstairs. I started loading sawdust to fuel the stove, then boiled a big pot of water and shoved in my brother's shorts and underwear. There were only four pieces. I hung them to dry. Meanwhile Di wore my school uniform, a green skirt I let him borrow to use around the house.

We had no clock in the house, so I asked Uncle
Eddie to lend me his watch. It was the only way I could
tell when to get up and give my brother his medicine.
During the night, I woke every four hours, as advised
by the doctor, and made him drink his medicine.
Occasionally, I got up two hours early, went right back
to sleep. I had to shake him awake, and hold him half
sitting to spoon the liquid medicine into his mouth. Then
we went right back to sleep. A couple of times, he was
in too deep a sleep and refused to sit up. At this point,
I, too, was in my deep sleep and missed an hour or two
of giving him his medication on time. But I'd promised
the doctor I wouldn't miss any, though so I pinched his
nose until he opened his mouth, and I popped the spoon
in. He coughed and sat up straight, irritated, snapped at
me for pinching his nose, turned around, lay down, and
went back to sleep.

By the fourth night, he started to feel better.
His fever was gone, and he was able to change the
dressings himself. I was beginning to feel relieved. The
medicine was working. I wanted to take a peek and see
if he was healing, but he turned away, angry and told
me I was a pervert. I laughed. To me this was a sign
that he was better.

I started to feel confident that our situation would
soon be back to normal—at least as normal as it got—
and I would get a decent night's sleep.

GRANDFATHER

Two weeks passed, Grandfather came to visit from the province. He stayed with Aunt C for a while since we no longer had room for him in our already cramped house. He was free to come and go as he pleased, as our house belonged to him, but he preferred Aunt C's, where he had his own room.

He had had a stroke and was supposed to rest a lot. He seemed old and frail, walking slowly with his cane, often stumbling, then mumbling, frustrated of his condition. He came to Manila to get better medical treatment than in La Union. I figured he might help with our school dilemma if he stayed around long enough. Since all he did was sit watching TV, maybe he could look after sisters Neneng and Weng, while Di, Wilma, and I went to school.

So I went to him and explained how Di and I had been missing school for weeks. He listened, looking like he understood our plight, so I hurried and got dressed for school. I gave him instructions about my sisters' meals and their bottles of milk which I had prepared earlier to make his work easier. After secretly giving Di his school money, I put on my school uniform. The skirt was losing a button and the zipper was broken. I was definitely going to be late. I found a big safety pin and fastened the waist

before noticing Weng crawling up the stairs. I yelled at
her to sit still.

"Stay down stairs. Don't come up!" I called out
to her, irritated when I could not get the safety pin to
close through the fabric. She continued climbing the
stairs. I let her be, knowing she had a strong grip on the
steps. I needed to gather my books into my school bag.
When Weng reached the ninth step, she paused, her feet
dangling. Nervously I tread down to grab her, but just as
I almost reached her to grab hold of her arm, her little
small frame tumbled down the stairs, head and face
hitting the concrete floor first. I screamed in disbelief, in
a state of shock, afraid she might not still be alive. Then
she cried out as I frantically ran down the stairs.

I picked her up, cradled her small, light body, as she
screamed hysterically. I danced around the room with her,
hushing her. She groaned and blood poured from her
nose and mouth. Her forehead was bruised and swelling.
I panicked and looked into Grandfather's face, standing
in front of me, leaning on his cane. He was speechless.
I did not know where he had been while I was upstairs
getting dressed, but I thought we had an understanding
that he was watching her. He said he could not move fast
enough to keep pace with her. I lay Weng on the wooden
bench. Her eyes were closed now and blood dripped
down her cheeks. She was gurgling on her own blood.

I told Grandfather to watch her and Neneng while
I went to Aunt C's for help. I rushed out and ran as fast
as I could, with no shoes. I pretended I was Darna, flying
through the air, my feet never touching the ground, not
caring if I bumped into people on the street.

As soon as I got to her house, I welcomed myself in, not bothering to clean my feet, despite her beautiful floor and her previous warnings not to enter without permission first.

I found her doing laundry, sitting by the entrance to her kitchen, scrubbing dirty clothes one at a time. Heaps of dirty clothes were piled around her—piles that would have taken her weeks to finish. "Help, Aunt C," I said frantically. "Weng fell down the stairs. I need money to take her to the doctor."

"You people are unbelievable," she said. "If it's not one thing it's another. Every time for help as if I'm made of money."

"She's bleeding," I said. "She needs to go to a hospital now!" I knew that without money, the hospital would do nothing. She stood up, rinsed the suds off her hands, looking grumpy, angry, and went upstairs. I assumed she went up there for money.

Please hurry Aunt C, I whispered to myself. I had to be patient in case she changed her mind. I was starting to panic, my mind with Weng. She might have broken her skull or her tiny bones. I did not know what was taking Aunt C so long to get the money and come down with it.

"Please hurry Aunt C! My sister is bleeding through her nose and mouth!" I shouted out loud so she would hurry down with the money. I wondered how much she was willing to give me this time.

Finally she came down and handed me some paper notes, mumbling something about "If your father wasn't such a hoodlum and your mother such a stupid fool, your family wouldn't be leading the life you live. Here!" She handed me forty pesos.

I grabbed hold of the bills quickly before she changed her mind and rushed home, not wanting to hear any more of her assessments. Her criticism meant nothing to me at this point. It went in one ear and came out the other. I knew she had more money. She was just frugal or did not want to waste a dime on us. My family was not her responsibility, and she did not wish for any of us to be a financial burden. Her expression of sharp disapproval whenever we asked for help was meant to discourage us from seeking future financial assistance, regardless of how miserable our condition happened to be.

I briefly thought maybe grandfather could have paid, but I thought he didn't have much money. I thought how it was Aunt's C's fault that my brother had had the circumcision, so she could hardly blame us for that. And who knows why it had been botched and got infected. Was our house too dirty? Or had she slipped the doctor extra bills for my cousin's good treatment?

As soon as I got home, Aunt Besse said she had to leave for work, as she was already running late. So, I asked grandfather again to keep an eye on Neneng and Wilma while I took Weng to the doctor.

"Don't let anyone climb the stairs!" I reminded him, pointing to him what had just taken placed. He nodded, and I picked up my sister, who was now drinking her milk bottle. I took it from her momentarily, added a bit more water and condensed milk, shook it and placed it in my bag.

I bundled her up in a pillowcase. She looked very sleepy and hungry, still sobbing, with her eyes closed, bloody nose and cheeks. I wiped them off with a clean t-shirt I found in the corner of the room. I gave her the bottle. She sucked on it as I held her and walked out the door. She let go of the bottle and gurgled. Clots of blood must be blocking her airway. She could not breathe. I wanted to breathe for her. I held her upright as we walked on the street, hurrying. Blood dripped out of her nose and mouth. I was freaking out. She cried and then fell back to sleep. My heart raced, thinking of which jeepney to take to the hospital. I hurried and tried to wake her so she would breathe, afraid she'd stop in her sleep.

I was fast up the street, carrying her cradled in my arms, baby bottle in one hand, blood all over her shirt. And mine.

At the depot, I waited for the right jeepney for the hospital, just like Di and I had recently done. When a jeepney stopped, all eyes were on us. I held her tight in my arms, trying to make her comfortable. Exhaust fumes made me choke. I prayed to the gods to take me instead of my sister.

"Let her live," I prayed.

The jeepney made several stops to let passengers out and in. The driver needed to make money, after all. He probably had a family to support. I desperately wished I could fly like *Darna*, rushing without pause, sister in my arms, to the hospital.

The hospital lobby was long, with many doors and signs. I searched desperately for the emergency clinic section.

Luckily, I remembered seeing it on the first floor when I brought Di here.

As the closest public hospital, it was always crowded, and it was first come first served. I sat and waited, trying to be patient, along with mothers with their sick children in their arms. Many looked as bad as my sister. There were very few fathers. Weng's shirt was now soaked with blood and still more gushed out from her nose, down to her neck. I wiped with the t-shirt I found earlier, as I surveyed the scene. Some children had tubes sticking into their noses and intravenous tubes attached to the backs of their hands.

A nurse came out of the exam room and checked the upper back of a girl sitting next to me. She removed a four-inch gauze bandage, exposing what looked like a flesh tube coming out of the girl's lung. The nurse pulled the tube with forceps and the girl gave a big, loud, "Ouch!"

The nurse apologized, still holding on to the clamp, pulling some more. The girl started to cry loudly, her voice echoing down the long, narrow corridor. The nurse covered the exposed hole with a clean dressing, apologized again, and left. Children and babies moaned, groaned, cried from fear, from hunger, from pain.

I was sick to my stomach, fearing our turn and fearing it would not come soon enough. The big round clock on the hall way said 10:45. A couple more people ahead of us.

When the nurse called us, she motioned us to follow her to the doctor's office where he sat behind his big, wooden desk. I sat on the chair across from the table, Weng on my lap. He asked what had happened. I told him my sister fell down the stairs.

"Where are your parents?" he asked.

"Dad is at work, and Mom ran away," I explained.

He shook his head, stood up, and came round the table, where I sat. He examined my little sister who tried to suck her bottle. Then she threw her bottle to the floor and started to cry, seeming irritated.

"Come with me," the doctor said. He picked up the bottle from the floor, and I followed him into the exam room.

"Put your sister down on the table," he asked. He examined her from head to toe.

I stepped aside and watched. He told me she had a broken nose and the dried blood made it hard for her to breathe and possibly to swallow. He said to keep her head elevated, and he would be back in a minute. A nurse came in and cleaned her face with a warm wet cloth. She explained that if Weng felt hot, if she developed a fever, to bring her back. Otherwise, she was good to go. She gave me a bottle of medicine to give to my sister for pain and explained the dosage and times to give it. I memorized it.

I bundled her again in the pillowcase, now caked in dried blood, and left the emergency room to find a jeepney.

I realized I did not pay the doctor a dime! And the medicine was free. I still had more money left over.

At home, I opened her milk bottle, tasted it, and spat it out. It was sour. I ran to the store and bought a can of condensed milk. At home, I made her a fresh one. As soon as grandfather saw me, he left for Aunt C's, probably eager to get back to the TV. Neneng tugged at me, saying she was hungry. She was sucking and chewing on something. "What is that in your mouth?" I asked. I reached for her mouth and pulled out a long, rusty nail.

"You've been chewing on a nail with poop and worms on it," I told her angrily, purposely to scare and prevent her from doing it again. Oh, God. I knew I could never leave the girls with Grandpa again.

I slapped her, saying never to put anything she found in her mouth. She cried, pressing her hand on her mouth. Waving my finger in her face, I chided her saying, "You know better than to put such things in your mouth!"

I'd had enough scares for the day. Who knew if I'd be able to keep Weng breathing with her broken nose?

"Do you remember the worms we pulled from your butt? That's what happens when you put things from the dirty ground in your mouth." I snapped. She nodded, looking scared—maybe of worms, maybe just that I might slap her again. I told her to sit in the corner with Weng and watch her. She nodded again, tears rolling down her cheeks.

I stared at her momentarily, surprised at my reaction. Watching her cry made me feel ashamed of myself. I was the oldest and should have known better than mistreat my helpless, defenseless, younger sister.

I ran back to the store. It seemed like more and more houses in the neighborhood had food stalls in front of their houses with meat stews, cooked vegetables, and steamed rice. I bought a couple of bowls of fish and chicken stews with the money left over from Aunt C and took them home for our lunch and dinner. My siblings and I gathered around the wooden table and ate with our hands while Weng slept in the corner.

When Dad came home from work, I told him what had happened. He handed over his month's salary and told me to go pay Aunt C, and then he said that the rest

of the money should be kept safe and used for buying
food and emergencies.

Pay her? No way!

THE TRUTH

Dad came home from work early one afternoon and
called out for me, Di, and Wilma to come downstairs.
I said we were upstairs. Dad sat by the top of the
stairs, drunk, and asked us if we had been seeing
mother secretly.

"Yes," I told him, speaking for all of us.

"Didn't I tell you not to meet with your mother?"
His voice was angry. How many times have I reminded
you about that? What will it take to put that into your
little heads, huh?"

With my head bowed, I told him she just wanted
to talk to us.

"What did she want?" he inquired.

"She wanted to find out how my sisters and brother
are doing. She misses us," I cried while thinking of our
sad, forlorn situation.

"You are just like your mother. Can't get things in
your head," he tells me. "You tell your mother to watch
out. I had better not see her around this place. You tell
her that. Do you hear me?"

"Yes, I hear you," I said.

"I better not see you accepting gifts from her," he warned.

"But my little sisters need their milk!" I cried.

"They are old enough to stop needing milk!" he replied and walked away.

I was lost in my own private hell and Father's warnings weighed heavily on me. Now he would probably never let me go back to school. I needed cans of powdered milk for my sister's nourishment. I needed to go to school to get the milk and money mother brought. There was no food in the house. We needed the money mother brought, for food and for school.

I LL TEACH THEM TO NOT LIKE MILK

The following day, Dad was sober again. He asked for milk bottles. He had a plan, he said. A very good plan. He should have thought of it months ago, he said, holding some type of vegetable in his hands. He instructed me to hand over two empty milk bottles. He started rubbing the nipples with what looked like hot chili peppers.

"Put water in the bottle instead of milk," he said as he continued spreading the hot chili peppers all over the nipples, top, sides, bottom, not missing a spot. Then he picked off small, yellow seeds left on the nipples.

"Here. Give these bottles to your sisters," he told me while handing over the bottles.

"No, Dad!" I protested in disbelief. "That'll burn their mouths!"

"Do as I tell you!" he insisted, raising his voice.

I did not know what to think. I started to cry, pleading for him not to do it. The strong pungent smell of red peppers permeated the room. It burned my nostrils, my eyes. I was down on my knees, one bottle on each hand, head bowed, begging Dad not to pursue his plan.

I wanted so badly to hurt him at that moment, but I was too small, too weak to take him on. He would only hurt me so that I wouldn't be able to care for my sisters. I wished he would disappear. Thoughts of the day when I was ready to chop his head off with a machete came back flooding my head. I should have done it then. I could not force myself to watch what was about to take place with baby sister. I was desperate for some type of miracle to happen or someone to stop this mad man. I thought of mother. Why was she not strong enough to defend us all?

Where was she right now anyway? I wanted her to come home. She could support us just fine without him. Why had we ever come back?

He told me to bring my sisters. My heart stopped, terrified for the two innocent babies.

"Dad, they're not asking for their bottles. I'll give the bottles to them later when they ask, okay?" I pleaded, thinking I could wash off the hot peppers when he was not around. I tried to sound convincing.

"Bring your sisters over here now!" he demanded, raising his voice even louder, sounding angry.

Trembling, I got up, still begging him to postpone his plan. "Please . . . it's not fair to burn their mouths. They don't know anything."

Dad gave Neneng her bottle. The moment she put the nipple to her mouth, she withdrew it, cried out, and threw it across the floor, one hand pressed to her mouth. She felt the sting, the burn, fire in and around her mouth. She kept crying as it burned and burned.

"Good. She learned her lesson. She's not going to ask for her bottle again," Dad predicted. "That was quick! Good for you, Neneng. You don't want a bottle any more, do you?"

Neneng just stared with hurt eyes, both hands pressed to her mouth, tears wetting her little cheeks, screaming for some relief for sure.

"Next," Dad said.

I felt sick.

"Bring your sister Weng here. Lay her down on her back," Dad instructed. Weng was not yet walking.

"Please don't do this, Dad, please!" I protested, desperate. He ignored my pleading. I tried to grab hold of Weng away from Dad's hands. He jerked the bottle away, looking at me with a hint of menace, as if to say, do that one more time and you will have a burn in your mouth, too.

Neneng watched, scared and crying. She understood what was going to happen to her baby sister. She became hysterical as she watched me lay our sister Weng on her back. Weng did not know what was going to happen. Neneng screamed louder, frightened for our youngest sister.

Dad forced the bottle to Weng's mouth. She sucked it in just a fraction and screamed out loud, so loud her face turned the same red as the hot chili peppers. Her mouth, too, was on fire. She started kicking her legs, screaming. Now both sisters were screaming, and there was no way I could stop the burning. I ran down stairs to get water. Neneng drank a big gulp, not removing the glass from her mouth. But the baby wouldn't stop crying.

"Do it once more," Dad said, handing the bottle to sister Weng who was crying hysterically. Weng sucked on her bottle and gave a very long cry, stomach heaving, mouth wide open, eyes shut, and face red. She was being given a lesson that a bottle would never be a comfort to her again. It would only give her pain. That those she thought loved her were treating her cruelly. I was crying, helpless, so sorry for both of them.

"This will train your sisters to stop asking for bottle, for milk," he reasoned.

I didn't care to hear him speak. I hated him so much. I wished anyone else on earth were there rather than him.

"Now you don't have to rely on your mother for milk," he said as if his reasoning was brilliant.

He wanted to teach mother a lesson. I kept my eyes away from him and picked up cardboard to fan their mouths

"Stop fanning. Let them feel the burn, so they will stop asking for their bottle!"

"If they ask, give them the bottle again."

At last he left, mission accomplished.

I hid away the bottles and gave Weng water, let her sip it, let it run over her swollen red lips. She had never drunk from a glass before. I let her hold it. They both held water glasses in their little hands.

That night when Neneng awakened, I whispered for her not to ask for milk. They were hungry because there was no food in the house. I had tried to get some from Aunt C, but she had instructed Grandfather to report to her if I came into her house and what I was doing. I usually went in, opened the refrigerator, and took two or three slices of white bread for my siblings and myself. I even noticed a pitcher of pineapple juice. I drank in a hurry. Grandfather saw what I was doing. The pineapple juice tasted sour. I resented Aunt C for leaving pineapple juice to sit around in the fridge for weeks instead of sharing them with us.

Weng had not had any milk since late afternoon, only sips of water, all day. In the evening, middle of the night, at dawn, her whimpering revealed her hunger and suffering. Dad woke and put the hot peppered nipple in her mouth, as if he enjoyed her pain. Maybe he was getting revenge on the wife he had chased away, by hurting a toddler. *How could I help her understand? How could I understand it myself?*

This went on for two days and two nights. I was reaching my limit. I tried to figure out how to fight against his cruel plan. The sight of my sisters, red in the face and betrayal in their eyes was more than I could endure. He didn't even bring cool soothing things to replace their milk bottles, as if he wanted them to suffer as much as possible. All I could do was hope for a miracle. The best miracle seemed like a life without father in it. Despite instructions from father, I continued to sneak warm milk to my sisters when he was not around. I made them drink it in a hurry, knowing at their age they still needed the calcium. I continued to meet Mother and told her everything that had happened, but now I feared for her safety and mine more than ever.

As I told her what he was doing, her eyes opened wide in shock and tears rolled down her cheeks. She had to sit as I told her everything. She broke down and cried on the street corner where we'd met. Passers-by looked at us, and I had to worry that one might know father and tell him. I begged her to stop crying, but she couldn't help herself. I hated embarrassing public scenes. One of my friends from school might see us.

"That demonic monster!" she seethed.

I told her how he threatened if we saw her or took anything from her. She was not allowed to talk to any of us. He forbade it. She got up and moved away to a less conspicuous place. I was glad. I hated the pitying looks we were getting. I wanted her to figure out a solution, to fix our lives.

Teary eyed, we soon said good-bye. It was lunchtime, and I had to get to class. She handed me forty pesos.

"Make sure you hide it well," she said. She handed me two 32-ounce cans of powdered milk. "Make sure your sisters drink their milk. Forget what that evil man told you." She told me she was going to get extra ironing work and find us a place to live.

"Why can't you take us now?" I asked hastily. "We could go where he can't find us."

"I only share a room with a maid, a very small bedroom where I also iron clothes," she explained. "There would not be room for all of us. Besides, the owners of the house would not let us all live there."

As usual, we conveyed our love through our eyes and then parted.

AUNT BESSE WANTS TO BE A MOTHER

Aunt Besse started taking more of a role in caring for us, giving special attention to sisters Wilma, Neneng, and Weng. Maybe because she wasn't having children of her own, she talked about adopting them, confident that she could support all three little girls.

One day she announced she was getting the paperwork started. I felt like a bucket of cold water had been thrown in my face.

"I don't know if Mother would like that idea," I tried to say calmly, worried that she really could file for adoption, without mother's permission. I thought she might pay someone underground to forge Mother's signature and file paperwork. Mother would go berserk! Why hadn't she already taken us! I told her cordially, offering a solution to hold her off from filing the paperwork, "But you can borrow them."

She kept having miscarriages. Everyone had heard her stories. A rumor spread that she was trying to cover up Uncle Eddie's homosexuality by making it appear that he was paying attention to her, that they were still celebrating marital bliss, in bed. The couple's rendezvous had fogged up my curious little mind, but I immediately brushed the thoughts aside as sick and disgusting.

Other times she announced she had not had her period in the past four months and, just as she was urinating, a fetus fell out. She said a brief prayer and buried it, out in the backyard. She dug up a grave using a tablespoon.

Then came inside the house saying it had tiny hands and feet, to make her story sound convincing.

For a week she did not go to work. I asked her why. She said she was taking a long vacation.

"Oh? How long?" I asked, thinking she might babysit.

"Three months," she answered, "possibly six."

My eyes lit up. She said her work had given her stress.

What could be more perfect than to make her a babysitter for my three sisters since she was talking about adopting them anyway? Surely it would do her good to have their company for the time she was off work. That way she would never get bored or worry about where Uncle Eddie was.

When I came home from school, Aunt Besse was carrying Weng on her hip, holding Neneng by the hand. She passed me my sisters, telling me to take them. She was exhausted. She complained that she needed to rest before she cooked dinner for herself and her husband.

After dinner, she helped him correct test papers and homework assignments from college students. She dozed off while still sitting in her chair, trying to correct papers. When her head dropped, she awakened and went back to work. When he finished eating, he brushed his teeth,

showered and went to bed. I assumed she'd gotten over
wanting to adopt my three sisters.

MAKEOVER

On the weekend, I decided to try to help Aunt
Besse win Uncle Eddie's affections. I thought I knew
just how to do so.

    Uncle Eddie happened to be staying around the
house gazing out the window with bored sighs as he
listened to music, read student essays, or took short naps.
During one of these naps, I thought it was an opportune
moment to propose a makeover. I told her I would make
her beautiful. I brushed and braided her hair, and then
I put make up on her and helped her pick out nice
clothes, telling her Uncle Eddie would fall in love with
her when he saw her. She smiled, liking the flattery. She
loved the attention.

    For days, I paid her compliments, and on the
weekends, I reminded her to dress up. I polished her
nails and gave her massages. I curled her hair with pliable
twigs. I told her we would leave the twigs curls on her
head for two days, and she walked around the house,
doing her chores with curlicues made of twigs and hair
adorning her head. When I took them out, I styled her
hair. The curls smelling of fresh mowed grass, but she did

not mind. I came up with new styles, assuring her this would revive her husband's interest and affection.

I made sure she got help with fetching water and with chores around the house. The plan was to keep her home to babysit, so Di and I could go to school. However, one night when Uncle came home grouchy, he found no water in the tank, and the house was a mess. I had been busy giving Aunt Besse her makeover that I had neglected doing other chores. Aunt Besse said she had no time to fetch water or clean or cook because she was busy taking care of my sisters.

Uncle Eddie blew up, asking her what the hell she had been doing all day. Looking in the mirror? Hearing the commotion, I rushed to their quarters and was greeted with a seething glare.

He pointed his finger at me. Enraged, he yelled, "I want you out of my house now!"

I was shocked. I took his words to mean literally. It was his house, his name on the deed. I ran to my room, packed my few belongings in a plastic bag and wrote Dad a note, folding it and placing it on the table. I paused and thought of my little sisters and brother. How will they be cared for? Will Aunt Besse be able to care for all of them without me to help around? But I had to get going. I had to get out. I had to find mother, help her earn money, and get our own place to live. I hesitated a moment, thinking maybe I should wait until dawn to leave.

I found Di, and I told him I was leaving for good, to be with Mom. But in the note I wrote that I had to leave to find Mother, that I wanted to be with her, never mentioning the fact that Uncle Eddie had thrown me out of his house. If I mentioned it in the letter, Dad would go beat his brother up. Uncle Eddie had no business throwing Dad's kids out of the house. That would only create havoc for everyone. I think I wanted to be pushed to make this decision and was glad Uncle Eddie had forced it.

When all my sisters and brother were settled in bed, I reminded Di that I would be leaving at dawn, while everyone was still asleep. I also told him he needed to keep an eye on the little ones while I was gone. He nodded, irritated, and went back to sleep. Perhaps he was glad I would no longer bear the brunt of the abuse and yet, at the same time, hated the idea he was left with the responsibility to care for our sisters.

THE GREAT ESCAPE

At 5 AM, I grabbed my plastic bag of clothes and walked quietly out of the house. The street was still dark, but a few lights left on outside people's houses illuminated my path. Here and there, an adult would pass me on the street as I walked away from the cluster and left Tatalon behind. The traffic was light. There were only a few jeepneys, rarely any tricycles, running. A chill passed through me. I was not wearing a sweater, just a sleeveless shirt, a skirt, and my flip-flops. I kept walking, not looking back.

I took a jeepney to *Malabon* where Grandmother lived. Soon it was morning rush hour, and the streets clogged with cars, jeepneys and buses by the hundreds, heading in all directions. Black smoke spewed into the air from tail pipes. I pulled my t-shirt over my nose as cars sped by, horns honked, a few jeepneys with stereos blaring, one playing *Air Supply,* John Lennon, Kenny Rogers, while another playing the *Eagle's* latest popular album, to energize morning commuters, all the city heading for work. Tatalon was no longer in sight. Running away seemed like a fun adventure. I asked the Jeepney driver to drop me off in *Malabon.*

I went and stayed with Grandmother.

Three days later, Mother walked into the apartment, frantic, asking if I was there. I ran down stairs as soon as I recognized mother's voice. All of the cousins raised down the stairs with me.

"I've been worried sick about you!" she blurted out the minute she saw me. "And how did you find this place? Never mind. As long as you are all right. That's all that matters." She sighed with relief.

We sat together, and I explained what had happened. She told me to get dressed, that I was going with her.

She insisted I go back to Tatalon to care for my younger sisters. I stopped dead in my tracks.

"Uncle kicked me out," I said. I was determined never to return. "Besides if dad sees me, he'll whip me for running away!" I told her and then suggested, "I can help you at your job and earn more money."

"Who's going to care for your sisters?" she asked wearily.

"Aunt Besse is still there. She can and will take care of them." I assured her. I could see she heard a new tone in my voice. She sensed I was desperate never to return.

Early morning the following day, we left. Mother and I travelled together to *Marikina City*, where she worked as a live-in laundry person, doing the laundry of two families. Because of heavy traffic, our morning was spent inside the bus and jeepney. We arrived at her employer's house late in the afternoon.

The house was located in a magnificent subdivision neighborhood. I'd never seen anything like it. We passed by big houses with swimming pools and manicured, park-like lawns, iron-wrought fences, coconut palms in front and backyards. We reached the house where mother worked. She let herself in, leading me through the gate, and down the private cobblestone driveway lined with rose bushes of magnificent colors. The scene was breathtaking, and intimidating.

We walked through the grand, marble-floored entry and into a luxurious living room with elegant furnishings, a shiny glass table in the middle with glass chandelier hanging above, a grand piano in one corner, custom lighting throughout. She instructed me to stand in the corner by the door and wait for her. She said to not sit on the soft couch as we were not considered important guests, so we had to show proper etiquette. She went to look for the lady of the house.

My eyes moved to the European style dining room with its huge glass chandelier over a polished cherry oak table with lazy Susan in the middle. I wondered what it would be like to sit on the blue, velvet-covered sofas in the living room and what kinds of foods do they have in the fridge.

Mother came back. "She's coming. Get ready to meet Mrs. Murita," she said anxiously.

I straightened, eager to make a good impression, hands clasped before me. Mrs. Murita looked very polished, elegant with her long, flowery, ironed dress as she came closer to meet us. No doubt mother ironed the clothes she was wearing at the moment. She smiled at me, then mother. I remained quiet. I felt uneasy. Shy. Dirty. Extremely poor. Desperate to be accepted in her big house. Hungry.

"She can help Norene with the household chores," Mother blurted out. "And help me with some of the ironing, after school. She won't be any trouble. She knows about hard work." She tried to sound convincing. Still wearing her friendly smile, Mrs. Murita looked in my direction. Her eyes scanned my tiny form from my head down to my feet, and then turned to face my mother. Mother added, "She'll get along very nicely with Norene."

Mrs. Murita gave a nod of approval and said, "Yes, she can stay. It's no problem."

I helped Norene prepare and serve the rich folks their meals and washed dishes everyday after school. Once a week, I scrubbed and polished the marble floors. During supper, I made sure no main dishes were empty on the table. I went back and forth from the kitchen to the dining table, refilling main dishes, rice plates, empty glasses with juice or water, and waited for anyone to ask something they wanted from the fridge or the kitchen because they were not supposed to lift their asses to get

the stuff wanted. I marched back and forth, serving like
a full time waitress for six people, and sometimes seven
when their cousin was staying over.

All they do was open their mouths and gave orders.
If someone dropped his knife or a slice of meat on the
floor, no one bent his or her back. It was my job to pick it
up. If a fly buzzed while they ate, I had get rid of it. When
the weather was hot while eating, one would call for the
ceiling fan switch to be turned on.

When they were done eating, I was exhausted.
Norene and I cleared and cleaned the table, washed the
dishes, swept the floor, and then have our own supper. We
ate their leftovers. By nine o'clock in the evening, I was
ready to drop dead. But I forced myself to stay up and
finish my homework while mother busily ironing clothes.
I had to wake up at 4:30 AM and be out of the house by
5:30 AM to beat the traffic so I could be in school by 7:30
AM. This routine went on for about a year.

LIFE AT THE GRAND HOUSE

A teacher, guarding the gate at the school entrance,
questioned me, asking why I arrived late everyday. When I
told him where I lived, he was surprised. I was always the
last student to arrive. He announced to his class that I was
a role model, and must be commended for the efforts I
put forth trying to get to school on time.

As soon as I arrived back at Mrs. Murita's house around 5:30 PM, I served the gardener his juice and snack and then helped Norene prepare supper.

The youngest teenage daughter scolded Norene for being slow.

"I'm not a robot!" Norene answered in defiant tone.

"Have you polished my shoes for tomorrow?" she asked Norene.

"Yes, I have." Norene replied.

"Well, where are they?"

"They're outside drying."

The youngest daughter of the house walked away to retrieve her polished shoes. Norene kept quiet as I helped her gather dirty clothes to wash later that evening. My mother was at Mrs. Chang's house doing laundry. I knew I would be going to bed around one or two o'clock in the morning with all those unfinished chores.

The youngest daughter came back, "I can't find my shoes. Can you get them for me?"

"I told you I put them outside to dry." Irritated, Norene dropped the dirty clothes on the floor and walked towards the door, mumbling. I trailed behind her. "I bet you if her vagina is not attached to her body, she would have lost it and ask me to find it for her."

Everyday, all six people, dump their dirty clothes and put on their house clothes. They, too, get washed the next day. Mother could not keep up with the mounds of laundry at Mrs. Murita's and Mrs. Chang's house, so Norene suggested she and I do the laundry every night. So, after serving dinner and washing the dishes, and eating our own meals, I stood next to Norene in the tiled sink, scrubbing away with our hands.

MOM S LITTLE HELPER

Mom and I helped each other, enduring the hard work in order to save money. We were determined to get an apartment spacious enough for all six of us. Occasionally, mom or I would alternately take turns visiting my sisters and brother in secrecy. Sometimes we asked a neighbor to deliver a can of powdered milk and cans of sardines to Aunt Besse since she had been in charge of looking after sisters and brother.

Other days, when Norene and I were the only people at Mrs. Murita's house, I snuck into the pantry and took out a can or two of SPAM. Other days, I took a can of spaghetti sauce. I stashed them in my school bag, rolled up in a t-shirt. I'd rearrange the rest of the cans in the pantry to avoid suspicions by the headmasters.

On Wednesdays and Fridays, when I had two hours of school recess, I took the jeepney to Tatalon, making sure ahead of time that dad would not be around. I cooked rice and fried slices of SPAM for my sisters and brother to eat. Some days, I arranged for brother to boil spaghetti noodles ahead of time, noodles that I had kept for a day in my bag and given to brother in school when we met. By the time I arrived in the house in Tatalon, I just boiled the spaghetti sauce. I always left them with plenty of food to eat.

STAYING TOGETHER

At fourteen, I was old enough to help mother look for a place for us to live. I asked my classmates if they knew of a room for rent, but through word of mouth mother found a spacious bedroom on the first floor of a house in a small town of *Singalong*. We would share the kitchen and one toilet with the owners and their three grown children. The room will be available in two days.

Mother paid the first month's rent and got ready to pick up my sisters and brother. She decided to get them herself on a Monday. She had earlier in the week requested a day off. When she arrived in Tatalon, she hid at Mrs. Opal's house, whose residence was facing our old house. Mrs. Opal sent one of her grown daughters to our old house to get Di, but Mother was greeted with the news that brother Di and my sister Wilma, were in school. They were being looked after Aunt C. Aunt Besse, however, had taken my two little sisters with her to live in another city. Dad, in his sober state, had given my sisters away to Aunt Besse. His verbal consent was just as good as signing a legal contract for adoption. Aunt Besse must have been thrilled since it had been her longtime wish to adopt little sisters. Aunt Besse and Uncle Eddie had taken my two sisters and left *Tatalon* for good.

Mother's mind was in a whirl with us all living in
different places. I was still living at Murita's house, and
Bebeng was at Aunt Li's in the province. Di and Wilma
were fending for themselves in Tatalon, and my sisters,
Neneng and Weng, were somewhere in another town
with Aunt Besse. Mother had only one day off a week
to look for them. Using the little time she had on a
Monday, mother had decided she would return to Di
and Wilma on another day, as soon as she could find her
other two children.

Wasting no more time, she rushed to Aunt C's
house to inquire of Aunt Besse's address, but Aunt C,
who came home very late in the evening after work, was
still asleep. Luckily, a visiting cousin, Aunt Ud's daughter
Hershey, was at Aunt C's house having breakfast in the
kitchen. Cousin Hershey and I were never close, never
even speaking to each other while growing up except
wave to or nod to greet each other. Mother had not seen
nor talked to Hershey for over a decade, and she was the
same age as Bebeng, twelve. Mother was surprised but
grateful to meet her again at Aunt C's house.

Frantic she may never see her babies again, mother
asked if Hershey knew of Aunt Besse's whereabouts.

"Yes. Mother, Uncle Eddie, and Aunt Besse bought a
piece of land in *Carmona, Cavite,*" she replied. In previous
conversations among grown ups, she overheard a town
called, *Carmona, Cavite* where parcels of land were being
auctioned at a low cost to people with low income. The
price was low enough for Aunt Besse to afford a down
payment, so she and Uncle Eddie bought a piece of land
and started building a house in order to start a family.
Aunt Ud was able to borrow money from a bank because

she had a stable income as a second grade teacher. She, too, bought a piece of land and had enough savings to afford to build a new house.

Mother was determined to find her babies. She thanked Hershey and ran out of Aunt C's house, going straight to the bus depot. After traveling by bus, she took a short train ride and then traveled by jeepney. As soon as she arrived in *Carmona,* mother stopped momentarily to look at mothers carrying their children, thinking perhaps that one of them might be hers, before continuing on. She passed by children playing on the streets. She stopped their playing and asked each one if they knew or heard of her little girls. She had no photographs of them, for she never owned a camera nor could afford to have their pictures taken. One old picture of Neneng was all she had kept in the safe, but she did not have it with her. It never crossed her mind that her babies would be taken away from her and brought to another town, that she may never see them again.

She had to find the little ones, and, once she did, she would bring all of her children together to live in the one room apartment she had rented. That was her plan, to start a new life with her small savings. Just being together with all her children, laughing, and enjoying freedom was all she could ever hoped for without a hint of fear or the expectation of psychological torture lurking around every bend. She wanted us to be free of domestic violence.

She asked strangers how to get to the address she was given. They pointed in the direction. Her heart racing, she quickened her pace in that direction. Anger, guilt, self-blame added to her longing to be reunited with all of her children. Overwhelmed by the instant replay of her life's tragedy, she reminded herself, she must keep going. She turned in another street corner, found the house, and knocked on the door. Aunt Besse's mother, an old lady with salt and pepper hair, opened the door. Mother introduced herself and told the old lady she came to pick up her daughters, Neneng and Weng. Mother knew she had the correct address, the right house.

"They are not here," the stooping woman answered suspiciously.

"Do you know where they are?" Mother asked anxiously.

"They're out on the street. Walking."

"Why are you letting them outside? They might get lost or kidnapped!" She did not bother to waste any more energy with the old lady. The old woman had been instructed to keep an eye on the two while Aunt Besse and Uncle Eddie went to work everyday.

It was already passed noon, and it was hot. Mother walked on a wider street where jeepneys came and went. On the street corners, she craned her neck for a better view.

Not too far ahead of her were two little girls, walking towards her. The rays of the sun hit her eyes, making it difficult to recognize the two small figures. She walked faster, using her hand as screen from light or heat.

"Nanay (Mother)!" Neneng shouted. They both came running forward, holding hands. Mother was overjoyed as soon as she recognized them. She dropped to her knees, her arms wide open.

RESOURCES

The following are a list of resources and reporting agencies in the Philippines for help with child abuse.

"THE SPECIAL PROTECTION FOR A CHILD AGAINST ABUSE, EXPLOITATION, AND DISCRIMINATION ACT"

-REPUBLIC ACT 7610
-18 YEARS UNDER AND OLDER

Report to: Department of Social Welfare and Development or (CHIPS) Child Health and Intervention & Protection Services.
Metro Manila: (632) 732- 4216

Anti-Child Abuse, Discrimination, Exploitation Division
National Bureau of Investigation
Metro Manila office: (632)525-6028 or 525-8231

Commission on Human Rights/Child's Rights Center
Metro Manila (632) 927- 4033

Philippine National Police Operation Center
(632) 721-8613 or (632) 722-0540

Department of Justice Task Force on Child Abuse
(632) 523- 8481 TO 89 LOC 378

For children in remote areas: Make reports to Provincial City or Regional Prosecutors, Local Barangay Council for the Protection of Children.

For other private organization located in various islands of the country such as: Bicol, Laguna, Cebu, Iloilo, Negros, Davao, and Zamboanga. Please contact:
ABS-CBN Bantay Bata: 163 (632) 411- 0856

Help in the United States and internationally:

National Child Abuse Hotline in the United States:
1-800-4-A-CHILD

National Domestic Violence Hotline in the United States:
1800-799-SAFE (7233)

Women's Link Worldwide (Western Europe and Latin America) website: www.womenslinkworldwide.org

Unifem, United Nations Development for Women
website: www.unifem.org

ABOUT THE AUTHOR

Born in the Philippines, **Victoria Mulato** entered the world in a way no child should ever have to; into a family and culture of poverty, neglect, and terrible abuse. As a young girl she had lived through too many horrible experiences. Even through these extraordinary challenges though, her spirit shined, always believing in and striving for something better, something more.

Through her determination and courage she eventually found her way to a better way of life in the United States. Here, like many who immigrate, she worked hard to educate herself and succeed, having a family of her own and developing a career as a Medical Assistant. Now, secure in her life, Victoria has discovered the power of her own voice and wrote *Sister Moon of the Philippines* so the world can know more about the dark side of Filipino culture and those that need help will find a compassionate voice.

In Victoria's words:

I have written this book to raise awareness of the wide spread domestic violence and child abuse that is so prevalent in the Filipino culture. All too often children in the Philippines are robbed of their basic human rights to an education because they have to become parents to their siblings or have been sold for money.

Through my writing and work, it is my passionate goal to help stop domestic violence and child abuse by educating the very young as well as adults about the effects of physical, emotional, and mental abuse, and show those in need how and where to seek help.

In addition to her career and writing, Victoria helps others by donating her time to volunteer organizations that focus on child abuse, parental stress hotlines, and natural disaster relief groups. She has also contributed significantly to medical missions to Zimbabwe, Africa assisting in surgical procedures.

Connect with Victoria Mulato via email: victoriam2sistermoon@gmail.com or visit her website at www.VictoriaMulato.com.